MW00736817

Performing Antiquity

Performing Antiquity

ANCIENT GREEK MUSIC AND DANCE FROM
PARIS TO DELPHI, 1890–1930

SAMUEL N. DORF

OXFORD
UNIVERSITY PRESS

OXFORD
UNIVERSITY PRESS

Oxford University Press is a department of the University of Oxford. It furthers
the University's objective of excellence in research, scholarship, and education
by publishing worldwide. Oxford is a registered trade mark of Oxford University
Press in the UK and certain other countries.

Published in the United States of America by Oxford University Press
198 Madison Avenue, New York, NY 10016, United States of America.

Library of Congress Cataloging-in-Publication Data
Names: Dorf, Samuel N., author.
Title: Performing antiquity : ancient Greek music and dance
from Paris to Delphi, 1890–1930 / Samuel N. Dorf.
Description: New York : Oxford University Press, [2018] |
Includes bibliographical references and index.
Identifiers: LCCN 2018016172 (print) | LCCN 2018038097 (ebook) |
ISBN 9780190612108 (updf) | ISBN 9780190612115 (epub) |
ISBN 9780190612122 (oso) | ISBN 9780190612092 (cloth : alk. paper)
Subjects: LCSH: Music, Greek and Roman—Performance.
Classification: LCC ML169 (ebook) | LCC ML169 .D67 2018 (print) |
DDC 780.938—dc23 LC record available at https://lccn.loc.gov/2018016172

9 8 7 6 5 4 3 2 1

Printed by Sheridan Books, Inc., United States of America

μνάσεσθαί τινά φαιμι καὶ ἔτερον ἀμμέων

Someone will remember us

I say

even in another time

—Sappho, *If Not, Winter*, frag. 147, trans. by Anne Carson

ἔλθε μοι καὶ, χαλέπαν δὲ λῦσον
ἐκ μερίμναν, ὄσσα δέ μοι τέλεσσαι
θῦμοσ ἰμέρρει, τέλεσον, σὺ δ' αὖτα
    σύμμαχος ἔσσο.

Come to me now again and deliver me from oppressive anxieties;
Fulfil all that my heart longs to fulfil, and you yourself be my fellow-fighter.

—Sappho, *Greek Lyric I*, last stanza from frag. 1, translated by David
A. Campbell

CONTENTS

FIGURES

MUSIC EXAMPLES

ACKNOWLEDGMENTS

It is with great humility that I thank all of my collaborators in this project, for what good is a scholar without artists, archivists, librarians, audiences, friends, family, and readers to work with and for? I acknowledge the work and the generosity of archives, museums and libraries that opened their doors to me. Thank you to the librarians, archivists, preservationists, curators, and staff at the following institutions: The Smithsonian Institution Archives (especially Tad Bennicoff); the Bibliothèque littéraire Jacques Doucet in Paris (in particular former director M. François Chapon); The Library of Congress Music and Prints & Photographs Divisions; The Bibliothèque-Musée de l'Opéra in Paris; the Special Collections Library at the University of Wisconsin, Madison; the Historical Archives of the Benaki Museum and the staff at Delta House in Kifissia, Greece (special thanks to Dr. Maria Dimitriadou), and the staff at the Delphi Archaeological Museum in Delphi, Greece. None of my trips to the archive would have been possible without the generous and continued financial support of the University of Dayton, including the University of Dayton Research Institute, the College of Arts and Sciences, and the University of Dayton Department of Music.

Colleagues at University of Dayton from upper administration to faulty, students, and staff to office workers and janitorial staff have supported me in this work. Special thanks go to my UD colleague Heather MacLachlan, and to department chairs Sharon Gratto and Julia Randel. I've been very lucky to collaborate with wonderful area musicians who helped me, namely my colleague at UD, Ryu-Kyung Kim, who sang the Reinach/Fauré version of *L'Hymne à Apollon* for me; instrumentalists Leslie Stratton, Christopher Chaffee, John Kurokawa, and Jeffrey Carwile for playing with her; and my former student Bobby Trick for recording. My colleague at UD Toby Rush is responsible for creating the special ancient Greek music fonts for this book.

I am thankful to the faculty and students at Tufts University and Northwestern University, where the initial ideas for this book were born out of my graduate work. Students and faculty at Case Western Reserve University, The University of South Carolina, Boston University, and Youngstown State University, invited me to share portions of the book with them while I was still beating around ideas and for that I am very grateful.

Other colleagues and friends have all contributed to this project in unique ways. Some read portions of the manuscript, some answered questions, some chatted over coffee, and all through their generosity provided encouragement and guidance in multiple ways: Carlo Caballero, Daniel Callahan, Christophe Corbier, Sam Dwinell, Karen Eliot, Louis Kaiser Epstein, Lynn Garafola, Sarah Gutsche-Miller, Elissa Harbert, Hanna Järvinen, Karla Jay, Marian Wilson Kimber, Cassandra Langer, Artemis Leontis, Jann Pasler, Mary Simonson, Suzanne Rodriguez, and the two anonymous readers of the manuscript. Thank you to the staff and production team at Oxford University Press: production editor, Tharani Ramachandran; copyeditor Sharon Langworthy; indexer Rachel Lyon; and especially my great editor at Oxford University Press, Norm Hirschy. Norm has made the whole process from start to finish enjoyable. I am grateful for his faith in this project from the very beginning!

Last I wish to thank my family. My parents Judy and Marty Dorf, my brother Ben Dorf, my mother-in-law Victoria Kisel Carman, and my amazing children Jonah and Lana have all been good sports while I worked on this project and showed me love even when I was boring them with details about ancient Greek music notation. This book would not have been possible without the constant love and support of my wife, Masha Kisel. She read every draft and talked through every idea with me over breakfast or dinner, much to the frustration of our kids. She has been my most trusted reader and my best friend through the whole process. Thank you Masha for everything, especially for convincing me to use the term *anaphrodisiac* in the final chapter of this book instead of the much more crude phrase I originally came up with. This book is for you.

1 | Musicology, Archaeology, Performance
MODELS AND METHODS

To ACCESS THE ARCHIVES of the Bibliothèque-musée de l'Opéra at the Palais Garnier in Paris, you have to enter on the west side of the building on rue Scribe. Flash your identification card to the guard, and you can skip the line of tourists and head up one of many elegant staircases in the building and find your way to the quiet hallways filled with some of the more visually appealing items of the collection. En route to the reading room you pass the expected volumes of luxuriously bound books and scores, portraits of former stars of the opera and ballet, and some memorabilia, but also an enchanting and unexpected collection of maquettes (scale models) of set designs smartly housed in wooden cabinets lining the wall. Most adults need to crouch down a bit to really take in their effect. Delicately constructed out of paper, thin pieces of wood, and paint, the model stages with painted curtains are like miniature worlds. Peering into them, you can imagine yourself on the stage of Wagner's *Tannhäuser* or Verdi's *Aida*. Some of these models have little paper cutout trees and mountains; others feature ships, temples, and towering cathedrals. You can also visit the gallery in the comfort of your own home via Google Arts & Culture, which provides an almost virtual reality "street view" of the museum. If you hold your face close enough to your computer screen or smartphone, you can imagine being there in the museum, being there on the stage.[1] Similarly, a visit to Athens, Greece, is not complete without a trip to the new Acropolis museum, where you can walk around a reproduction of the exterior of the building and see at eye level the remaining marbles preserved from the building. Google also provides a "street view" of this exhibit allowing a "being there" experience similar to that of the models in the Bibliothèque-musée de l'Opéra in Paris.[2] The museum in Athens has models of the archaeological site as well, similarly protected by glass (even one made entirely of LEGO bricks, populated by tiny ancient Greek minifigures). You can similarly press your nose up to the glass (the protective shield of the model or the glowing smartphone screen) and imagine being there. You could even use the

Google app to tour the British Museum's Elgin Marbles while walking around the Parthenon itself in Athens. With a smartphone and a little imagination, you could perform a virtual repatriation of the contested bas-reliefs: the virtual marbles inserted into their real surroundings as an act of historical correction/ completion. The doubling effect of the models (reproductions) standing so close to the real thing (archives) reinforces the distance between the archives or ruins that scholars consult and the performance of those materials on an opera stage, in a concert hall, or in a museum. In both scenarios, someone else, an artisan or a performer, needs to work with the scholar to bring the past to life. The models are constructed for various purposes. While the ones at the Bibliothèque-musée de l'Opéra are blueprints for set constructions, the LEGOs in Athens are the reconstruction of a ruin. Today, both types of model function similarly for their audiences as miniature spaces for imagination, fantasy, and dreams of a constructed past. The models help us to not only see the past but also imagine ourselves as part of this past, to engage in play. They allow museum visitors and curators, scholars and performers, to experience and perform their own visions of the past in their minds just by pressing their noses against the glass.

This book examines the moment in archaeology and musicology at which performance, experimentation, and play served as critical heuristics in the production of scientific knowledge. It does this by examining the collaborations between French and American scholars of Greek antiquity (archaeologists, philologists, classicists, and musicologists) and the performing artists (dancers, composers, choreographers, and musicians) who brought their research to life. This book takes a comprehensive view of the collaborative process of reconstruction within the Parisian community of artists and scholars interested in Greek antiquity. It does not seek to formally analyze the music, the dance, or the costumes of ancient Greek revivals in isolation. I highlight several representative examples of the performance of ancient Greek music and dance culture, including public performances at the Paris Opéra, public festivals staged in ancient amphitheaters, and private performances at the Parisian home of the lesbian American writer and patron Natalie Clifford Barney (1876–1972), whose salon became a site for archaeologists, classicists, musicians, and dancers to embody, perform, and observe ancient Greece in modern France. Such musical and dance collaborations are built on reciprocity: the performers gain new insight into their craft while learning new techniques or repertoire, and the scholars gain an opportunity to bring theory into experimental practice; that is, they have a chance to see/hear/experience what they have studied and imagined. The performers receive the imprimatur of scholarship, the stamp of authenticity, and validation for their creative activities. The scholar imagines the past, the performer/artist helps bring it into the present, and they can both press their noses to the glass to "be there." History informs performance, and performance informs history. By re-examining century-old collaborations between scholars from across the humanities and artists, this book enriches our understanding of the methodologies of musicology and the uses and abuses of archives and historical performance. It does not shy away from asking what it means to love the past as a scholar, a performer, and a scholar/performer.

Musicology has always had a problem with the past. Scholars of music history have traditionally engaged in the project of historical writing not to affect policy, redraw borders, create social change, or earn fame and fortune. Those may be added benefits, but the primary beneficiaries of the musicologist's slog through the archives are performers who discover forgotten repertoires through scholars' research or reinterpret familiar ones in new ways in light of their scholarship. Similarly, many scholars of music find inspiration in the performances of their scholarly work. The discovery of a new Mozart work may make news, but its public world premier after being lost for centuries is an event—a cause for celebration. These interdisciplinary encounters are intoxicating for both scholar and performer and have sometimes led to a shared illusion of time collapsing, of a corrosion of borders separating the past and the present. Here I examine the blurred lines between scholarship and performance in the recreation of the past. The larger questions seek to understand the relationship between works from the past and performances of works in the present, as well as the relationship between the scholar (specifically the archaeologist and musicologist) and his or her object of study (be it archival or living). Or in other words: How do performers and scholars re-enact the musical past together? This will bring up long-ignored ethical issues. How have past scholars positioned themselves in relation to their objects of study? What happens when the scholar also performs or the performer practices historical work? What happens when sexual politics enter the mix?

Make no mistake, this project is not just another opportunity to explain how previous generations of scholars "got it wrong"; the book examines the ways history has been performed in the past and also tries to imagine ways it might be performed in the future. Also, I do not generally approach the works in this book as a musician or dancer. For the most part I have not performed the compositions studied. That said, the approach here owes much to Elisabeth Le Guin's "carnal musicological" study of Luigi Boccherini's cello works that bring fleshy, sensual, passionate, bodily knowledge to the composer's compositions. Her readings of and "trysts" with Boccherini produce vividly personal analyses informed by static scores and her own fleshy body.[3] Preemptively defending her readings against those who might dismiss her work by claiming "that what appears above is not musicology, not history, but an exercise in narcissistic free association by a particularly verbose performer," she proposes performance and analysis as two faces of interpretation that pile on readings to smother out the idea of an authoritative reading.[4] Like Le Guin's study of Boccherini, this book also seeks to answer the calls by Suzanne Cusick and William Cheng to forge a reparative musicology: a musicology that not only is not paranoid, or accusatory, that accepts all kinds of scholarship (and performance), that can be personal, intimate, and even political, but also does some of the work of mending, repairing, and reconciling.[5]

The paranoid and reparative modes of reading, concepts discussed by Eve Kosofsky Sedgwick since at least the early 1990s, are not necessarily antithetical.[6] While a paranoid reading values the revelation of hidden meanings, the belief that the exposure of the hidden will itself solve problems, and the belief that the audience of the criticism would be unable to discover this on their own, a reparative reading suits the reader and the object being read; it is an act of love and concerns itself less with standing out from other voices.[7] For Sedgwick, a reparative mode of reading was "[n]o less acute than a paranoid position, no less realistic, no less attached to a project of survival, and neither less nor more delusional or fantasmatic."[8] The paranoid and reparative are impulses toward objects of study and the ways readers situate their own authority. We should not outright dismiss the paranoid. Criticism (the product of the paranoid reading) offers privilege to the critic, proudly stating what the thing is, whereas those pursuing a reparative reading seek, as Robyn Wiegman has written, "new environments of sensation for the objects they study by displacing critical attachments once forged by correction, rejection, and anger with those crafted by affection, gratitude, solidarity and love."[9] Throughout this book, and most important, in the conclusion, I perform both modes of reading but am drawn to the reparative, not because I believe reparative strategies of scholarship will save us from the abyss of hermeneutic meaninglessness, but because I believe that reparative strategies are useful when writing about fellow scholars and performers (living and dead). Reparative readings of reconstructions also shift discussions away from what others did wrong and toward what we can do with reconstruction.

While it may seem self-evident to many that reconstructions (be they musical, choreographic, personal, intimate, or political) are inherently revisions, this was not always a foregone conclusion. Examining the nexus of performance and history at the birth of modernism may also provide insights into the ways the act of performance and the idea of antiquity shaped the modernist project in the first decades of the twentieth century. At the end of the nineteenth century new technologies seemed to offer the promise of bringing back the dead. Building on theoretical and historical studies on music and dance performance practice, as well as research on historical re-enactment and performance studies, this book explains how scholarly methods (new empirical approaches to music history) and technologies (mainly photography) altered the performance and, ultimately, the reception of music and dance of the past. As scholars from a variety of disciplines continue to join together to reconstruct the past anew, fin-de-siècle France offers lessons on potential relationships among scholars, performers, and their objects of study. Acknowledging and critically examining the complex relationships performers and scholars had with the pasts they studied does not undermine their work. Rather, under-standing our own limits, biases, dreams, obsessions, desires, loves, and fears enriches the ways we perform the past.

In the late nineteenth century both musicology and archaeology were dominated by men. This book, however, is primarily focused on women: women who read Greek, women who danced antiquity, women who sang antiquity, and women who lived an antiquity-inspired lifestyle. The an-tiquity most often invoked by the participants of this book is very often a woman-centered version of ancient Greece in which Sappho's works take precedence over Sophocles's and Penelope is the hero, not Odysseus. These women who engaged with antiquity performed the Greece they wanted. It is not an issue of correct or incorrect performances of antiquity, but rather of my performance of antiquity versus yours. In this story, women are most often performers but also performer-scholars, writing and enacting the narratives of antiquity that resonate with them. These women's narratives of antiquity, performed in private or published in smaller presses, differ from the more traditional narratives of antiquity found in histories and monumental stage works written and performed by men. While they differ in their focus, they also helped shape the dominant narratives of antiquity written by the men with whom they collaborated.

The women in this book are mostly women who loved other women. Barney identified as a lesbian, and Eva Palmer Sikelianos (1874–1952) had an on-again, off-again sexual relationship with her for many years before she married Angelos Sikelianos and moved to Greece. Together they traced a female lineage, a queer history of antiquity that resonated with their modern hopes and dreams for a brighter queer future. Sappho (c. 630–570 BCE) was their guide. Since she had been dead for millennia, they could only commune with her through the fractured remains of her lyrical oeuvre. Barney always loved Sappho's fragment 134: "I conversed with you in a dream Kyprogenia [Cyprus-born]."[10] In this fragment, sung by the lesbian Sappho dozens of centuries ago, the Cyprus-born is Aphrodite herself, the goddess of love and beauty. For out lesbians like Barney at the turn of the last century, Sappho's fractured poetry, with its open acknowledgment of same-sex relationships, pro-vided a unique model for both life and art. Completing, dramatizing, singing, rewriting, and translating fragments enabled Barney to keep Sappho alive, to converse with her.

While Barney and her circle constructed a private haven for the resurrection of their own army of Amazons, men curious about these alternative versions of antiquity sought access. The women loved each other and ancient Greece far away from the prying eyes of the male gaze, but glimpses here and there from male scholars of antiquity were just enough to spur the imaginations of later scholars hoping to fill in the gaps of our understanding of ancient sex and gender.

In each story of this book, someone is using modern tools to re-enact, reperform, or repair the ancient world—to converse with Aphrodite in their dreams. The storytellers apply the tools of translation to make the past come alive in the present, to make the score, the tablet, or the ruin into a living thing—adored by the ones who created it because they breathed life into it with love. As Pygmalion's story reminds us, "love," whether she's called Venus or Aphrodite, can bring the models of the past to life, but it can also blind us to the fact that at the end of the day we're only staring at LEGO bricks, cut-up pieces of paper, piles of paper, or just cold, hard stone.

This introduction provides historical and theoretical context and sets up the key questions explored in the book. In an interdisciplinary project such as this, it is nearly impossible to provide a standard literature review. I have opted instead to outline a few of the most important voices across a variety of disciplines that have informed this work. Here I highlight the theoretical methodologies by examining in parallel the historiography of musicology, archaeology, and photography in Paris in the 1890s and the first decades of the 1900s. I look at the tools and methods that I use as well as those of the late nineteenth- and early twentieth-century scholars to bring our dreams to life.

Performance Practice and Performance Studies: Re-enactment and Reperformance

This project takes as its premise that "performing" is another form of scholarship. While the academy has established the value and position of performance as postmodern scholarship since at least the 1960s, I set out to unearth the collaborative, creative, and performance-like (or performatic) aspects of historical study (namely reconstructions) that took place at the birth of modernism.[11]

In the 1980s and 1990s Anglo-American musicology wrestled with the waning interest in a "history of style," manuscript study, and other more positivist trends and the blossoming of new approaches to musicology: the "new musicology" that embraced Adorno, gender and sexuality studies, Foucault, hermeneutics, reception history, psychology, and so much more.[12] Essentially, the "new musicology" sought distance from strictly formal analysis of music. Along with new feminist and queer readings of famous musical works, debates about performance practice, namely "authenticity," took center stage in musicological circles.[13] Practitioners of the early or historically informed performance (HIP) movement sought archival sources to inform their performance practice decisions in the reconstruction of familiar works. Musicians experimented with tunings, instruments, tempi, placement of musicians, ornamentation, and venues in attempts to reproduce the conditions of performance at a work's creation. These two seemingly different approaches to musicology are linked. It was only through a broadening of musicology to include areas such as reception studies that scholars could discover some of the conditions of performance informing the HIP movement.

In his critique of the early music movement of the twentieth century, Richard Taruskin makes a distinction between the "authentistic" and "authentic": "The former construes intentions 'internally,' that is, in spiritual, metaphysical, or emotional terms, and sees their realization in terms of the 'effect' of a performance, while the latter construes intentions in terms of empirically ascertainable—and hence, though tacitly, external—facts, and sees their realization purely in terms of sound."[14] That is, Taruskin sees a difference between those in the early music movement who seek to tell history as it "really was" and those who tell it as they "really feel it." "Performers," he writes, "cannot realistically concern themselves with *wie es eigentlich gewesen* [how it really was]. Their job is to discover, if they are lucky, *wie es eigentlich uns gefällt*—how we really like it."[15] Those who claim specialized knowledge about the way Bach might have performed his cello suites could no longer boo the cellist who relied on modern accommodations—an endpin, too much vibrato, and so forth; the way it really was wasn't always right and was not always best. Taruskin's historicizing of authenticity seemed to put the matter to bed in the 1990s. That also means that in this project I do not need to concern myself entirely with which scholar or performer was most authentic in recreating ancient Greek music or dance. Instead I am more interested in performance. Antiquity in this study is to ancient Greece as medievalism is to medieval Europe; that is, antiquity is merely the modern imagined Greek past.[16]

But unlike musicology today, musicology around 1900 centered on performance. Describing the place of musicology in France in 1900, Katherine Bergeron writes:

> It is not stretching the term too far, I think, to consider the idea of musicology as a mode of performance, a particular way of executing music by a body of players—in this case, scholars who would call themselves musicologistes. [. . .] To do musicology requires, in effect, [. . .] a tacit cooperation among players—that underlines all musical performance, a cooperation that rests on established modes on interaction, standards by which players learn to measure their behavior and play in tune.[17]

This early acknowledgment of the performative aspects of *musicologie* (a portmanteau of *musique* and *philologie*) and its uniquely French influences has gone uncommented upon for too long.[18] Now that the "new musicology" is no longer so new, the field can look back on the foundational French methods from the 1880s and 1890s and place them in conversation with those written a century later, the feminist, queer, and performance practice scholarship of the 1980s and 1990s.

One way to bridge the gap between the 1980s and 1990s interests in performance practice and the "new" musicology is by looking at them through the lens of performance studies. The field of performance studies offers new avenues for understanding musical performance. Peggy Phelan's famous insistence that "[p]erformance's only life is in the present"[19] opened the door for scholars to dig into the past and future iterations, reverberations, reperformances, and re-eanctments of performance as works that exist only in the moment. Performance, Phelan states, cannot be saved or recorded. Once documented, the traces of performance are merely a representation, not a performance.[20] While fundamental to a wide range of theoretical positions surrounding performance, Phelan's work has of course been questioned and challenged, notably by Philip Auslander and more recently by Rebecca Schneider, both of whom have questioned the status of the "live" as processed through mass media culture and the durational limits of "liveness."[21] Nonetheless, building upon Phelan's work, Diana Taylor argues for a historical understanding of performance through the use of the archive and the repertoire. In her examinations of traditions of performance throughout the Western Hemisphere Taylor identifies a distinction between an archive and a repertoire as such: "Archival memory works across distance, over time and space[.] . . . What changes over time is the value, relevance, or meaning of the archive, how the items it contains get interpreted, even embodied."[22] The repertoire, "enacts embodied memory: performances, gestures, orality, movement, dance, singing—in short all those acts usually thought of as ephemeral, nonreproducible knowledge."[23] While performance studies may have initially viewed singing (and by proxy all musical performances?) as nonreproducible, the discipline of musicology rests on the reproducibility of fixed musical works and our ability to work concretely with song and dance as archival material. "The rift [between the archive and the repertoire]," Taylor explains, "does not lie between the written and spoken word, but between the *archive* of supposedly enduring materials (i.e., texts, documents, buildings, bones) and the so-called ephemeral *repertoire* of embodied practice/knowledge (i.e., spoken language, dance, sports, ritual)."[24]

Diana Taylor's notion of the archive and the repertoire as analog sites of knowledge and ultimately performance informs my understanding of the performance of ancient Greece in the early twentieth century. While I focus on issues of authenticity and fealty to archival sources in some chapters of this book (the traditional interests of musicology), I offer alternative studies that draw from embodied practice, or what Taylor calls "the repertoire."

One might call the works that primarily draw from the archive "reperformances" and those from the repertoire "re-enactments"; however, just as the archive and the repertoire aren't fixed categories, neither are reperformances and re-enactments. The two examples of models discussed at the opening of this chapter illustrate the differences between these two modes of performance. The miniature opera sets are guides, archival tools for the reperformance of an opera, whereas the LEGO Acropolis is a re-enactment, an imagined reconstruction with LEGO minifigures doing things we can only imagine. Both, however, draw from archival data and embodied practice.

Musicologists and musicians are familiar with reperformances of old works; they do it all the time. The vast majority of music performed in concert halls by major orchestras has been performed before. That is to say, the vast majority of the music we hear live is being reperformed rather than being re-enacted. While we are comfortable trying to embody the structure, feel, and emotions of a musical work, we rarely try to embody the feel, emotions, and movement of a long-dead performer. We do not track the re-enactments of past performances, the occasions when musicians seek to re-embody and re-construct past bodies making music.[25] These are different acts that draw upon different sources. No matter what primary sources the performers use to bring the past (work) alive—be it a musical score (as in a concert performance of a Haydn symphony) or a past musical moment (e.g., the procurement of pe-riod instruments, period clothing, and site-specific performance of a Haydn symphony in a specific room in Esterháza palace lit by candlelight)—both performances draw upon archival and embodied knowledge to build a mean-ingful experience for all participants. Much is lost, but much is also gained in the translation of static or archival knowledge into a performed, dynamic knowledge. Similarly, the codification, measurement, and arresting of move-ment into static data require a translator's talents. Even the most diligent and faithful of performers cannot bring to life a work from the archive without "tainting" it or adding a "patina" to the "work" with our own lived experience and imagination.[26] But again, that isn't necessarily a bad thing; it is essential when performing a work from the past.

When discussing performances of long-dead musical cultures, I propose that although performances rarely draw exclusively from either the archive or the repertoire, we should draw some distinctions between works primarily informed by the archive and those of the repertoire. Performances drawn pri-marily from the archive exist in the form of a blueprint somewhere in a fixed place. Performances drawn primarily from the repertoire require bodily pres-ence in the transmission. Or as Diana Taylor puts it, "As opposed to the sup-posedly stable objects in the archive, the actions that are the repertoire do not remain the same. The repertoire both keeps and transforms choreographies of meaning."[27] This is not to say that archives provide a clear window to the past. They are, as Taylor writes, only "supposedly stable." Michel Foucault earlier questioned the archive's impartiality, writing in 1969 that through its archives, history tries to "'memorize' the *monuments* of the past, transform them into *documents*, and lend speech to those traces which, in themselves, are often not verbal, or which say in silence something other than what they actually say."[28] Even the archive does not remain the same. Re-enactments, I argue, follow different rules and draw upon different inspiration than those works primarily reperformed from the archive. Re-enactment, through its embodied transmission, often has the ability to give participants and nonparticipating viewers a sense of tripping time, of being there, something that reperformance often (but doesn't always) lacks. Re-enactments allow one to converse with the past as if in a dream (Sappho, frag. 134: "I conversed with you in a dream").[29]

In her study of Civil War re-enactors, Rebecca Schneider writes that many feel that "if they repeat an event *just so*, getting the details as close as possible to fidelity, they will have touched time and time will have recurred."[30] The comparison to Civil War re-enactors also highlights the high stakes of their performances. Re-enactors are invested in their performances in ways that traditional stage actors and musicians might not be.[31] As Rebecca Schneider has written, however, it is not just about touching time: "[Re-enactors] also engage in this activity as a way of accessing what they feel the documentary evidence upon which they rely misses—that is, live experience. Many [Civil War re-enactors] fight not only to 'get it right' as it *was* but to get it right as it *will be* in the future of the archive to which they see themselves contributing."[32] Schneider's argument here is quite similar to that of Richard Taruskin (discussed previously) when he sees a difference between those who tell history as it "really was" and those who tell it as they "really feel it." Authenticity in music is not fidelity to the scientific evidence from the past, but rather fidelity to one's own imagined past. It is an authenticity to the self: a willingness to think independently, critically, and creatively. Taruskin's critiques of musical authenticity movements lay the blame squarely at the feet of the twentieth-century modernists. In "The Pastness of the Present and the Presence of the Past," Taruskin has no patience for those seeking complete accuracy who wish to strip modern performances of the "dirt" of the present. He concludes:

> What is thought of as the "dirt" when musicians speak of restoring a piece of music is what people, acting out of an infinite variety of motives over the years, have done with it. What is thought of as the "painting" by such musicians is an imaginary rendering in which "personal choices" have been "reduc[ed] to a minimum," and ideally, eliminated. What this syllogism reduces to is: *"people are dirt."*[33]

Analyzing what he deems "authentistic" performances of early music, Taruskin notes the modernist aesthetics—emotional distancing, execution versus interpretation, and an antihumanist agenda—applied to the music of the past. In the performance of early music in the first half of the twentieth century, Taruskin contrasts what he determines as positivists conducting scientific research (including Nadia Boulanger and her disciples) with those more interested in expression and feeling of early music (Arnold Dolmetsch and Wanda Landowska).[34] These early practitioners and preachers of authenticity in early music carried out their work in France at the same time that the figures in this book embodied, imagined, and played with ancient Greek music and dance. This book applies this friction to the classicism of ancient Greece rather than the classicism of eighteenth-century music, also popular at the birth of modernism.

"Authenticity" exists on a continuum. Some artists try to repeat an event, an artifact, or an act exactly as possible. Others, according to Schneider, "feel that the true spirit of reenactment should be to 'artistically' and 'creatively' *interpret* a precedent act, event, or artwork to make it 'original' again, not to replicate it or 'slavishly' repeat it."[35] The importance of the body in enacting and re-enacting is also critical. In an archival-based musical reperformance, the knowledge source is fixed; it can be reinterpreted, but the notes on the page do not change. The old violin doesn't magically grow an extra string, and the score doesn't spontaneously sprout a new movement. That is to say, on a creative whim, we don't decide to play the Hallelujah chorus from Handel's *Messiah* in a minor key just because we feel like it. Our referents in the archive limit performance possibilities.[36]

Separating the scholar's passions, imagination, and fantasies from the objectivity of historical research poses a problem, but scholars and artists have to create even when they intended to merely recreate or realize. For example, it is often necessary for a dance scholar or a musicologist to imagine the missing notes of a musical score or fill in missing steps in a dance notation score if they ever wish to see the work performed. In dance, theater, and performance art, the bodies of the performers play a critical role in determining the final state of the reperformed work. Choreographers regularly alter choreography in dramatic ways to suit the bodies of those dancing the work. It is not at all uncommon to play with music, plot, and choreography in canonic works like *Swan Lake*. If Odette dies at the end, or the Prince, or both, or neither, it is still the same ballet (it is hard to imagine a *La Traviata* in which Violetta lives).[37] This is not the space to rehash the "authenticity wars" of 1990s musicology, but reframing the question of authenticity in terms of motivations rather than fidelity or outcomes allows us to shift the conversation to the "so what." What are the limits of experimentation, performance, and musicology?

Archaeology, Musicology, and Experimentation in the Belle Époque

In the field of archaeology "performance" also constituted a critical methodology for late nineteenth-century scholars.[38] I see the performance-like aspects of archaeology as a critical concept in my own work on reperformances and re-enactments of the past. The three-dimensional models of archaeological sites popular from the 1870s through the 1930s provided windows into the past and made their way into museums and private collections in the early decades of the twentieth century. The act of constructing visual representations of the past blended art and science and attracted scientists and connoisseurs equally.[39] Like the models of stage sets on display at the Opéra and the LEGO model (among others) of the restored Parthenon in the Museum of the Acropolis in Athens, to take these archaeological models in one had to walk around them, to put one's face up close, to squint and visualize oneself within them. They are miniature stages or playgrounds for a drama or game of the viewer's own fantasy.[40] Models and other visualizations of archaeological data as performed at the end of the nineteenth century, as well as their interpretation, are foundational to modern archaeological practice.[41] The discipline's interest in visualizations of the past mirrored the public's interest. Models of sites found their way from universities to museums and private collections in the early decades of the twentieth century.

The models, however, are also symbolic of an antiquarian strain that many institutions wished to shed in the early years of the twentieth century. For example, the curator, collector, and model maker Hippolyte Augier was employed at the Musée d'Archéologie Méditerranéenne from 1863 to 1889 and created at least seventy-nine such models. Subjects ranged from models of sites as they existed at the time of excavation to dioramas of reimagined and reconstructed villages. Augier and his colleague Abel Maître, who worked at what is now the Musée d'Archéologie Nationale in Saint-Germain-en-Laye, found inspiration for their model designs in existing archaeological sites, recovered and purchased artifacts, and popular science books.[42] While the models were undoubtedly important artifacts in the history of archaeology, twentieth-century archaeologists were forced to admit that they might be more theatrical than archaeological. The fact that many models and other archaeological visualizations remain uncataloged in museums reveals that some modern scholars view these older ways of seeing as commercial rather than scholarly and not worthy of an acquisition number in their own collections.[43] We must also take into account the theatrical nature of these archaeological reproductions; the process of excavation itself was turned into a performance. International congresses of archaeologists abandoned Latin in their official communications and purposefully tried to draw journalists' and nonspecialists' attention to their work. Major excavations were timed for congresses at which tourists and scholars rubbed shoulders. Chateaubriand wrote of the excavations of Pompeii as a "living antiquity" versus the museum of Rome, and models, artifacts, and ruins became important symbolic resources and attractions for tourists.[44] Within a generation the models and dioramas lost their appeal to scientific archaeologists. The new curators at the Musée d'Archéologie Méditerranéenne in the twentieth century openly discredited Augier's work and his models.[45] By the mid-twentieth century one could no longer be an antiquarian and an archaeologist. Models and other archaeological visual media are nonetheless important ways scholars of the past communicated with their nonprofessional peers as well as with future generations of scholars.[46]

Like archaeology, French musicology had an awakening in the waning years of the nineteenth century. On the eve of the twentieth century, Pierre Aubry defined "musicologie" as "all the various manifestations of musical science [. . .] relating to musical history and philology."[47] His research centered on the work carried out by the Benedictines at Solesmes, who stood at the forefront of collecting, transcribing, and printing photographs of antiquarian musics. His work also focused on performance, and as Bergeron has argued his musicology constituted a performance.[48] Similar to archaeology, musicology in France also drew from a more public discourse. Articles penned by critics/musicologists such as Louis Laloy, Romain Rolland, and Émile Vuillermoz populate the early twentieth-century musicological journals as well as the more popular press.[49] Popular journals like *Comœdia Illustré* and *Musica* regularly took up music's history as a topic of interest for its general readers, as did French periodicals like *Le Figaro* and *Candide*. During the Paris World's Fair in 1900, Louis-Albert Bourgault-Ducoudray presided over the Congrès international d'histoire de la musique. Early French musicologists such as Romain Rolland, Julien Tiersot, Jules Combarieu, Pierre Aubry, and Maurice Emmanuel straddled scholarly and public realms just like their colleagues in archaeology. Musicology, slower to take off in France than in German-speaking lands, did not have a chair at the Sorbonne until 1903, with Romain Rolland.

The Germanic roots of American musicology have dominated the narrative of the field's formation, historiography, and methodology. American musicology grew out of the Austro-Germanic tradition of *Musikwissenchaft*—a field of study founded by Guido Adler and primarily concerned with musical paleography in the Austro-German tradition—and to date, American scholars have paid less attention to the French historiography of our own discipline. Whereas the Austro-German musicological tradition in Europe and America concentrated on the creation of critical editions of music of the sixteenth-century Catholic Church, J. S. Bach, Mozart, and Beethoven, the first generation of French musicologists employed an entirely different set of methodologies to explore a far more distant repertoire of musical works: the performances of music and dance in ancient Greece. While nineteenth-century early practitioners of *musicologie* such as Fétis, the Benedictines of Solesmes, and Pierre Aubry followed trends of German musicology, a new generation of French musicologists (Maurice Emmanuel, Théodore Reinach, and Louis-Albert Bourgault-Ducoudray) employed a combination of quantitative experimental procedures (photography, archaeology, and kinesthetic analysis) and their imagination to understand the musical past.

As Jann Pasler has shown, these early French explorations into musicology were able to "embody and recall the past" and "empower a notion of race as an imaginative projection." Music tied to these notions of race was a nationalist project able to construct and document the classical and ancient Greek origins of French musical culture and its centrality to Western civilization.[50] In 1867 François-Joseph Fétis argued to the Société d'Anthropologie and then again in his *Histoire de la musique* that ancient images of music and music making can allow scholars to assess ancient musical cultures, stressing their similarity to modern music.[51] It is still tempting to see ourselves in the past. In our desire to find the historical forbears of our musical traditions, we often mistake what is new or different for something old.

Photographic Authority, or Build Your Own Antiquity

We tend to view photographs found in archives as neutral chroniclers of moments: the photo proves a special occasion (performance, meeting, honeymoon, etc.) that necessitated documentation happened. However, photographs, and the photographers who take them, are not neutral indexers of history and are not purely empirical tools of documentation. Photographs are simultaneously scientific tools and works of art. Photography makes visible, in ways similar to other visualizing strategies explored in this book, imagination and fantasy. In English, *imagination* comes from the Latin (*imaginare*, "to form an image or to represent"), whereas *fantasy* is Greek (Φαντασία, "making visible"). All make images that seem real. The Google Arts & Culture website and smartphone app contain some amazing features, but neither replaces going to the Bibliothèque-musée de l'Opéra or the Acropolis Museum oneself. The digitization of history's treasures makes research easier, but nothing replaces the encounter with "the document itself." Held in one's hands, the treasures of the archive offer more than a microfilm or 300 dpi digital scan can. The latter two often miss marginalia, signatures, but also the important "feel" of the paper, the binding, the light underlines, and other difficult to discern markings.[52] As Natalie Zemon Davis put it, "In their handwriting, their occasional doodles and asides, [. . .] I have in my hands a link to persons long dead: it strengthens my historian's commitment to try to tell of the past with as much discernment, insight and honesty as I can."[53] Technology can aid the work of scholars, but it cannot fully substitute for the archival pilgrimage.

The documentation of performances with photography is often critical in deciphering their meanings after the fact. While musicology has traditionally relied on the documents containing musical notation, dance has tended to rely on film and photography. The musical sources are blueprints; the dance sources most often document past performances. However, in the early days of musicology in France, musical notation (an ancient form of documentation) was tied to photography (a new form of documentation) as the science of scholarship explored new tools. Late nineteenth-century developments in the use and availability of photography as a tool of research and documentation spurred growth in both the sciences and the arts and humanities. In the 1890s the use of photography spread beyond a circle of specialists, allowing anyone to "point and click." By 1900 Kodak had opened processing and manufacturing sites throughout Europe to handle the demand for professional and amateur photography on the continent. I have examined thousands of photographic images for this project: personal photos taken by insiders/participants in private performances, professional photos meant to document performances of ancient Greek–inspired music and dance, photos taken by archaeologists in the field, and photos taken by musicologists and dancers. The availability of photographic and film technology and its power to capture performance were also critical to the performative and scholarly work of the individuals discussed in this book. Katherine Bergeron discusses the importance of photography as a musicological tool in the work at Solesmes. Dom André Mocquereau endeavored in the late 1880s to publish a series of facsimiles of chant manuscripts "to prove it all, *through the sources themselves*."[54] Similarly, archaeologists used photography, models, dioramas, and other visual representations to make manifest the archaeological past.

To deal with the dualities of photographs as works of art and historical documents, Christopher Pinney proposes that anthropological methods may help:

> If an image that appears to do a particular kind of work in one episteme is able to perform radically different work in another, it appears inappropriate to propose inflexible links between formal qualities and effect. Instead, we need a more nuanced reading of the affinities between particular discursive formations and image worlds that parallel them, as well as sophisticated analyses of their transformational potentialities.[55]

Making photographs is not as simple as "pointing and clicking," but rather involves complex relationships among objects, photographers, and viewers that allow for the image's meaning to constantly shift. Just as the photograph is not an impartial witness to history, it is not always a function of a violent disciplinary "framing" and "exposure."[56] Such approaches, embraced by a group of anthropologists, offer a novel way for musicologists to engage with the parallel indexical and the artistic functions of photographs in our own work. It is not merely enough to acknowledge that a scholar employs a new technology or methodology; it is critical to understand that new tool from a multidisciplinary perspective. That is, a facsimile is not just musicological, but also artistic, historical, anthropological, and more. Photographs are not simply indexical; they carry myriad meanings for their viewers.[57]

The performance of music from the past is a lot like the practice of photography. The sustained encounter with the sonic presence of music written by the dead constantly bombarding our bodies in a concert hall can feel as real as seeing a photograph of the dead. To observe the photographic or musical work as an authentic relic of the past requires a willful denial of reality. Carolyn Abbate casts doubts on the familiar musicological tools and questions our understanding of historical sonic experiences. Questioning acoustic perception and human hearing, she argues, allows us to reconsider "the degree to which historical informant's assertions about sound or listening or hearing are to be taken as realism, rather than as inventions or feints, or (put in a better light) as utopian buoyancies, warding off despair."[58] Similarly, technologies of sound can be "mischief-makers, fabulists, liars."[59] We can't hear the past, but we can enter an imaginative experimental plane of play and understanding. But to lose oneself in the musical plane distorts the fact that we are in a constructed space—a photographic tableau, staged for the viewer.

The camera is *the* truth-telling device, the way to prove you were there and linked to the modern activity of tourism.[60] Tourist photography, like professional musicology, provides an opportunity for a safe amount of distance. As Susan Sontag notes, "Most tourists feel compelled to put the camera between themselves and whatever is remarkable that they encounter. This gives shape to experience: stop, take a photograph, and move on."[61] Those who do archival work are not just scholars but also tourists. Even when traveling across town or across campus to thumb through the archives, they are visitors: at home and yet strangers. Feelings of nostalgia for the worlds that produced the artifacts can mask the position of the scholar in the archive. To document the desired object is, in a sense, to own it or acquire it. One can acquire a work through the embodied reperformance of the work or through the ownership of its physical traces. Rebecca Schneider explains how acquiring another person's movements (a live performance) in "the museal context means acquiring the rights to disseminate the gestures across bodies. That is, the right to the interval—the right to jump across bodies. This is the right to determine whose body will host the work, or whose body will ingest the work as guest."[62] Schneider then opens the door to let us think of the ownership of a document of bodies as linked to the control of real bodies (past and future). As with a pornographic image (digital or analog), owners of photographs can look back at them in the privacy of their homes or offices. They are now theirs.[63] With digital photography, our ability to capture images, manipulate them, and carry gigabytes of archival data around with us has substantially changed the ways we think and work with archives.

If we look at musicology as relational, what happens when we become passive voyeurs? Unlike the ethnomusicologist or the performer/scholar, in the archive musicologists/archival scholars do not typically position themselves as participants-observers, but typically carry out their work as passive observers.

I have peppered this book with my own stories and memories of working in and with archives, not merely to tell anecdotes of my adventures (although that is fun), but primarily because I approach the archival work as ethnographic (often autoethnographic). The archival experiences are critical components of the performance of writing and thinking and of living this project. As a scholar in an archive I participate in the stories I tell, although most often I participate by taking pictures with a smartphone. Sontag again notes:

> Although the camera is an observation station, the act of photographing is more than passive observing. Like sexual voyeurism, it is a way of at least tacitly, often explicitly, encouraging whatever is going on to keep happening. To take a picture is to have an interest in things as they are, in the status quo remaining unchanged (at least for as long as it takes to get a "good" picture), to be in complicity with whatever makes a subject interesting, worth photographing—including, when that is the interest, another person's pain or misfortune.[64]

That is all true as long as the scholar does not tamper with the archive itself. Modern archives have safeguards against such meddling. There are the white gloves to prohibit greasy fingers from damaging the fragile papers and inks. Layers of security ensure that only qualified and verified readers gain access to the holiest of holies. Scholars often need letters, seals, business cards, or a friend to get access to what is needed or what they just want to look at. One archive I visited outside of Athens had three heavily armed police officers protecting a building that housed only a handful of employees. Gatekeepers often prohibit access without reason. One day the documents are too fragile to handle; the next day a different librarian unceremoniously dumps the crumbling pages on your desk. There is safety for both parties (past and present) in the voyeur scenario. You can watch the past dance for you in all its denuded glory, but you can't touch it. As badly as you want to rub the manuscript against your cheek, to feel the paper that Mozart's hand left its mark on, to caress it as if it were Mozart's body itself, you cannot. Tourists and voyeurs are not allowed to do that, but sometimes (when no one is looking) they do. When scholars and performers use the camera to cover up their relationship with their subjects, and when they put down the camera (the scholarly distancing device) and step onto the ruins, the relationship changes. These are the types of ethical considerations and problems that arise in musicology that the discipline is only starting to confront.

Although many of the scholars, artists, and performers discussed in this book perceived photography to be merely an indexical tool, I consider how the photographic image can be a malleable material for the creation of one's desired fantasy of the past. Some scholars discussed relied on high-resolution photographs and on facsimiles, like the Benedictines of Solesmes. In other chapters, personal collections of photographs offer tantalizing evidence of performances imagined and staged and tell stories that the photographers and their subjects may never have intended to tell. When musical sources are silent, photographs of musical performances can sing.

The following chapters all examine performances of ancient Greek music and dance in Paris, France, along with visits to Lesbos and Delphi in Greece. The chapters proceed mostly chronologically, starting in the 1880s with the discovery of ancient Greek music notation in Delphi, Greece, and concluding back in Delphi with performances of ancient Greek theater with music and dance in the Theater of Dionysus in the years between the two world wars.

Chapter 2 focuses on the archaeologist and music scholar Théodore Reinach's (1860–1928) collaboration with composer Gabriel Fauré (1845–1924). In 1894 Reinach asked the composer to create an instrumental accompaniment to a recently discovered second-century BCE hymn dedicated to Apollo in Delphi. Reinach, along with other scholars from the French school of Athens, deciphered the Greek notation from the marble tablets but remarked that "the instrumental accompaniment was missing from the stone: it needs to be supplied."[65] Fauré obliged with a modern accompaniment to the original melody. For Théodore Reinach, the need to re-enact antiquity transcended scholarly interest in his private life. Reinach built a replica ancient Greek villa in the south of France (with a modern piano hidden behind an ancient cabinet) in order to live out his ancient Greek fantasies. This chapter uses the metaphor of the modern piano hidden behind the ancient veneer of the cabinet to explore the ways modern aesthetics lurk underneath the scientific reconstructions of ancient music carried out by Théodore Reinach in the 1890s and 1910s.

Chapter 3 excavates the remaining traces of pseudo-ancient Greek musical and dance performance that took place in Barney's Parisian home at 20 rue Jacob in the first decades of the twentieth century. Barney's discovery of Greek antiquity came about at the same time that she became aware of her own sexual identity. She saw a freedom in the culture of ancient Lesbos and Athens that she felt was lacking in early twentieth-century American and French culture, and she used her passion for studying ancient Greek poetry under the tutelage of the best Greek scholars in Paris to channel both her creative and erotic interests in a very public way. This chapter focuses on the alterity of queer performance and reception within Barney's Parisian circle by exploring how queer influence and identity were mapped in her cultural salon. I apply Elizabeth Wood's concept of "Sapphonics" to the few available musical descriptions chez Barney.[66] The evidence of these performances remains in fragments, scattered across public and private collections, preserved in photographs, memoirs, letters, and anecdotes told thirdhand. I draw on theories of performance and queerness to make sense of the archival materials relating to re-enactment of ancient Greek dance and music hosted at the heiress's home. This illustrates the role of ancient Greek–inspired music and dance in defining queer subjectivity in early twentieth-century Parisian salons.

In piecing together fragments, this chapter offers new ways to think about performance and the archive for musicologists.

Chapter 4 brings dance into the discourse by examining an opera on an ancient Greek subject created by two scholars of ancient Greek music, dance, and history: Maurice Emmanuel, a composer, musicologist, and dance historian specializing in ancient Greek music and dance, and Théodore Reinach, a librettist, archaeologist, musicologist, classicist, and numismatician. It begins by outlining and critiquing Emmanuel's relevant scholarly contributions to the reconstruction of ancient Greek dance and to music history. I then demonstrate how tensions between conflicting trends were manifested in the 1929 production of Emmanuel's opera *Salamine* with a libretto by Théodore Reinach and choreography by Nicola Guerra and based on Aeschylus's *The Persians*. During this time the Opéra had a eurhythmic dance section, a style that Emmanuel and critics such as André Levinson viewed with skepticism. In contrast to the Greek inspirations of Duncanism, Delsartism, and eurhythmics, Levinson used Emmanuel's research to argue that classical ballet was the true inheritor of the ancient Greek tradition. Exploring Emmanuel's aesthetics of dance (ancient and modern) affords a unique opportunity to see how these creative media were theorized and practiced during the eurhythmic years, while illustrating some of the conflicts between abstract and embodied knowledge.

Dance remains the focus in chapter 5. Eva Palmer Sikelianos, along with her husband, the poet Angehlos Sikelianos, founded the first modern Delphic Festival in 1927 in an effort to revive the ancient Greek rites that had been performed on that spot over twenty-five hundred years before. The couple invited the world to convene in the holy city of Delphi for a re-enactment of the performance of *Prometheus Bound* by Aeschylus in the ancient amphitheater, an Olympic-style athletic contest, and an exhibition of Greek crafts. This chapter explores Palmer Sikelianos's choreography, rituals, music, and dramaturgy for her reconstructed *Prometheus Bound* in light of her research on ancient Greek culture, conducted in both Paris and modern Greece. Based on silent film records of Palmer Sikelianos's 1930 festival, her own autobiography, her collaborations with Barney on Greek-themed theatricals in the early 1900s, and comparisons to the movement vocabulary and other contemporary stagings of ancient Greek festivals and sport, I demonstrate how Palmer Sikelianos navigated between the needs and methods of the archaeologist and those of the performer. She blended the oldest sources on ancient Greek ritual music and dance that she could find with what she saw as an authentic "spirit" of Greek culture that she observed in modern Greek society. Her performances drew from archival/archaeological sources (ancient treatises, dance iconography) and lived practices (folk song, modern dance, Byzantine chant traditions). Like the Ballets Russes's re-enactment of ancient Greece in Michel Fokine's *Daphnis et Chloé* and Vaslav Nijinsky's *L'Après-midi d'un faune* (1912) and of pagan Rus' in Nijinsky's *Le Sacre du printemps* [*The*

Rite of Spring] (1913), Palmer Sikelianos's project to re-enact "authentic" Greek theater and choreography illustrates that theories of theatrical historical reconstruction in the early twentieth century were heavily influenced by contemporary theatrical, political, and social events. And like the Fokine and Nijinsky models, Palmer Sikelianos's staging redefines ancient dance through the prisms of ancient sources and modern concerns.

The concluding chapter directly addresses the relationship between the scholar and his or her object of study. In two parts, I look at the relationship between the Parisian archaeologist and art historian Salomon Reinach (1858–1932) and Barney before turning to analysis of contemporary collaborations between musicologists/dance historians and performers. In order to better understand ancient Greek artistic and social life, Reinach (the scholar) attached himself to Barney (the living embodiment of the past) and the queer women who performed pseudo-ancient Greek music and dance at her Parisian home (namely, the dancers Régina Badet and Liane de Pougy). Their correspondence reveals a complex system of reciprocity in the relationship of the scholar, his object of study, and the individuals with the power to embody the past through performance.

The Barney-Reinach relationship reminds us to continually interrogate the ways we perform our scholarship today. As musicologists engage more in the creative realizations of their scholarly projects, and as musicological arguments find their way into performances, the negotiations between the performer and the scholar in the days when the discipline of musicology was forming will prove insightful. Recent calls for a reparative instead of a paranoid musicology emphasize the role of love in the work of music studies. The conclusion echoes calls for a reparative mode of scholarship, but one that doesn't ignore the blinding powers of that love.

2 | Gabriel Fauré and Théodore Reinach

HIDDEN PIANOS AND *L'HYMNE À APOLLON*

A GLEAMING WHITE PALACE, VILLA KÉRYLOS in Beaulieu-sur-Mer (an aptly named town on the French Riviera) sits on a bluff overlooking the crystal-blue waters of the Mediterranean. Like its neighbor, Villa Ephrussi de Rothschild, Villa Kérylos showcases the splendors of an age of wealth and prestige. For six years beginning in 1902, the ancient historian, numismatician, classical philologist, librettist, and musicologist Théodore Reinach worked closely with the archaeologist and architect Emmanuel Pontremoli to build his very own second-century BCE Greek nobleman's villa. Reinach spared no expense and attended to the smallest details: delicately veined and soft white Siena and Carrera marble covered the walls, and rose-wood and Ceylon lemon furnishings inlaid with ivory and coral decorated the rooms. Each step in the building and design of the house was an experiment in historical reconstruction. Craftsmen meticulously recreated tables, chairs, and beds based on ancient models. Reinach supervised the work, seeking to create "a model of archaeological recovery"; nothing was left to chance.[1]

Built around a peristyle, the villa contains a library and a *triklinos* (banquet hall) as well as private chambers.[2] Théodore called his own bedroom the "Erotès"—dedicated to Eros—which featured mosaics of Dionysus; he decorated his wife's chambers with peacocks and swans in honor of the goddess Hera. Modern reproductions stand next to examples from Reinach's own collection of ancient treasures: amphorae, Tanagra figurines, and other relics. Historically appropriate low tables and beds furnished the rooms; authenticity was not sacrificed for modern comforts. Of course certain hygienic concerns had to be addressed; in the otherwise authentic *balaneion* (men's bathhouse) were discreetly hidden modern faucets and plumbing behind grills. One other modern device remained concealed from view: in the *oïkos*, or family room, a lemonwood cabinet contained a specially designed Pleyel piano built to Reinach's specifications in 1913 (see figures 2.1a and b). Once the cabinet doors are opened, small knobs allow the player to pull out the keyboard, a

FIGURE 2.1a AND b Hidden Pleyel piano in lemonwood cabinet built for Théodore Reinach's Villa Kérylos (1913), shown open and closed. © Colombe Clier/Centre des monuments nationaux.

small box on the floor is pushed aside to reveal the pedals, and a wrought-iron music stand unfolds. The cabinet is beautifully inlaid with Greek geometric patterns and sunburst designs, and is signed in Greek by Pleyel (ΠΛΕΙΕΛΟΣ ΕΠΟΗΣΕΝ).

Today the secret piano stands against the wall in the small room, its authentic ancient veneer disguising its modern interior. Théodore Reinach's piano reminds us to look underneath the hood of historical reconstructions. It reminds us to dig deeper into how scholars of antiquity, musicians, composers, dancers, choreographers, and their patrons sought to reenact the musical past through performance and modern technologies.

This musical contraption can also be seen as the inverse of Carolyn Abbate's *tombeaux* (the musical and architectural containers that house a mysterious past, a musical work written in memory of someone who has died). In Abbate's configuration, *tombeaux* are like phonographs, or other musical machines that bring back something that is gone—the style of a beloved teacher, for example, as was the seventeenth-century tradition. The musical past is made manifest through some modern device in the present.[3] However, Reinach's piano (as "musical *tombeau*") does not bring back something from the past into the present, but rather hides the present from the past. Reinach's home, with its mixture of ancient artifacts and hidden modern modifications and reconstructions, provides the ideal domestic environment to consider the scholar's own methodology for editing and performing the music of ancient Greece, as seen in his edition of the first of two second-century BCE hymns to Apollo discovered in Delphi in 1893. Reinach's treatment of the musical sources—his diplomatic transcriptions, and performing editions with musical accompaniments composed by Gabriel Fauré—demonstrates how a modern scholar employed modern methods and aesthetics for the preservation and performance of ancient musical works. Reinach's editions perform two tasks: like the hidden piano at Villa Kérylos, they are presented as accurate, diplomatic reproductions of musical works, but examination of the editorial process and accompaniments reveals an obfuscation and reinvention of the ancient musical source material to align with contemporary understanding of modern French and ancient Greek musical aesthetics. This is not to say Théodore Reinach was a bad scholar, or sloppy, or dishonest (he may have been). Perhaps he loved his objects of study too much (Is there such a thing?) and was unable to see the faults in his argument within his own creations. Reinach's scholarly revisions emanate from his desire to re-enact the past, to perform it, to surround himself with his object of study, which may be an inclination modern academics share with their scholarly progenitors. If mistakes were made, why? What led Reinach to see the musical past in this way?

Neoclassicism and Historical Performance

The performance, reproduction, obfuscation, and reinvention of the past in modern music are perhaps the most significant features of musical neoclassicism. But composers have memorialized the musical past in so many diverse ways. As Tamara Levitz has argued in *Modernist Mysteries: "Perséphone,"* defining musical neoclassicism requires a more nuanced understanding of the subjectivities that comprise it.[4] And so Reinach's piano, with its uncanny combination of past and present, represents just one image amid the myriad ways one could be neoclassical in the early decades of the twentieth century. A catch-all term used by historians of musical form and theorists to describe all sorts of works written in the twentieth century that reference earlier musical forms, *musical neoclassicism* does not have a unified aesthetic and may not be a genre at all.[5] Scott Messing, Richard Taruskin, Martha Hyde, Carolyn Abbate, and Tamara Levitz have all underscored the cacophony of voices trying to edge their way into the neoclassical debates when they have asked, each in his or her own way, "What does it mean to invoke the past? What past? How? When?"[6]

Challenging notions of what musicology thinks of as neoclassicism (the Stravinsky-Schoenberg traditions of the post–World War I years), Théodore Reinach and his colleagues sought not to encase the past in tombs, but rather to re-enact antique sensibilities in the present. Unlike neoclassical works from the fin de siècle and early twentieth century, Reinach and Fauré's collaboration attempts to bring long-silent ancient Greek music to modern audiences in traditional performance venues and in scholarly colloquia. It does not evoke Greece, it does not borrow old styles or forms; it *is* the real thing (at least in the minds of its editors). The ancient notes are deciphered and made manifest through performing bodies. The dead have come alive.

A traditional understanding of musical neoclassicism posits that underneath the surface of these uncanny, "emotionally detached" musical works lurks the past with all of its nostalgia and melancholy. In the modern performance of ancient Greek music it is not the outside containers—for example, the lemonwood cabinet—but the inner workings of the machine that remain uncanny, the modern hand of the editor and the commissioned accompaniment lurking underneath the false patina of the past. The lemonwood cabinet performs the same double duty: it protects the past from the hand of the present by maintaining the authenticity of Reinach's ancient Greek villa. Reinach's piano begs us to ask what kind of past this is that hides the comforts of the present, to preserve a fantasy of the past.

During the fin de siècle, ancient Greek-themed art, music, and dance often took on a notoriously decadent and erotic character, and many of the artists and scholars mentioned in this book took part in these activities, either on public stages or in private salons;[7] however, scholars of ancient Greek dance and music, such as Théodore Reinach and his older brother Salomon, discussed their work in terms of "science" and "research" in order to protect images of antiquity from being seen as a cipher for their subjective motivations for resurrecting the past. For the most part, Théodore Reinach's academic work was rooted firmly in the methods of social science and philology rather than in performance.

Théodore Reinach was the youngest of three brothers, all distinguished in the fields of archaeology, history, and classics. Known collectively as the know-it-alls ("**Je**-**S**ais-**T**out," representing the first initials of their names), Joseph, Salomon, and Théodore Reinach shaped French humanistic thought in the Third Republic. Ancient Hellenic and Jewish culture was the family business, but each brother approached the ancient world from different disciplinary perspectives. Joseph Reinach (1856–1921) was a lawyer, historian, and politician and an ardent supporter of Alfred Dreyfus.[8] Salomon Reinach (1858–1932) studied archaeology, but his academic interest in the ancient world focused on Greek art as well as philology. Like his brothers, he was also involved in Paris's Jewish community, served as president of the Alliance Israélite Universelle, and was active in the Société des Etudes Juives.[9] A world-renowned authority on ancient Greek art, Salomon led digs at Myrina, Lesbos, Carthage, and Odessa; taught art and archaeology at L'École du Louvre; and directed both the Musée d'Archéologie Nationale at St. Germain-en-Laye and the journal *Revue Archéologique*. His contributions to the performance and reimagining of ancient Greek will be dealt with in chapter 6. The youngest brother, Théodore Reinach edited numerous scholarly journals (e.g., *La revue des études grecques* and *La Gazette des beaux arts*). He taught comparative religion and numismatics at the Sorbonne (1894–1901), L'École des Hautes Études (1903–1928), and the Collège de France (1924–1928). Along with Joseph and Salomon, Théodore was very active in Jewish causes and was a leader of the Parisian Jewish community. In addition to important translations of the works of Josephus—histories of Asia Minor, early Christianity, and Judaism—Théodore also contributed to musicology, serving as chair of La Société française de musicologie (an offshoot of the Société International de Musique), collaborated with Albert Roussel and Maurice Emmanuel on music for "Greek" operas and chamber works (see chapter 4), studied archaeology and musicology, and became an important scholar of ancient Greek and Jewish coins as well as ancient Greek music, publishing numerous books on both subjects.[10] Aside from their academic credentials, lists of publications, and awards and recognitions, Théodore and Salomon took a keen interest in the private salon of Natalie Clifford Barney and the courtesans who passed through her garden (see chapters 3 and 6).

One of Théodore Reinach's scholarly projects involved the transcription of ancient Greek musical notation. The 1893 discovery in Delphi of new material for decipherment yielded a little-known collaboration between scholar Reinach and composer Fauré. Perhaps inspired by Fauré's pseudo-ancient Greek work *Pavane* Op. 50, written in 1887,[11] with its languid harp-like strings and sinuous woodwind lines, Reinach approached the composer about creating an authentic, "real" instrumental accompaniment to a hymn dedicated to Apollo that was discovered at Delphi in May 1893. Reinach and other scholars deciphered the Greek notation and text from the marble tablet but remarked that "the instrumental accompaniment was missing from the stone: it needs to be supplied"; Fauré obliged, supplying an accompaniment for harp and harmonium (or flute and two clarinets).[12] The first complete performance took place in Paris on April 12, 1894, at l'École des Beaux-Arts under the auspices of the Association for the Promotion of Greek Studies.

Delphic Hymn to Apollo, ca. 127 BCE

Since the discovery in 1893 of the two inscriptions—the longest and most complete extant examples of ancient Greek music—generations of scholars have re-examined them. The fractured remains of the pair of paeans to Apollo were found on the south outer wall of the Athenian treasury at Delphi. Today the Delphic Museum proudly displays the hymns fixed in cement and permanently installed in the museum, but over the past century, due to handling, transportation, and study, the fragments were badly damaged, and the edges of the stones have been lost. Early photographs from when the fragments were first unearthed, squeezes, drawings, and later photographs have aided later generations of scholars such as Egert Pöhlmann and Annie Bélis in the preparation of transcriptions, but there are discrepancies of interpretation and format among these modern transcriptions.[13]

To understand the evolution of Reinach's editorial hand, it is important to first assess, as best as we can *today* in the twenty-first century, what these stones have to say. The distance between the stone markings discovered in Delphi from the second century CE and Fauré and Reinach's *Hymne à Apollon* is great, but the discovery occurred at an opportune time, when it was suddenly possible to hear music from the ancient past using a combination of new technologies and methodologies (namely, photography), imagination, and new sources unavailable to previous generations of scholars and artists. Photography, again, is the technology that allows the scholar to travel to another time.

What do we know about these two hymns today? Interestingly, the two paeans use different notation systems: the first hymn uses vocal notation and the second uses instrumental notation. Both appear to have been written for the Pythic Games of 128/127 BCE, the first hymn composed by Athenaeus, son of Athenaeus, and the second by Limenios, son of Thoinos.[14] In both paeans the melodic line carefully follows the accents of the text, and it is assumed that the melody's rhythm would correspond to the poetic meter. Both hymns are clearly paeonic (the third rhythmic genus recognized by Aristotle and Aristoxenus), that is, in quintuple time.[15]

Due to the damage to the original source, lacunae remain in the transcriptions. In 1893 Reinach provided supplements to the text of the first hymn through line 24, and further scholarship has provided supplements through line 26, but lines 27 through 33 and the two additional smaller fragments, while clearly belonging to the hymn, are lacunose.[16] Despite these gaps a lot can be said for the remaining music. The notation is in the ancient Phrygian and Hyperphrygian modes, and the majority of the extant fragments sound familiarly pentatonic. Sections within the poetic text seem to dictate modulations in the vocal line's key or register. For example, as Pöhlmann and West point out, the opening section (lines 1–8) in Phrygian prepares for a modulation to Hyperphrygian in the next section (lines 9–16) with the insertion of a D♭ in line 7.[17] The second section uses a chromatic tetrachord (C, D♭, D, F) and also employs an accidental B-♮ ten times. The third section (lines 17–24) returns to the notes used in the first section (E♭, G, A♭, C, D, E♭, F, G, A♭), but also has a Hyperphrygian D♭ (more on this note later) and an accidental B-♮, recalling the tonality of the second section.[18] Based on the extant fragments, the severely damaged fourth section (lines 25–34?) most likely shares the Phrygian scale of the first and third sections.[19] Text painting appears throughout the setting. The melody climbs up to reach the words "δικορυνβα Παρνασσιδος [double-peaked Parnassus]" (lines 4–5), chromaticism colors the incense smoke wafting from altars and the "weaving shimmering tunes" on the aulos in the second section (lines 9–16). A dramatic octave leap opening the third section washes away the chromaticism as the text invokes the "τεχνιτων[20] [chorus of professional singers]" and their glorification of Zeus.[21] The last few lines of the stone are too damaged to render a reasonable reading of the text or music.

Fauré and Reinach's *Hymne à Apollo*, 1893/1894

Over the course of two decades, Théodore Reinach published a series of editions of this work, the first hymn to Apollo. His first edition and essay on the musical text appeared along with Henri Weil's edition of the poetic text in the 1893 issue of the *Bulletin de Correspondance Hellénique*.[22] Later editions appeared in 1894 (with an accompaniment by Fauré),[23] a significantly revised edition appeared in 1911 in the scholarly *Foilles de Delphes*,[24] and Fauré's accompaniment was reworked to fit the revised edition in 1914.[25] Most significantly, the revised editions of 1911 and 1914 reordered the two largest

TABLE 2.1 Comparisons of Editions of the First Delphic Hymn to Apollo

PÖHLMANN AND WEST (2001)	REINACH (1893)	REINACH, FAURÉ, AND WEIL (1894)	REINACH (1911)	REINACH, FAURÉ AND WEIL (1914)
Col. i, lines 1–8	"B" mm. 67–95[a]	"B" mm. 23–52, and "E" mm. 86–113	"A" mm. 1–28	"A" mm. 1–31 and mm. 88–117
Col. i, lines 9–16	mm. 96–123	"C" mm. 53–81	"B" mm. 29–57	"B" mm. 32–60
Col. i, line 17	mm. 124–127	"D" mm. 82–85	mm. 58–61	"C" mm. 61–64
Col. ii, lines 18–23	"A" mm. 1–21	"A" mm. 1–22	mm. 62–83	"CHŒUR" mm. 65–87
Col. ii, lines 24–25	mm. 22–27	not set	mm. 84–91	not set
Col. ii, lines 26–33	mm. 28–62	not set	not included	not set

[a] Reinach mistakes the title inscription for poetic text in this edition, which appears as text with musical lacunae in mm. 63–66.

stone fragments (See table 2.1). Studying the evolution of Reinach's *Hymne à Apollon* reveals the way modern aesthetics creep into the reconstruction of ancient music—how the scholar seeks to conceal the modern under the cloak of the past. And while Théodore Reinach did edit other fragments of ancient Greek music throughout his career (e.g., *L'hymne à la Muse* in 1896 and the second Delphic hymn in 1897), the first Delphic hymn with Fauré's accompaniment most clearly illustrates Reinach's method of updating antiquity for modern performance.

Dwarfed by Fauré's large-scale "ancient Greek" endeavors, namely *Prométhée* (1900) and *Pénélope* (1913), Fauré's contribution to the *Hymne à Apollon* has been ignored or dismissed by scholars.[26] While by no means his most inspired contribution, it is not without its charm. It does not neatly fit into our narratives of Fauré at this time, and its absence from the critical literature emphasizes this work's marginal status. We can't look at it as another Fauré *mélodie* if the melody was written two millennia ago; moreover, the accompaniment is not like other works in Fauré's œuvre. Compared to contemporary works such as *Cinq mélodies "de Venise"*, op. 58 (1891), and *La bonne chanson*, op. 61 (1892–1894), Fauré's *L'Hymne à Apollon* is backward looking. Thus, it is easy to relegate it to the periphery or dismiss it outright, as in the following example from Graham Johnson's study of Fauré's songs:

> Fauré harmonises this strange work (mainly in the Phrygian mode) more successfully in the hymn's first three pages, when the accompaniment is in simple chords. This dubious result is hardly helped by the extraordinarily long sentences in the French translation of Eugène d'Eichtal. Everything attempts

to be so faithful to what was then perceived as authentic Greek performing practice that this work, impossible to shorten, is unsustainable on the concert platform—outside the kind of specialist seminar in which it was first performed.[27]

Fauré's purported faithfulness to authenticity appears to prohibit a credible concert performance. Johnson here exaggerates the gulf between the audience of archaeologists and musicologists at a specialist seminar and a concert hall of music lovers. And while these arguments conjure up debates in musicological circles about the limits of hermeneutics,[28] I think we can safely say that it is indeed possible to appreciate musical works both as a scholar and as a performer or listener. Or as Karol Berger has said, "We cannot help it: We are hermeneutic creatures through and through."[29] That, however, does not diminish the power of listening and performing, and the ability of music to transport us to a different time and place. This phenomenon is not limited to the listener, but yes, even musicologists get caught up in the performance, and Reinach (as evidenced by his own home) was prone to get caught up in the performance of ancient Greece.

We can imagine Théodore Reinach stepping aside at the April 12, 1894, meeting of l'Association pour l'encouragement des études grecques to let Mme. Jeanne Renacle "faithfully" sing this purportedly authentic Greek work, accompanied by Fauré on harmonium and M. Robert on harp.[30] After delivering his lecture on the first Delphic hymn, Reinach most likely left the stage to listen, and like the rest of the scholarly audience in attendance, he probably imagined himself transported to ancient Delphi. Perhaps he imagined Mme. Renacle draped in a Greek gown accompanied by kithara and aulos players leading a procession of supplicants up the steep slope of Mount Parnassus. Maybe they paraded along the sacred way past the Sibyl Rock, weaving among cypress trees toward the Athenian Treasury and to the Temple of Apollo. Did Reinach close his eyes during the performance? It is almost difficult not to imagine its original setting upon listening to it. That, Nick Wilson argues in *The Art of Re-enchantment*, is one of the reasons we perform music of the past, to find that sense of authenticity lost in our modern life: to negotiate the drive to make art and to bring art into our lives.[31]

On the other hand, we could also imagine that Reinach experienced the performance of his hymn the way a historical re-enactor may seek out "period rush": the desire, as described by Rebecca Schneider, to "try to bring that time—that prior moment—to the very fingertips of the present."[32] For re-enactors, it is not just about touching time; they "also engage in this activity as a way of accessing what they feel the documentary evidence upon which they rely misses—that is, live experience. Many [American Civil War re-enactors] fight not only to 'get it right' as it *was* but to get it right as it *will be* in the future of the archive to which they see themselves contributing."[33] Performance has the power to fix ideas about the past in the present, but also to facilitate messy interactions between real and imagined pasts and presents.

While Reinach clearly fell deeply under the spell of re-enactment at home at Villa Kérylos, in his professional life the Parisian scholar viewed his work as rigorous and scholarly. He most likely viewed *L'Hymne à Apollon* from three intricately interwoven perspectives, as scholar, musician, and fan. While Reinach never admitted to the last perspective, his dedicated collection of archaeological specimens from the ancient world and the careful construction of new ones (i.e., Villa Kérylos) attest to the re-enactor's fanaticism. What does it mean to be all three at once (scholar/musician/fan)? In his *Divas and Scholars*, Phillip Gossett opens with a preface on the "three elements of [his] operatic being," which are now "hopelessly merged."[34] The resulting study shares insights from his triple position, something scholars today feel comfortable doing. Gossett's fanboy honesty is refreshing and begs the question: Why shouldn't we be "fans," "enthusiasts," "supporters," or advocates of what we study?[35] Théodore Reinach's deep and profound love for Greek antiquity takes fandom to new heights, allowing us to view his editing and transcription of *L'Hymne à Apollon* as not only his object of study, but also a creative work and a collectible relic.

As editor, Reinach engages in a textual criticism that seeks to mediate between an ancient music-maker and a modern music-making audience. His emphasis is for the most part on performance. His criticism, annotations, and corrections emphasize the *performance* of this music, even when his editions are not traditional performing editions. Reinach's transcription and completion of the damaged sections of the ancient Greek melody is simple in its shape and rhythm; he retained the quintuple time and the Greek text setting. His scholarly editions, however, illustrate the scholar/musician/fan's hand in the reshaping of ancient Greek music in a number of places. The restorations of text (in the lyrics and music) may be the most obvious opportunity to see Reinach's approach to this music, but his editions also contain critical apparatus to help the reader peek behind the curtain of scholarship, and it seems just as suited for a scholarly audience as it is for the concert platform.

Reinach acknowledges and explains the complexities of the notation. With multiple realizations of the tetrachord in the Phrygian mode (the ancient Greeks offered three flavors of each mode: diatonic, chromatic, and enharmonic), he concedes that it is difficult to be completely certain which to use here. He dismisses the use of the enharmonic scale for this example because it was out of fashion at the time of composition, and he favors the chromatic and diatonic interpretations. The secondary arguments show a clear preference for a realization that conforms to modern musical sensibilities and performance. He explains his reasoning as follows, "However, in this case I am inclined to favor the *chromatic* mode, not only because this is the only one playable on our modern-tempered instruments, but also because it is less difficult to sing, and in a piece like this the composer can't accumulate difficulties."[36] Whereas ease of performance may not seem like a reliable argument today, Reinach connects it to the ease of performance in antiquity. It should have been easy to perform then; ergo, it should be easy to play today. Reinach also relies on a "modern ear," a tool used by other music antiquarians, to reperform music from distant pasts and to help solve epigraphic musical problems.[37] Later in the same essay, Reinach notes that this modern ear can help identify an ancient mode when working with an incomplete melody, as is the case with the first hymn to Apollo. When missing musical text, he offers a method to identify mode based on three elements: "1) the tonal impression produced in a modern ear; 2) the last pitch of phrases and important occasions; and 3) the most frequently used note."[38] Here Reinach observes that a section of the hymn gives a tonal impression of C minor: "[I]f you wanted to harmonize the melody, the three chords that would consistently fit harmonically would be C minor, F minor, and G major, that is to say, precisely the three basic chords in the key of C minor."[39] In his discussion of mode and harmony, Reinach continues to emphasize the similarity to C minor, leading him to conclude that the range of this example "is not only similar, but identical, to our C-minor scale. It is a remarkable coincidence here that proves the antiquity and the persistence of the present musical sentiment."[40] The emphasis on "modern" music elevates the example. Reinach notes that the complexities of the chromatic section and modulations are "newer and more unfamiliar, than our usual modern music."[41] The comparisons to modern music lead Reinach to make some unorthodox analogies, in the hope (one imagines) of securing a place for this newly discovered ancient repertoire in the canon. If one were to compare the ancient hymn to modern music, Reinach suggests it most closely resembles certain naïf and melancholy shepherd's songs, but also asks listeners to recognize "a direct ancestor of European music" in the hymn and to seek out "analogues between this air and modern contemporary music." His comparison climaxes in a reference to the English horn solo in the opening of the third act of *Tristan und Isolde*.[42]

Although characterizing the music of the hymn as "naïf," and at times "étranger," Reinach does not view it as particularly foreign. He points out that the hymn "has nothing in common with the vague and floating chants of modern Oriental music, of which a superficial theory would approximate the music of the Greeks."[43] Thus, when Reinach's "modern ear" hears functional harmony in C minor beneath the ancient hymn, and echoes of *Tristan*, that is acceptable. When another modern ear picks up strains of "modern Oriental music," that is (according to Reinach) a superficial theory. Ancient Greek music thus anticipates modern music: a theory of music history shared by Reinach's contemporary and sometime collaborator Maurice Emmanuel (see chapter 4).

He concludes: "But whatever the value of these connections [between the past and the present], one fact remains certain, which gives the discovery at Delphi its high historical and aesthetic value: It is that the musical ideal of the Greeks of the third century BC [*sic*] was very similar to our own: we could not suspect until now, our ideal melodic current principles are the same: the same processes offer surprising similarities."[44] One would think the length and completeness of this very old example of notated music would be enough to demonstrate its importance to fellow scholars, but Reinach argues that not only is it in remarkable condition, it is a direct ancestor of modern music.

We see a further modernization and Hellenization of the hymn in Reinach's discussions of performance practice. Due to the work's range, Reinach discounts the idea of a choral performance; this is most likely intended for a solo voice.[45] He does suggest that an instrumental accompaniment might consist of flutes and a kithara, as referenced in the text (αείολοις and κίθαρις),[46] and justifies the addition of the modern accompaniment to the ancient text, noting the deficiencies in the original:

> The Greek's orchestra was no less flawed than their harmony. Admittedly, they did not designate purely instrumental music; like us, they had concert halls and applauded virtuosi, and their authors have left us the names of a variety of instruments. But under the labels look at the things you will see that all these instruments—at least those commonly used—boil down to just two types: the lyre or kithara, and the flute. However, their lyre had a smaller range than our harp, and their flute less sonority than our clarinet.[47]

Reinach's discussion of instruments, though introduced in a scholarly context, nonetheless speaks to a modern audience. It also prescribes Fauré's instrumentation for the accompaniment.

Reinach divided his transcription into four parts, allowing Fauré to add color and contrast to the structure of the somewhat repetitive ancient melody (see table 2.2). In the 1894 edition sections A and B are accompanied by the harp alone; section C is more chromatic, and this is reflected in a contrapuntal accompaniment for clarinets and flute (or harmonium), with numerous neighbor tones and passing tones emphasizing the contrast to the first two sections; and section D is very short and more declamatory, with the return of the harp and a short addition of the flute before the final E section, which repeats B, but now with a simple flute adding eighth-note movement to the line.

For the accompanied version, the music has been transcribed up a major sixth to suit a mezzo-soprano voice rather than a tenor. Fauré's accompaniment consists of mostly simple arpeggiated triads on the harp. In the first and second sections Fauré stays in A minor with a few enharmonic chords, namely B♭ major chords and a dominant E-major chord, before an inverted authentic cadence at the end of section A and a half cadence at the end of section B. Awkward intervals within the melodic line (e.g., dissonant tritones) are

TABLE 2.2 *Hymne à Apollon: Chant Grec du IIIe Siècle avant J. C.* (1894)

	FRENCH TEXT (1894)[a]	MUSIC
Section A	Dieu dont la lyre est d'or, O fils du grand Zeus! sur le sommet de ces monts neigeux, Toi qui répands sur tous les mortels d'immorales oracles, Je dirai comment tu conquis le trépied fatidique, gardé par le dragon, Quand de tes traits tu mis en fuite le monstre affreux aux replis tortueux.	Mostly stepwise, nonchromatic melody. Accompanied by diatonic chords on the harp.
Section B	O Muses de l'Hélicon aux bois profonds, Filles de Zeus retentissant, Vierges aux bras glorieux Venez par vos accents charmer le dieu Phébus, votre frère à la chevelure d'or, Le dieu qui sur les flancs du Parnasse Parmi les belles Delphiennes Sur la roche à double cime, monte vers le cristal pur Des eaux de Castalie, Maître étincelant du mont à l'antre prophétique.	Style similar to section A: mostly stepwise, nonchromatic melody. Accompanied by diatonic chords on the harp
Section C	Venez à nous, enfants d'Athènes, Dont la grande cité, grâce à Pallas, la déesse au bras vainqueur, Reçut un sol ferme, inviolable. Sur les autels brille la flamme, qui des jeunes taureaux consume les chairs Vers le ciel monte l'encens d'Arabie . . . Le doux murmure des flûtes Sonne en chants modulés, et la cithare d'or la cithare aux doux sons, répond aux voix qui chantent les hymnes.	Chromatic melody with a contrapuntal accompaniment for flutes and clarinet (or harmonium).
Section D	O pèlerins de l'Attique chantez tous le dieu vainqueur!	Style similar to section A: mostly stepwise, nonchromatic melody. Accompanied by diatonic chords on the harp.
Section E	Same text as section B.	Section B, with obbligato flute adding eighth-note movement to the line.

Greek text restored by Henri Weil; translated by Théodore Reinach, accompanied by Gabriel Fauré.
[a] French translation from the Greek by Eugène d'Eichtal.

smoothed out through the accompanying harmony. In music example 2.1, a tritone between mm. 4 and 5 sounds less jarring through the tonicizing triads underneath. A few bars later, between mm. 10 and 11, another tritone appears. The errant B♭ is treated as a ♭II harmonically, thus smoothing out the awkward tritone in the vocal line (see music example 2.2). Last, a G♯ in the vocal line of m. 20 that seems to come from nowhere is employed as part on a B diminished seventh chord in first inversion. This leads us toward the cadence at the end of m. 22, where a G♯ is reintroduced in the E-major chord before resolving to A minor (music example 2.3).

While melodic modal irregularities have been smoothed over by healing tonal harmonies before (see J. S. Bach), Fauré and Reinach's 1894 work does not claim to correct or update the music for the sake of modernity, but is rather offering a suitable accompaniment to showcase the work of the past.

MUSIC EXAMPLE 2.1 Théodore Reinach and Gabriel Fauré, *Hymne à Apollon* (1894), mm. 3–6.

MUSIC EXAMPLE 2.2 Reinach and Fauré, *Hymne à Apollon* (1894), mm. 9–13.

MUSIC EXAMPLE 2.3 Reinach and Fauré, *Hymne à Apollon* (1894), mm. 18–22.

Reinach has not updated or changed the melody (at least not yet); he has only cast it in a different light via the accompaniment in order to best present it to his audience. Like the new museums of the late nineteenth century, the archaeologist's presentation of the hymn is not part of a jumble of curiosities, but sits on its newly created pedestal and is folded into a narrative of contextualization.[48] Reinach pulls another sleight of hand in the 1894 edition. In his 1893 article for *Bulletin de Correspondance Hellénique*, Reinach transcribes only the deciphered musical notation visible on the existing fragments, leaving note stems in the place of pitches for the lacunae. He gives rhythmic values to the lacunae based on stresses in the poetry as completed by Henri Weil (see figure 2.2).[49]

FIGURE 2.2 Théodore Reinach's transcription of *Hymne à Apollon* from *Bulletin de Correspondance Hellénique* (1893).

In the collaboration with Fauré not only are the lacunae completed, but Reinach makes no mention of them in the opening editorial note. The musical score does not give any editorial indication that many of the pitches were not contained in the original source. Reinach only mentions that Henri Weil reconstituted the text and that the accompaniment had been lost. Reinach's melodic completion of 1894 moves primarily stepwise, borrowing gestures from the original source material with leaps of a third, and the occasional fourth or fifth, but those are usually reserved for lacunae at the end of a line or for cadences (see figure 2.3).

The 1894 version not only passes off Reinach's musical completion as part of the original work; it leaves out portions of music and text that had been successfully transcribed in the *Bulletin de Correspondance Hellénique* essay but that for some reason Reinach (or Fauré) deemed unworthy of accompaniment, namely the severely damaged and more chromatic portions of what Reinach had identified as the first part of the hymn (Reinach and Weil later realized they had the stones in reverse order; see below). As the lacunae get larger and the remaining notes become more chromatic, Reinach stops filling them in. After m. 21 in the 1893 transcription, Reinach simply moves on to the next stone, leaving out some particularly interesting chromatic fragments at the end of a predominantly Phrygian section. In the contrasting chromatic section, Fauré replaces the harp with a flute and two clarinets, or alternatively a harmonium on a reedy setting, whose chromatic contrapuntal lines neatly balance the craggy chromaticism in the vocal line (see music example 2.4).

Like Fauré's earlier *Pavane*, op. 50 (1887), the accompaniment to the hymn evokes both the plucked strings and low winds of imagined/idealized antiquity. Where *Pavane* took a pseudo-Verlaine text written anonymously

FIGURE 2.3 Théodore Reinach and Gabriel Fauré, *Hymne à Apollon* (1894), mm. 1–4. Editorial completion of lacunae in m. 2 not indicated.

by Robert de Montesquiou and set it as a baroque dance with a pronounced antique feel, *L'Hymne à Apollon* took a real ancient text and turned it into a courtly and elegant melody with a most traditional harmonic and contrapuntal accompaniment. Despite *Pavane*'s French origins, its text and its early performance history place it closer to Delphi than seventeenth-century Paris. The text opens with an elegy to Greek women—"C'est Lindor! C'est Tircis! et c'est tous nos vainqueurs! / C'est Myrtil! C'est Lydé! Les reines de nos cœurs!"—highlighting its classical origins.

In addition, after *Pavane*'s premier in 1888, the work's dedicatee, the Comtesse de Greffuhle—a friend of the Reinach family—organized a performance at one of her nocturnal parties in the Bois de Boulogne on July 21, 1891, with miming and dancing, and then on December 29, 1895, it was performed as part of a display of "ancient dances" at the Paris Opéra.[50] And so, while its inspirations might have been French, its reception was often antique and seems to anticipate Fauré's *Hymne à Apollon*'s stately harp and the distant, muted flute and clarinets in their low-tessitura. The major difference is that while *Pavane* was written as stylized pseudo-antiquity for after-dark parties for the salon that was the inspiration for Marcel Proust's Duchess de Guermantes, the Comtesse de Greffuhle,[51] Reinach asked Fauré to write "authentic" music to accompany an ancient text for performance at a scholarly conference under the auspices of the Association for the Promotion of Greek Studies.

What is also very striking is how conservative Fauré's accompaniment to *L'Hymne* is in comparison to works like *Cinq mélodies*, op. 58 and *La bonne chanson*, op. 61. In both of these publications Fauré experimented with independent accompaniments, executed novel harmonic turns, and set Verlaine's evocative and decadent poetry. As Carlo Caballero argues, the "stylistic novelty" of works like *Cinq mélodies* helped doom his chances of membership in the Institut de France in 1894.[52] *L'Hymne à Apollon* shares none of these stylistic traits. What might have been Fauré's motivations for taking such a commission form Reinach? Money surely helped. He had a family to support in the 1890s and needed some sort of official, steady income. The setting could also help burnish his academic résumé; after all, Théodore Dubois's election to the Institut de France that year was partly owed to his academic contributions as well as his status as an official musician.[53] Despite this fruitful exchange, when the second hymn in Delphi was discovered, Fauré declined the opportunity to harmonize it.[54] Perhaps he was no longer interested in collaborating with Reinach or no longer felt the need to burnish his academic pedigree or appeal to the academy (he earned his seat in 1909), as he was starting to gain fame through the salon circuit and receiving major commissions, such as *Prométhée* for Béziers.[55]

Fauré and Reinach's *Hymne à Apollo*, 1911/1914

The significantly revised edition of 1911 that appeared in the *Foilles de Delphes* reorders the fragments with the realization that the section with the most missing text followed the more complete tablet (see table 2.1). Reinach notes that at first he thought the opening letters across the two large fragments, ΙΣΤΟΝΘΕΟΝΟ [. . .] ΗΝΑΙΟΣ, were part of the poetry with their musical notes above missing. On closer examination, these letters resemble the title of the second hymn, indicating that it is not part of the text at all, but rather a title: [Παιὰν καὶ ὑπόρχημα] εἰσ τὸν Θεὸν ὃ ἐ[πόησεν | ᾽Αθήναιοσ.[56] With a re-organization of the melody, changes in transcriptions, and a rewriting of some of the lacunae, Fauré's accompaniment had to be tinkered with as well; this was republished in 1914.

In the critical apparatus to the edition for *Foilles de Delphes* Reinach explains more about his methodology nearly two decades later. He credits the poet Eugene d'Eichtal with help in completing the musical lacunae, which now appear in the edition.[57] For the most part, these completions are the same as those seen in the 1894 edition with accompaniment by Fauré, leading one to assume that d'Eichtal assisted Fauré and Reinach then as well. Later that year Fauré would stay at d'Eichtal's home while he worked on his sixth nocturne. Fauré subsequently dedicated the work to his poet friend.[58]

The most significant differences between the 1911 and 1893 editions occur in the second half of the newly revised hymn (what was section A in the 1893 and 1894 editions and now section C in the 1911 and 1914 editions; see table 2.3).

In this section Reinach altered two of the dissonant downward tritone leaps in the vocal line, the first at mm. 3–4 and the second at mm. 9–10 (see music examples 2.5 and 2.6). The first alteration in the first line of col. ii (now known as block "B") (line 18) corrects the Greek symbol I (Db) to a Γ (F). Reinach provides little explanation of this change, but one can presume he based his decision on a closer examination of the sources (better photographic prints and new squeezes).[59] Reinach's correction of the more consonant pitch upon revisiting the source has been accepted by later scholars (including Bélis, Pöhlmann, and West). New pressings and photographic techniques allowed Reinach to determine that a portion of the musical symbol had been broken off.[60] The most surprising alteration occurred a few measures later, where Reinach rejects the clearly engraved symbol Λ (Db) and replaces it with a far more consonant ⋏ (♩). Unlike the previous change, Reinach acknowledges the indicated pitch but insists that the Db was a mistake; the engraver meant to write ⋏ (Ab) (see example 2.6).

Reinach writes, "The Λ (Db) is correct, but it is certainly a stonecutter's error for ⋏ (Ab). Moreover, in this example, the symbol for ⋏ is just like the Λ with a line through it."[61] The argument lacks evidence (the stonecutter didn't appear to have made any other errors), and no other edition retains Reinach's correction. My own appraisal of the extant marble sources in Delphi supports this reading. With my nose millimeters from the exhibit in the Delphi Archaeological Museum, I minutely scrutinized the stonecutter's work. I wanted to find a way to reconcile the source with Reinach's new conclusions; however, the two musical symbols as cut by the engraver are not even remotely similar. ⋏ is not just like the Λ with a line through it. The character that looks like the Greek letter lambda Λ has a narrower angle than that of the upside-down psi ψ; furthermore, it is clear that the stonecutter made a vertical line for the ⋏ first before working the two angles, making Reinach's argument of a supposed error

TABLE 2.3 *Hymne à Apollon: Chant Grec du IIe Siècle avant J. C.* (1914)

	FRENCH TEXT (1914)[a]	ENGLISH TEXT (TRANSLATED FROM THE GREEK)[b]	MUSIC
Section A	O Muses de l'Hélicon aux bois profonds, / Filles de Zeus retentissant, / Vierges aux bras glorieux / Venez par vos accents charmer le dieu Phébus, votre frère à la chevelure d'or, / Le dieu qui sur les flancs du Parnasse / Parmi les belles Delphiennes / Sur la roche à double cime, monte vers le cristal pur / Des eaux de Castalie, / Maître étincelant du mont à l'antre prophétique.	Come forth, ye (Muses) that were allotted deep-forested Helicon, loud-booming Zeus' fair-armed daughters: come to celebrate your brother in songs, Phoebus of the golden hair, that over the twin peaks of this crag of Parnassus, accompanied by the famous maidens of Delphi, comes to the waters of the fair-flowing Castalian spring as he attends to the mountain oracle.	Mostly stepwise, nonchromatic melody. Accompanied by diatonic chords on the harp.
Section B	Venez à nous, enfants d'Athènes, / Dont la grande cité, grâce à Pallas, la déesse au bras vainqueur, / Reçut un sol ferme, inviolable. / Sur les autels brille la flamme, qui des jeunes taureaux consume les chairs / Vers le ciel monte l'encens d'Arabie . . . / Le doux murmure des flûtes / Sonne en chants modulés, et la cithare d'or / la cithare aux doux sons, répond aux voix qui chantent les hymnes.	Lo, famous Attica of the great city is here at prayer, whose home is Athena's invincible ground; and on the sacred altars Hephaestus is burning the thighs of young bulls. At the same time Arabian incense-smoke spreads up to heaven, and the clear-braying pipe weaves shimmering tunes into the singing, while the sweet-voiced golden kithara takes its part in the song of praise.	Chromatic melody with a contrapuntal accompaniment for flutes and clarinet (or harmonium).
Section C	O pèlerins de l'Attique chantez tous le dieu vainqueur! / Dieu dont la lyre est d'or, / O fils du grand Zeus! sur le sommet de ces monts neigeux, / Toi qui répands sur tous les mortels d'infaillibles d'éternels oracles, / Je dirai comment tu conquis le trépied fatidique, gardé par le dragon, / Quand de tes traits tu mis en fuite l'affreux reptile aux replis monstrueux	The whole company of Artists of Attica glorifies you, the son of mighty Zeus, who granted you this snow-capped crag, where you show forth immortal oracles for all men. [We sing] how you took possession of the prophetic tripod that a fearsome serpent guarded, when you removed the earth-born, shimmering, coiling creature, and with charmless hissing it expires.	Style similar to section A: mostly stepwise, nonchromatic melody. Accompanied by diatonic chords on the harp.
Section D	Same text as section A.	Same text as section A.	Section A, with obbligato flute adding eighth-note movement to the line.

Greek text restored by Henri Weil; translated by Théodore Reinach, accompanied by Gabriel Fauré.

[a] French translation from the Greek by Eugène d'Eichtal.

[b] English translation by Martin L. West in *Ancient Greek Music*, 289–292.

MUSIC EXAMPLE 2.5 Editorial changes avoiding tritones in 1911 edition (mm. 62–66) of *Hymne à Apollon* compared to 1893 edition (mm. 1–5).

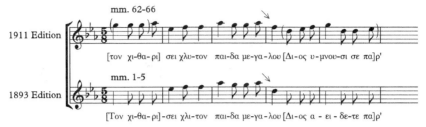

MUSIC EXAMPLE 2.6 Editorial changes avoiding tritones in 1911 edition (mm. 71–73) of *Hymne à Apollon* compared to 1893 edition (mm. 9–11).

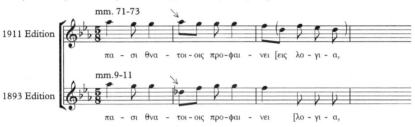

unconvincing. What could then account for the scholar's certainty in the face of such clear evidence? It is literally written in stone.

The source of Reinach's professed certainty most likely comes from the accompaniment, Fauré's tonal panacea to the modal and chromatic melody. Moreover, the reordering of the tablets seems to have inspired a further reworking of the melodic completion that better fits the 1894 accompaniment. The 1914 corrected edition retains Fauré's accompaniment to the newly edited melody. Reinach's new completion of lacunae does not reflect some new evidence; he did not discover new material to fill the gaps. His completion instead uses his favorite tool in the musicological tool chest, the "modern ear."[62]

We have seen this before in the 1894 edition of the hymn. Although col. ii, lines 24–33 are lacunose, Reinach could very well have supplemented lines 24–26. These two lines on the stone are no more incomplete than the first two. Lines 18–19 are missing thirteen syllables of music and text. Lines 24–25 are missing only twelve. Fauré and Reinach most likely did not set these lines, not because so much is missing, but rather because of what remains. In a predominantly pentatonic section (especially in the 1911 version without the tritones), the melody moves chromatically, reaching a high A-♮ on the word "Γαλαταν [Gaul's]" (see music example 2.7). The 1894 and 1914 accompanied editions only set the first two measures of this example, leaving out the remaining chromatic line and the insertion of a new pitch (A-♮). The text does not introduce a new idea either, but rather comments on the previous material.[63] Thus, the only

logical reason to omit these measures is to avoid unwanted chromaticism that might not fit the imagined, idealized, ordered aesthetic of antiquity.

Siren Songs

Let us return to Reinach's piano. For Reinach, the preeminent scholar in his time of ancient Greek music, the modern piano remains hidden in the antique cabinet but fits right into the decor. Fauré's accompaniment functions as a tomb, like Maurice Ravel's *Tombeau de Couperin*, yet whereas in Ravel the tomb makes the relics seem out of place and vulgar, Fauré makes its relics seem less vulgar, less antique, less thorny: counterpoint as aspirin to the headaches of the past. Here the contrapuntal accompaniment blends the craggily ancient melody into the fabric of a popular and accessible music discourse. Remodeling the past to fit the aesthetics of the present was not new; however, Théodore Reinach carried out this process in search of what he envisioned as the real past, not a modern fantasy of it. After all, Reinach and Weil had science on their side; photographs of the stones support their arguments. In his discussion of the hymns, Weil makes numerous references to the power of photography to preserve the damaged stones. Photography "provides physical evidence" supporting the argument that the stone fragments belong together. While textual similarities (argued by Weil) and musical consistency (discussed by Reinach) support these claims, it is photography that ultimately "provide[s] physical evidence" for their editorial adjustments.[64] Reinach's historiographic sleight of hand is obvious to us now. From our vantage point, his teleological thread from ancient melody to Fauré feels slightly forced, and these experimental methodologies do not always stand up to the standards of some modern performers and scholars, as Graham Johnson indicated. That is to say, the curtain is easily pulled back.

That Reinach's *tombeau* at Villa Kérylos takes the form of piano is no coincidence either. As Richard Leppert has argued, the home piano represents domesticity—an "object to be looked at beyond being heard or played upon" and a "visual-sonoric simulacrum of family, wife, and mother."[65] But the eccentric designs and forms of nineteenth- and early twentieth- century pianos could also manifest "reflected and produced associations, both sonoric and visual."[66] A concert grand pianoforte by Alexandre Charpentier from 1902 with scenes from the *Odyssey* around its body and an enraptured nude woman under its lid invites Leppert to recall the Siren Song from the *Odyssey*. "Odysseus [. . .], despising the weakness his desire unleashes, avoids the erotic dangers promised by the Sirens' music. He has his men tie him to the mast so that he can hear the enticing melody but cannot act on it, then commands his men to row close to shore. His sailors are ordered to place wax in their ears and are thus denied access to the melody's enticements, to prevent the boat's loss on the coastal shoals."[67] The seductive Siren's song of the hidden piano is not the beauty of mythical creatures, but of the past itself, or is it the present? Odysseus's Sirens sing to him of his own past: "Odysseus! Come here! You are well-known from many stories! Glory to the Greeks!" they loudly sing:

"Now stop your ship and listen to our voices.
All those who pass this way hear honeyed song,
poured from our mouths. The music brings them joy,
and they go on their way with greater knowledge,
since we know everything the Greeks and Trojans
suffered in Troy, by gods' will; and we know
whatever happens anywhere on earth." (XII.184–191).[68]

Singing of the past, the Sirens tell Odysseus about his own adventures in the *Iliad*. They are omniscient and omnipresent eyes with an omnipotent voice. These inverted musical tombs sing their own luring siren songs of the past. As Judith Peraino writes of the Sirens' song in the *Odyssey*, they invite Odysseus to "wallow in a nostalgia" for his past heroic adventures before heading home. "The lure of the deceptive Sirens points a finger at all 'tellers of tales,' Homer included, and implicates the audience in their own desires to suspend time with bardic songs."[69] Reinach's piano—as well as his editions of the *Hymne à Apollon*—can thus be seen as a siren song. It traps the listener in the seductive aesthetic of their own history. It mesmerizes with its purported authenticity, its ability to tell us the history we want to hear, and in so doing, makes us forget to question our subjective idealizations of that past.

Tamara Levitz makes a similar argument in *Modernist Mysteries*. Igor Stravinsky's neoclassicism is melancholy. It is taking the uncanny, the painful, the hurt, and finding kinship in the past. Music becomes a ghost, something we are desperately trying to grasp. Stravinsky's process is not entirely different than that of an archaeologist like Reinach, for they are both seeking the same thing, albeit in different ways. Stravinsky explains that love reconnects the living with the dead. "I remake Pergolesi's music not because I want to repeat it or correct it but because I feel that I am the composer's spiritual brother.

[. . .] It is a phenomenon of love [*amore*]. There's a love affair [*un incontro d'amore*], the union of two spirits between Pergolesi and myself. Just as a man physically needs a specific woman whose qualities arouse the flame of passion in him, I too need Pergolesi or another musician of that time in order to create music."[70]

Reinach's desire to retreat to the past, to live and play in his own historical laboratory as scholar/musician/fan, may be a similar act of love (see figure 2.4). As Rebecca Schneider reminds us, performance is just another way to do history. Thus, for Reinach, enabling the performance of a long-lost relic of the past, his careful working through the piece, coming back to it, re-editing it, commissioning accompaniments for it, and sharing performances of it with colleagues, allow him continual connection over a twenty-year period with a piece he loves. Through constant editorial tinkering and performance, the

PORTRAIT DE THÉODORE REINACH
PEINT PAR M. ERNEST LAURENT DANS LA VILLA KÉRYLOS
(Collection Théodore Reinach.)

FIGURE 2.4 Portrait of Théodore Reinach in Greek costume at home in Villa Kérylos by Ernest Laurent. Reproduced from Jamot, *Théodore Reinach (1860–1928)* (Paris: Gazette des Beaux Arts, 1928).

ancient musical past can always be experienced "live." Reinach's editorial corrections are meant to help the ancient melody fit onto its modern accompaniment better. To smooth out unexpected dissonances in a vocal line or to add a stabilizing accompaniment to a fragile fragment helps fix the past into the fabric of the present. Paradoxically, altering the historical sources permits preservation through the act of performance (i.e., the modern instruments, which Reinach argues are equivalents of ancient ones, and the modern analysis of the melody that allows it to function alongside canonical works like *Tristan*). These actions, while potentially damaging to archaeological knowledge, can be seen as reparative in that despite their faults they permit those in the present to continually commune with the remains of the past. As we will see in chapter 3, fragments do not get performed. It is through re-enacting the music through modern devices (musical and archaeological instruments) that the past can even be accessed at all and thus reperformed and made live once again. Reinach is not merely resurrecting ancient Greek music just for the novelty of performing it; he is trying to fit it into a respectable musical lineage, to show that the classical past, and specifically his discovery, is lasting, significant, in line with our understanding of musical evolution, an important forebear of musical history, and that is indeed an act of deep and profound love for the scholar's object of study: for the crafts of philology, musicology, and archaeology. A critical reading of Reinach's work would dismiss the previous scholar's errors, blind spots, and assumptions. Seen through a reparative lens, Reinach's approach to the *Hymne à Apollon* becomes an opportunity for the contemporary scholar to engage with his world rather than to critique it. The past can be performed. I have performed it. In September 2013 I gathered colleagues from the Dayton area to record the 1914 version of *L'Hymne à Apollon* in the version for voice, harp, and woodwinds. I conducted the chamber group, coached the singer, and on the day of the recording I basked in the opening broken chord of the harp. I too stepped back, and closed my own eyes to imagine the feeling Reinach himself may have felt upon hearing that chord.

Edited by Reinach, *L'Hymne à Apollon* becomes a living artifact for Villa Kérylos, something complete that was previously incomplete, a fulfillment of the scholar's fantasy. Perhaps it is just another vanity project, like the villa: something to make him feel more Greek. Fauré's silence on the matter is further evidence that it isn't his work; it was and always will be Reinach's. Reinach crafted it, I posit, for his own edification. His hope was for others to perform it (as I have, and perhaps you will), to have a taste of the manufactured antiquity he is lucky enough to own. As we will see, his older brother, Salomon Reinach, held similar ideas about collecting and fandom. He also practiced a similarly questionable ethics in his encounters with living and dead objects of study (see chapter 6). Théodore Reinach's scholarly interests were idealistic. We as a community of contemporary scholars (like Théodore

Reinach) study what we study because we sincerely believe others need to hear it. This is an opportunity for all to embody antiquity in the privacy of their own homes, at their own uncanny pianos: to open their own pianos to hear the sirens' song.

3 | Performing Sappho's Fractured Archive, or Listening for the Queer Sounds in the Life and Works of Natalie Clifford Barney

E XPLORING THE FORMER BEDROOM of your object of study can be a dis-
concerting experience. In the summer of 2007, by happenstance, I found
myself exploring the abandoned remains of Natalie Clifford Barney's famous house at 20 rue Jacob in Paris, located in the heart of the 6th arrondisse-
ment. I was in Paris for the thirtieth annual conference of the Society of Dance
History Scholars that June. Between sessions, my wife and I took a little ex-
cursion to the Ladurée patisserie on rue Bonaparte. A quick glance at my trusty
pocket edition of *Le petit parisien* (pre-Google maps) informed me that we
happened to be only a block or two away from Barney's famous Left Bank
home and garden. As we walked up to the house, a young woman on a moped
parked right in front of us. She turned out to be a neighbor who just happened
to have a spare key to the property. Barney never actually owned the house;
she rented it for over fifty years, and when Michel Debré purchased the home
in 1966 he wanted Barney out as soon as possible. The new landlord began
renovating the home while the ninety-year old woman still lived there, making
her life miserable until she had had enough and moved across the river into
a suite at the Hôtel Meurice. Subsequently, under the ownership of the Debré
family the home fell into disrepair. It was sold again in 2007, and the new
owners handed an extra key to the neighbor so she could let the landscapers
and remodelers in to do their work before the new residents moved in. So
there I was with the neighbor at Barney's house almost a century after she had
moved in.

Climbing through the ruins of her home, looking through the keyhole at
her garden's Temple à l'Amitié, and standing in her bedroom, I could not
help but feel a giddy sense of excitement, familiar to many scholars as they
uncover a lost document in a box of papers or unearth a terra cotta statue from

the ground, but I also felt shame and an uncanny awareness of my role as a historian trespassing on the ruins of a life (see figure 3.1). This is my conundrum with Barney. I, like scholars before me, am fascinated not just by her life, loves, and exploits, but also by her own writings (nonfictional and pseudo-nonfictional) about her life, loves, and exploits.[1]

Barney stands at the center of this project due to her unwavering interest in staging fantasies of Greek antiquity in her writing and the private performances at her Parisian homes. Her patronage supported dancers, composers, and artists, and she used her home to bring together scholars of antiquity and the performers who brought the past to life on the opera and ballet stage. Throughout her life, Barney's poetry, plays, and other writings exhibited a fealty to the traditions of the ancient Greeks. I have read her works and worked in archives of her letters, photographs, and other belongings for well over a decade. I feel as though I *know* the woman in the fragments of conversations I have read in letters, the pieces of her life she wrote about in her published and unpublished writings, and the numerous photographs of her and her family and friends that I have studied. These moments in the archive, however, are not that different than those spent walking through her old home in Paris or around the blocks of downtown Dayton and Cincinnati, Ohio, where her childhood homes once stood. Both are rooted in some sort of tangible or physical traces of Barney, but where the fragments in the

FIGURE 3.1 The author in front of Natalie Clifford Barney's "Temple à l'Amitié," at 20 rue Jacob, 2007. Photo by Masha Kisel.

sanctioned archives demand a reasoned and clinical, scholarly approach, the pretense of scholarly objectivity is absent when standing in front of a former home that is devoid of precious archival materials. The spaces are instead magic circles in which past and present are free to mingle in the scholar's imagination.

There are huge lacunae in our understanding of the Sappho-inspired musical and theatrical performances that Barney created in the early years of the twentieth century. Like those of Sappho herself (fl. 600 BCE), Barney's writings about antiquity and female homoerotic and lesbian identity seem far ahead of their time. And also like Sappho, Barney has attracted a cult of devoted followers—a progeny of influence. I am interested in her efforts to reenact ancient Greek music and dance, as well as the difficulties in separating identity and history in reconstruction, then and today. I write about her because she fascinates me. I want to piece together her world; I want to hear and see these neo-Grecian rites. They are intriguing to me primarily because of the incomplete, fractured, and unheard status of her archive.

Trained as a musicologist, I nonetheless want to write about this woman who was at best an amateur musician. She didn't compose in the formal sense;[2] she didn't perform music publicly after her adolescence. I write about her as a musicologist despite and because of these challenges. She is of interest due to her early exploration of ancient Greek–inspired female homoerotic performance aesthetics, but also for what we might now identify as queer voices, queer time, and queer spaces. Like other characters in this book, she sought to revivify ancient Greek performances in a modern world, and in so doing, engaged with scholars. This led to the creation of her own theatrical works—blending music, poetry, and dance—and eventually resulted in an embodied or lived performance of a queer ancient Greek ethos. Her lesbian "lifestyle antiquity" ultimately became the object of study for a prominent archaeologist (Salomon Reinach), but I'll save that story for a later chapter. This chapter is about the ancient Greek–inspired performances Barney created and their fractured remains.

No one exhibited more creativity in the performance of ancient Greek music in the belle époque than the American-born writer, musician, and heiress Natalie Clifford Barney. While Théodore Reinach (see chapter 2) built a palace for himself far from Paris among the super-rich on the French Riviera, Barney built her fortress in the heart of Paris. She was devoted to ancient Greece, although that was not her only passion. She wrote poetry and plays, hosted a famous salon, played violin, and rode horses. Sappho's poetry and the imagined female homoerotic utopia of ancient Lesbos, however, resonated with the young Barney and established in her a lifelong interest in ancient Greek culture. Her Sapphic poetry and plays drew the attention of Remy de Gourmont and Pierre Louÿs, but her performance of her unique vision of Greek antiquity made her a celebrity.

This chapter looks at the remaining traces of ancient Greek musical and dance performances that took place in Barney's Parisian homes in the 1890s and early 1900s—real and imagined maps of performance spaces, playscripts, photos and memories of performances, and fictionalized reminisces of performances—fragments of lives reconstructed, reimagined, and reperformed. It is not a coincidence that Barney's discovery of Greek antiquity came about at the same time that she became aware of her own sexual identity. She fueled her passion by studying ancient Greek poetry under the tutelage of the best Greek scholars in Paris, preparing to perform ancient Greece in modern Paris. The ways Barney drew from archival (the poems of Sappho) and imagined (embodied) sources of queer identity and the fact that so little of both the ancient past and Barney's past remain for *us* provide an opportunity to re-evaluate the ways we navigate past and present, fact and fiction. Barney's interest in Sappho stemmed from her contemporary understanding of lesbianism, not a historical understanding of female homoerotics in ancient Lesbos. That is to say, Sappho of Lesbos was a Lesbian, but was not a "lesbian." Today, we may view Sappho's relationships through the lens of queer studies and thus call them queer in the ways that they queered standard narratives of sexuality and gender. Sappho and Lesbos's reputations developed after the real Sappho died.[3] To understand the competing methodologies by which Barney reperformed and re-enacted Sappho's life and work and other aspects of ancient Greece, I draw upon some work in performance studies and queer studies to illustrate Barney's unique methods of performing and embodying an ancient past.

The methodologies of performance studies, with foci on embodied knowledge and nontheatrical performances, can help us make sense of the types of materials left behind from Barney's musical and theatrical performances that musicological tools serve poorly. The archival traces of performances Barney created or participated in lack the traditional objects of musicological study (gasp, no scores!). In particular, Diana Taylor's binary understanding of the archive and the repertoire inform the way I treat sources Barney drew upon. As a reminder, for Taylor,

> the rift [. . .] does not lie between the written and spoken word, but between the *archive* of supposedly enduring materials (i.e., texts, documents, buildings, bones) and the so-called ephemeral *repertoire* of embodied practice/knowledge (i.e., spoken language, dance, sports, ritual). [. . .] Archival memory works across distance, over time and space; [. . .] What changes over time is the value, relevance, or meaning of the archive, how the items it contains get interpreted, even embodied. [. . .] The repertoire, on the other hand, enacts embodied memory: performances, gestures, orality, movement, dance, singing—in short all those acts usually thought of as ephemeral, nonreproducible knowledge.[4]

As I will show, Barney drew upon both types of knowledge to build a uniquely queer past and present.

This chapter examines how Barney built new lesbian (queer and/or homoerotic) works out of the fragments of ancient Lesbian (of Lesbos) works to make space for temporal slippage and play. All the while I remain keenly aware of the role scholars (myself included) play in telling her fractured story from Sappho's fragments. I am primarily focused here on Barney's earliest performances and writings about the female homoerotics of ancient Greece: her childhood training in music and ancient Greek in the United States and Europe, amateur performances at her parents' country club in Maine, and her first plays in the first decade of the twentieth century in Paris. This part of her life has not been as thoroughly documented, and retelling her early life as a *musical* and theatrical life reframes her interests in Greek antiquity. I conclude this chapter with a reading of Barney scholar and translator Anna Livia's novel *Minimax* (1991), in which the author casts the queer archival object of her desire, Natalie Clifford Barney, into the role of an immortal vampire. This chapter examines how we reconstruct queer times and places, and specifically queer musical time and space.

What We Know

> Finding out and writing about people, living or dead, is tricky work. [. . .] Getting too close to your subject is a major danger, but not getting to know her well enough is just as likely.
>
> —Jill Lepore, "Historians Who Love Too Much"[5]

Born on Halloween 1876 in Dayton, Ohio (where I am now writing this study), Natalie Clifford Barney's family moved to Cincinnati, Ohio, when she was in her teens and soon after settled in Washington, D.C. Regulars on the social circuit there, they also played an active role in the summer social scene in Bar Harbor, Maine, where they had a summer home. Barney was sent to boarding school in France and upon graduation rented a home in the Parisian suburb of Neuilly-sur-Seine in the mid-1890s. By 1909 Barney had moved to 20 rue Jacob on the Left Bank, where she held a literary salon every Friday afternoon until 1968. Her weekly meetings included regulars such as Colette, Liane de Pougy, Renée Vivien, Djuna Barnes, Jean Cocteau, Isadora Duncan, James Joyce, Gertrude Stein, Edna St. Vincent Millay, and Romain Brooks. Events took place in her salon or in her backyard pavilion, which housed a small stage and her own ancient Greek "temple of friendship." The temple served as a site for her neo-Sapphic rites, including plays, dance, and music.

What did these look like? How did they sound? Like music in ancient Greece itself, scant evidence remains. Physical traces of ancient Greek music exist—scraps of papyrus, fragments of poetry, shards of pottery—but the embodied experience remains hidden, buried under layers of time or conducted in private. By collecting traces, physically or through scholarship, can we really experience the past? That is, what are the limits of archival work? How does one break free from the tyranny of the document? Barney collected traces of antiquity (fragments of Sappho's poetry) and performed them with her friends in mock ancient Greek costumes, accompanied by the sounds of reconstructed lyres and flutes and while moving in Delsarte-inspired gestures across a small stage. She made archival sources into performances. Barney, fascinated by Sappho's homoerotic past, sought to hear its music. She sought ways to reconstruct the milieu, the social and physical spaces where ancient rites may have taken place. She wondered if a trip to Paris or Delphi or Lesbos would bring one closer to the real ancient Lesbos or the imagined performance of Sapphic/lesbian/Lesbian music.

Sapphonics Reconsidered

It is impossible to separate Barney's work from her lesbian identity.[6] To understand what she created, one first needs to examine why she chose antiquity and what made it queer—that is, nonheteronoramtive and radically antinormative. Perhaps we need to first ask, how and why we do (and did) queer musicology in the first place? Barney's motives were similar to the first generation of musicologists' work in queer studies in the 1990s; both were looking for their own history, a sense of historical presence, or as Mitchell Morris writes, "In the case of LGBT studies of music, the personal investment, the quest for some kind of historical presence, increases those satisfactions in abundant if unpredictable ways."[7] I ask this to find a space for Barney's understanding of queer time and queer space and in so doing place her performances and musical activities into this matrix of queer possibility. As Suzanne Cusick has illustrated in countless essays, queer musicology forms an important link between queer history and the ways that we as musicians make sense of our world—that is, through engagement with music.[8]

Barney built a modernist space from the past for the future: a queer utopia for performing the reverberating legacy of Sappho of Lesbos. Sappho is both past and present. Her poetry, twenty-five hundred years old, is irrevocably linked to her life and vice versa. The fictions of Sappho allow an extra degree of freedom in navigating her often reimagined life. Sappho was not just a lover of women, the most famous lover of women of the ancient world and the namesake of "lesbianism," but she was a musician—a singer—whose surviving lyrics on scraps of papyrus demand a melody. None of Sappho's melodies exists today. Concerning her music, we really know absolutely nothing. As Jane McIntosh Snyder has lamented, "Theories abound, but hard facts are in short supply."[9]

Musicologist Elizabeth Wood, in her seminal essay on lesbian musical aesthetics, coined the term "Sapphonics," which she defines as "a mode of articulation, a way of describing a space of lesbian possibility, for a range of erotic and emotional relationships among women who sing and women who listen."[10] For Wood, "Sapphonic" encompasses numerous techniques of performing, listening, and writing; Sapphonics is not only a way of describing and creating a realm of lesbian musical aesthetic possibility, but also a way of "trac[ing] the history and biography of a lesbian music," "a particular voice that thrills and excites me," whether the voice comes from a living body or from an imagined past, and Sapphonics is a "metaphor," and a "vessel of desire."[11]

The voices of performers as disparate as Hildegard von Bingen, Mary Martin, Ethel Merman, Julie Andrews, Barbra Streisand, Kate Bush, Annie Lennox, Patti Smith, and the actress Zarah Leander have been described as "Sapphonic."[12] Countless operatic stars and composers have joined the legions of Sapphonic voices as well, including Pauline Viardot, Emma Calvé, Clara Butt, Ethel Smyth, Joan Sutherland, Marilyn Horne, and even a man, Victor Capsoul.[13] In many cases authors apply the Sapphonic rubric to mark their own subjective attraction to the voice, which may signal a Sapphonic presence. Following Wood (and Wayne Kostenbaum), Samuel Abel, Terry Castle, Suzanne Cusick, and Stacy Wolf have used a similar model of mapping their subjective (and often queer) sexual excitement onto the past to explore Sapphonic possibility.[14] Sapphonics also connotes a sense of clandestine intentions. Wood discusses the problem of "lesbian invisibility" in music and the Sapphonic voice's ability to make visible and "give voice to forbidden desire."[15] Judith Peraino, in *Listening to the Sirens: Musical Technologies of Queer Identity from Homer to Hedwig*, approaches Sappho both historically and as imagined by nineteenth-century French and English writers. In Peraino's discussions of the historical Sappho, the poet of Lesbos, "song" becomes a vehicle for queer subjectivity in ancient Greece, not only in the meaning of the words; the singing and sharing of song presents a realm of erotic possibility.[16] Sapphonics, as practiced by musicologists in the 1990s, was a hermeneutics of clandestine intentions, codes, and ciphers. Sapphonics is about potential, not labels.

Like Sappho's music, Sapphonic voices are also inherently lost. If the Sapphonic voice, writes Wood, "is no longer audible as material sound, it is visible and resonant as presence in historical contexts and imaginary representations that once shaped and projected it: in performance records and auto/biographies of singers with this voice."[17] However, as Diana Taylor reminds us, these archival sources are no substitute for the repertoire. Like Sappho herself, they exist merely as fragments, incomplete shards of meaning demanding reconstruction, a filling out, and imagination. Barney was particularly attracted to the fragmentary nature of Sappho's work, famously inviting her peers in 1910 to "faire des fragments" ["make fragments"].[18] Unable to time travel back to Sappho's

Greece, Barney sought to re-enact it in fin-de-siècle Paris. Sapphonics, if it is to remain useful for musicology, thus needs to acknowledge the limits of the archive while opening itself up to alternative queer temporalities.

Queer musicology, in part, serves to make music queer and to make queerness more musical. It is a scholarly pursuit as it is a musical pursuit, and within the scholarly frame those two ways of knowing do not need to be mutually exclusive. Identity informs scholarship, music informs identity, music informs scholarship, and scholarship informs music. But these are not exclusively queer ways of knowing. Although Barney was not a scholar or a musician by trade, she took upon herself a project of queer musical historiography through her performances of Sappho. Performing Sappho for Barney was not purely musical, as queer musicology's goals are not purely musical either. It was a process of learning, discovering, and treating performance as scholarship.

Learning/Performing Greek: Natalie Clifford Barney and Eva Palmer

Barney's interest in Sappho materialized in the early 1890s. During a family visit to Bar Harbor, a young man with literary tastes, whom Barney refers to only as Alcée in her memoirs (a character in Sappho's poetry), introduced her to the Lesbian poet's works.[19] Around the same time Barney met Eva Palmer (later known as Eva Palmer Sikelianos),[20] a young socialite from New York City, who shared her love of Sappho. The two vacationed near each other in Bar Harbor during the 1890s; participated in theatricals written by Barney's mother, Alice Pike Barney (1857–1931), and recited Sappho's poetry with harp accompaniments at their fathers' country clubs.[21] A notice in the *New York Times* mentioned a "tableau" titled "Sappho" performed by Palmer among entertainments organized by Barney and her mother.[22] In private the two were lovers; they explored the woods of Bar Harbor, photographed each other nude, studied, read, and wrote poetry. As Barney wrote in her unpublished memoirs: "A liaison ensued where poetry, Plato's *Symposium*, and nudism, all had a part in our Arcadian life."[23]

Self-study in the woods with an intimate friend suited Barney; she detested formal education. After she left boarding school she found it far more convenient to just pay for knowledge or skills from tutors, mentors, and intellectuals with financial, social, or cultural exchanges. She did not want to be forced to learn "useless things" when she already knew how to read, feel, and love on her own.[24] She was not an amateur historian or hobbyist-archaeologist, either. She never considered herself to be a historian, a classicist, or a literary scholar, let alone a musicologist or dance historian. She certainly is not best known as a musician. She was an amateur musician but a professional poet and a memoirist, a hostess and collector of intellectuals.

Back in Washington, D.C., where the family eventually settled, Barney studied violin, then later traveled to Dresden for more advanced musical training and opera going. On her early trips to Europe she sent home annotated programs and photographs of her favorite musicians (many autographed), and she regularly attended the Bayreuth Festival throughout the 1890s and early 1900s. She often brought lovers, or women she hoped to seduce, with her to the festival. She also continued (although intermittently) to study ancient Greek. Encouraged by Palmer, Barney pursued these studies in order to read Sappho in the original.[25]

Barney sought out Jules Cambon, the American ambassador to France, to help her find an instructor of French poetry and classical Greek.[26] He introduced her to Jean Charles-Brun (1870–1946), a poet and professor of Greek and literature at Lycée Henri IV. Barney sought Charles-Brun as a tutor and confidant. Soon the other women in her circle, the courtesan and dancer Liane de Pougy (1869–1950; later the Princesse Ghika) and then the poet Pauline Tarn (1877–1909; known as Renée Vivien), sought his advice. When the young lovers Barney and Vivien broke up in 1901, Vivien wrote to Charles-Brun for advice.[27] When Pougy was caught in the middle, she wrote to Charles-Brun as well. Jean-Paul Goujon, in his biography of Vivien, cites a staggering five hundred letters between the poet and Charles-Brun.[28] As Goujon writes: "For Vivien, this man [. . .] became her literary adviser, faithful guide, and a friend. . . . In the eyes of Vivien, Charles-Brun possessed an intellectual influence which made him much more than a high school teacher [; . . .] he became a confidant."[29] With their tutor's help, Vivien, Barney, and Palmer devoted the summer of 1900 in Bar Harbor to learning Greek.[30] Barney used this model throughout her life. She realized while under Charles-Brun's mentorship that she never needed to be an expert herself; she just had to spend time with scholars to learn what she needed to learn.

Palmer and Barney had a fraught relationship.[31] Friends before they were lovers, and then friends again, they corresponded throughout their lives. In her biography of Barney, Suzanne Rodriguez writes, "They were each other's 'home port,' a safe place to dock, replenish spiritual stores, and venture out again."[32] Both benefited from Charles-Brun's mentorship. Once they had exhausted his knowledge of Greek, they moved on to more learned sources, such as the poet Louÿs. Vivien, Palmer, and Barney, as lesbian/bisexual women in 1900, were seeking their ancestors, and ancient Greek language and culture provided a gateway.

In lieu of a family tree of queer mothers and fathers, they sought historical sources; to commune with them, they performed them, re-enacting Greek poetry, music, dance, and drama. Louÿs's pseudo-Greek *Les Chansons de Bilitis* (1894) gave Barney license to perform her own Greek antiquity as her mentor did. Louÿs, relying on his scholarly investigations of ancient Greek poetry, created his own literary past for the future. As Karla Jay writes, "Works such as *Bilitis* suggested that Greek culture could be brought forward and recreated in the modern world."[33] Barney did not just recreate Greek culture in print; most important, she performed it with her friends in Paris in ways that blended scholarship on ancient Greece, dance, music, poetry, and female homoerotics.

To recreate Sappho, Barney wrote and staged plays involving improvised music and a free movement vocabulary inspired by Delsarte; however, these performances are extraordinarily difficult for the modern scholar to recreate. A recreation of a recreation or a performance of a performance can never attain complete fidelity to its original. Due to the paucity of archival sources pertaining to Barney's Sapphic performances in Paris during the 1900s, a careful study of performance practices, surviving photographs, and playscripts can help us re-imagine (not reconstruct) Barney's own reimaginings of Sapphic performance.

The Influence of Alice Pike Barney: Music and Movement for Ancient Greek Poetry

Barney's early theatrical work was heavily influenced by her own mother's amateur productions. Alice Pike Barney avoided traditional choreography. Instead, she preferred a more plastic, Delsarte-inspired movement in keeping with other late nineteenth-century amateur performance practices such as elocution, pantomime, and tableaux vivant. Natalie Clifford Barney was well versed in all of these practices from her childhood experiences. Alice Pike Barney organized theatricals for decades at the family's summer residence in Bar Harbor, in their adopted home of Washington, D.C., and later in Southern California.[34] Alice Pike Barney's guest books from the 1890s and the first decade of the 1900s reveal frequent visits by professional musicians and theatrical personalities, notably Walter Damrosch, Emma Calvé, and Mrs. Patrick Campbell.[35] Natalie benefited from her mother's artistic connections. She remained a lifelong friend of famed soprano Emma Calvé, and like Isadora Duncan, she and her mother collaborated with the famous conductor Walter Damrosch.[36] Artistic support and attention from well-connected and respected European artists like Calvé and Damrosch helped burnish the Barneys' artistic pedigree.[37]

Like other patrons, the Barneys engaged in an exchange of economic capital for social and cultural capital. Alice Pike Barney had been financially supportive of Duncan and Ruth St. Denis and later Anna Pavlova, for whom she created a ballet in 1915.[38] Building upon the fame and draw of these artists, Alice Pike Barney expanded the audience for her own amateur theatricals. She began staging these theatricals (mostly pantomimes and vaudevilles), often starring her daughters and their friends, at Bar Harbor's Kebo Valley Club in the summer of 1897.[39] Theatricals, often drawing upon ancient Greek themes, took place at Bar Harbor and at Alice Pike Barney's Washington home for decades.

In pantomimes for Bar Harbor devised by her mother, Natalie appeared as "Fair Rosamond" and "La Cigale." She also arranged for Palmer to perform

Henry Thorton Wharton's English translation of Sappho's First Ode (frag. 1) at her mother's theatricals. According to Barney, her mother was ignorant of the poem's significance. And so Palmer appeared on stage dressed *à la Grecque*, in white sandals with straps crisscrossing her legs, her red hair cascading down to her ankles and a gold band around her temples. Standing beside several broken Greek columns and accompanied by an arpeggiating harpist, she recited Sappho's verse to an enthusiastic albeit ignorant audience. Palmer left the stage to find an embrace in Barney's waiting arms.[40]

Natalie and Alice Barney's ancient Greek–inspired performances in Bar Harbor took place during a nationwide craze for the art of elocution set to music. As discussed by Marian Wilson Kimber, while male elocutionists were better known, the women practitioners of the art popularized the genre between 1880 and 1935. "In America, the chief practitioners of accompanied recitation were women, and their performances came to influence melodramatic pieces created by female composers well into the twentieth century."[41] The Barney women also appear to have blended a healthy dose of Delsarte into their theatrics. Delsartism, developed by French voice and acting teacher François Delsarte, had its own American flavor when it found root in American oratory schools; later at "ladies' matinees"; and then eventually in dance, theater, and silent film.[42] American Delsartism was both a technical system of dramatic expression for actors and singers and an aesthetic theory that students applied to all aspects of life. The technique emphasized tensions between stasis ("classical and mythic" attitudes and poses) and motion.[43] Genevieve Stebbins further popularized the Delsarte-inspired Greek statue pose within women's elocution circles in the 1880s. The Delsarte technique helped make the women's performing bodies acceptable as high art, lending their performances a sense of grace, fitness, and beauty.[44]

The musical components to Natalie Clifford Barney's performances also appear to have grown out of the elocutionary traditions. Descriptions in the American women's press of music for elocution are very similar to Barney's own performances. Kimber cites a writer in 1891 who found pleasing "a union of the reciting voice with delicate strains of music—chords and arpeggios played soft[ly] through and between certain lines of the poem."[45] The fact that no musical notation survives from these performances is also not surprising. In 1897 *Werner's Magazine* mentioned that accompanists for recitation needed to have skills in improvisation.[46] I can easily imagine Palmer's recitation of Sappho's first fragment in Wharton's translation accompanied by limpid arpeggios improvised on the harp.

Performing Sappho *en plein air*: Inventing the Repertoire in Barney's *Équivoque*

For Barney, Sappho was not a passionate and forgotten victim of a male lover (as told by Ovid) or a dangerous, corrupting succubus (as told by Alphonse

Daudet), but rather an almost messianic symbol of poetry, music, and feminine love.[47] Barney's rewriting of Sappho for her theatricals stripped the latter of the eighteenth- and nineteenth-century baggage. Barney and her friends not only dispensed with previous scholarly interpretations of Sappho, they did away with their translations, opting to study the musician's lyrics in the original language. No longer hampered by the rules of her family's country club, Barney could stage Sappho in ancient Greek and on her own terms.

While Barney's interest in Sappho has been well documented, only fragmentary information exists on the role of music in Barney's salon. She may have taken cues from the introduction to Wharton's 1885 edition of Sappho. Imagining the melodies to Sappho's songs, he gives an example of the church mixolydian mode as appropriate. He also described an instrument, the finger-plucked pēktis (πηκτις), cited by Sappho herself in fragment 156, that could accompany the melodies.[48] Photographs and reminiscences about Barney's temple at 20 rue Jacob and the more formal Friday salons provide the majority of the information. The Sappho-inspired performances began around 1900, when Barney still resided in the Parisian suburb of Neuilly. A photograph from one of the early performances (from her play *Équivoque*) from around 1906 depicts a group of women in ancient Greek costume, hands raised, circling a raised platform on which are an unidentified flute player, Penelope Duncan playing harp, and Palmer in the center as the singer or orator (see figure 3.2). Pougy appears on the far left side of the image looking at the camera, and Barney is in the center (in white in half profile).

The writer Colette discussed one early Greek-inspired performance in Neuilly, where she and Palmer dramatized Louÿs's *Dialogue au soleil couchant* (a simple Arcadian tale of a Greek shepherd who falls for the beautiful Greek maiden, who at first remains hesitant but then succumbs to the shepherd's voice). In Barney's garden the aspiring actresses, Palmer as the maiden to Colette's shepherd, performed this homoerotic fantasy for friends adorned in ancient Greek costumes, accompanied by a group of violinists hidden behind a boulder.[49] A mix of professional and amateur performances took place at Neuilly and later at rue Jacob over the next decades, with many, if not most, involving music. Calvé sang, Mata Hari danced, Palmer procured Lesbos-inspired costumes and props (harp, turtleshell lyre, sandals, and flowers), and Raymond Duncan (Isadora Duncan's older brother) choreographed.

June 1906 saw the production of Barney's *Équivoque* (Ambiguity), a reworking of the famous tale of Sappho's leap from the Lecudian cliff after being spurned by her lover. In Barney's tale, Sappho does not lament the betrayal of Phaon (her supposed male lover), but rather of his bride and her student (Timas). Featuring an impressive cast, Barney's published version of the play lists women who went on to become famous stage and film actresses. Marguerite Moreno played Sappho, and Jeanne Delvair made a cameo at the end of the play as a stranger. Delvair's younger sister Germaine Dermoz played one of Sappho's

FIGURE 3.2 A gathering of women, from *Équivoque*, including Eva Palmer, Natalie Clifford Barney, and Liane de Pougy, in Barney's garden in Neuilly. Smithsonian Institute Archives, SIA2017-061364.

friends, as did Sacha Guitry's wife Charlotte Lysès (another famous actress of stage and screen).[50] The ballet dancer and teacher Marie Rambert[51] played the dancer Lato, and Penelope Duncan played Artista, a lyre player. Palmer played Sappho's lover (Timas), now engaged to a man (Phaon).[52] Strikingly, Palmer's poses closely resemble those found in Anna Morgan's widely popular 1889 publication, *An Hour with Delsarte*. The illustrated plates by Rose Mueller Sprague and Marian Reynolds only depict women, most of whom are dressed in Genevieve Stebbins–inspired Greek costumes (see figures 3.3 and 3.4).

Likely photographs of the production housed at the Smithsonian Institute Archives only include the female participants, none of the men. They mostly feature Palmer, who not only starred in the work, but also most likely played an important role in helping Barney conceive it.[53] The photos also show another important collaborator, Penelope (née Sikelianos) Duncan (playing harp, although the published playscript indicated she played flute), standing near a short classical pedestal holding a tiny statue, both women draped in ancient Greek costume. Palmer's distant gaze and Duncan's focused attention seem to evoke Orphic overtones, with the iconic harp adding support to this reading. The resulting images weave the loss associated with the partial fragmented œuvre of Sappho's poetry with the loss of the beloved Eurydice, which mirrors the plot of *Équivoque*.

Rambert described her role as a dancer in Barney's theatrics in her autobiography. Raymond and Penelope Duncan first brought her to Barney's place in 1905. Rambert mistakenly notes that Barney lived with Palmer at the time and that Palmer ended up marrying Raymond Duncan's son (he was actually Raymond's brother-in-law and Penelope's brother).[54] Acknowledging the false recollections throughout the book, we should keep in mind that Rambert's descriptions of Barney's theatrical event may be colored by her notably vibrant imagination. After all, she was only seventeen when she danced for Barney.

In her book Rambert describes the setting (Barney's lawn in Neuilly) and the cast ("actors from the Comédie Française to act the speaking parts") and recalls one line: "Et Sappho de Lesbos où est-elle? Nous ne le savons plus, elle est morte." The choruses were "sung to what was supposed to be Greek music, played upon pipes, a flute and other suitable instruments." Rambert also notes that sections such as the chorus, "Levez haut les poutres, charpentiers, évoé," may have come from classical sources and not from Barney directly. In Rambert's telling, Raymond arranged the dances; he did not properly choreograph them. He mostly told the barefoot, tunic-clad dancers where to go, "so everything looked Greek to him."[55]

The production was not without controversy. According to a lengthy article in one of Barney's hometown newspapers, the *Dayton Journal*, her landlord in Neuilly objected to the play in her garden. This led to her eviction and move to the Left Bank. The article not only praised the hometown girl who had successfully written verse in French, but also defended her play against the accusations of the French press and the landlord. Apparently Barney originally

FIGURE 3.3 Eva Palmer and Penelope Duncan, possibly performing *Équivoque*, in Natalie Clifford Barney's backyard in Neuilly (ca. 1906). Smithsonian Institute Archives, SIA2017-061362.

titled the drama *Sapho*, which was confused with the famous modern novel by Alphonse Daudet about the depraved model Fanny Legrande and her many male lovers.[56] The anonymous author of the Dayton, Ohio, newspaper article from November 1909 related the plot and cast of the drama, corroborating the cast list published in Barney's *Actes et Entr'Actes* in 1910; however, the author missed the critical plot twist, in which we learn in act 2 that Sappho's death was a result of her jealousy not over a man, but over a woman:

> Whether it was the incense fires or the strange marriage ceremony or the frisky dances or the weird lamentations or the vague knowledge that Sapho wrote erotic poetry, or all combined, which induced the landlord to become aggressive against the American girl it is hard to say. [. . .] [Furious,] Miss Barney waxed indignant that a mere layman should dare to object to her beautiful

FIGURE 3.4 Illustrated plate from Anna Morgan, *An Hour with Delsarte: A Study of Expression* (Boston: Lee and Shepherd, 1889).

creation. She cancelled her lease, paid for the remaining term of years, left the villa in high dudgeon, shook the dust of Neuilly off her feet and took up her quarters in an old ivy-covered house not far from the famous École des Beaux Arts.[57]

The *Dayton Journal* article also included two photos from the garden production of *Sapho/Équivoque*. The first is the often reproduced image seen in figure 3.2. The other image does not exist in any other source. It depicts the male characters, Phaon and presumably the carpenters, as well as some children and women involved in the production (see figure 3.5).

Interestingly, all of the photos of Barney's drama feature musicians playing instruments (lyres or flutes), leading me to believe that music was possibly improvised throughout. The *Dayton Journal* review described Penelope Duncan's flute music as an authentic link to the drama's Greek origins: "Mrs.

FIGURE 3.5 Image of garden production of *Sapho/Équivoque*. From "Why Miss Barney's Sapho Had to Move," *Dayton Journal*, 2nd ed., November 14, 1909, 13.

Raymond Duncan, his fascinating Greek wife, [. . .] played the airs of her native land upon the flute. These she picked up from the mountain peasants and are the same as were sung in the days of Sapho."[58] The lyre playing would most likely resemble standard low harp arpeggiations employed in many elocutionary performances, since neither Palmer nor Duncan had any formal training as harpists.[59]

The body carriage and gestures also point to a Delsarte-inspired movement. The Americans (Duncan, Palmer, and Barney) involved were familiar with Delsarte movements popular in women's clubs and amateur society theatricals, like those produced by Alice Pike Barney. Genevieve Stebbins's popular Delsarte manuals emphasized the connections between poses in her books and those found in ancient Greek and Roman art.[60] I can imagine that the gestures and music performed for *Équivoque* found inspiration in what Barney viewed as authentic source materials: Wharton's descriptions, Penelope Duncan's rustic Greek melodies, conventional and simple harp figurations, and classical and Delsartian gestures.

In the play Barney crafted her own French verse around actual fragments of Sappho's poetry, which she dutifully cited in a series of endnotes. She filled in the missing pieces of these Sapphic fragments with fantasy, revivifying them through her connections, power, and wealth. But while she incorporated these fragments into the play, the plot is completely her own. Sappho is woven into

Barney's own life, in which the American poet gets to direct, produce, and control the narrative. *Équivoque* is about the pleasure of absence, the excitement of loss, and the enjoyment of despair.

Barney's performance of a new/authentic Sappho "corrected" centuries of male scholarship in a number of ways. Orthographically, she aligns her "Sappho/Psappha" with the ancient home of Lesbos and far from the European men who have rehabilitated her oeuvre over the centuries. Throughout the drama Barney's characters refer to their heroine as "Psappha" (from the Aeolic Greek, ΨΑΠΦΩ), or "Sappho" (a variant from the Attic spelling, ΣΑΠΦΩ, that became more popular in the twentieth century), but never as "Sapho" (the favored eighteenth- and nineteenth-century French spelling).[61] Truer to the Greek pronunciation, Barney's French play does not cast her heroine as part of the previous French legacy of Sapphic scholarship and reception, but rather as someone simultaneously antiquely unfamiliar and new. Her shift in spelling signals a rejection of the past (and the patriarchal lineage) for a new future of Sapphic study created by women (granted, with the assistance of male scholars) for women.

In the first scenes of the play two male carpenters chat idly with some of Sappho's students in a garden next to the poet's school in Mytilene on the isle of Lesbos. The group believe that Sappho is jealous because her lover Phaon is set to marry Timas. At the wedding, Sappho watches the ceremony from a short distance. The act ends as Sappho curses the couple, drops her poems to the ground, and throws herself off a cliff. When Sappho's followers Gorgo and Eranna read the poems left by their teacher, they realize that Sappho loved the bride Timas, not Phaon the groom. Timas, left at the altar, follows her lover to her grave. Karla Jay writes, "In this play, Barney challenges the stubbornly reiterated notion of Sappho's death. . . . If Sappho did kill herself for love, in Barney's view, she was far more likely to have done so for the love of a woman than for a man."[62]

Sappho is not just a character in the play; the lines of her poetry appear throughout, diligently cited and listed in an appendix with original Greek sources (an idea that Artemis Leontis posits came from Palmer).[63] The format is reminiscent of Louÿs's faux scholarly apparatus in *Les Chansons de Bilitis*, but instead of deceptively leading the reader to an imaginary fabricated Lesbos, Barney reverses the project. Her footnotes root her fabricated, imaginary Lesbos to the real shards of poetry. The appearances of Sapphic fragments abound in the work of Barney and her lover, Vivien. The fragments appear as precious Gospel. For example, in *Équivoque*, act 1, scene 4, Eranna and Gorgo warn Sappho not to attend the wedding of Phaon and Timas. They urge her to spare herself the humiliation and pain, but Sappho insists:

ERANNA: Their nuptial looks will humiliate you
  If you stay . . .

SAPPHO: I'll stay . . .

GORGO: You believe you can forget!

Thinking of the approaching nuptials your brow looks troubled.

SAPPHO: I don't know what to do for I am of two minds.[64]

Barney's Sappho's line, "I don't know what to do—I'm of two minds," is a direct citation of Sappho fragment 51.[65]

Setting aside for a moment the novel reconfiguration of the love triangle and the frequent citations, Barney's Sappho stands at the center of a school of adoring female students. They heap praise on her in the same way Barney may have wished her female followers to do. In act 1, scene 4, friends of Sappho try to cheer up the despondent poet:

GORGO: Your life is your poem

Most beautiful; Your eternal masterpiece is yourself.

ERANNA: And your songs, messengers of your glory, will say

For centuries to come your greatness.[66]

For Barney, Sappho's life itself was her greatest masterpiece.

Barney's Queer Temporalities and Spaces

Sappho's life was not just a great masterpiece to celebrate, but also an ancient ruin to explore. She was an entry point for Barney to construct a new temporal and geographic space for queer performance.[67] Barney created a space (a garden in Neuilly or at 20 rue Jacob) and a time outside of the rhythms of her nonqueer neighbors and peers, a place where one could engage in queer historical play. Barney's written work centers on "the potentiality of a life unscripted by the conventions of family, inheritance, and child rearing."[68] In *Équivoque* Sappho's suicide not only ends her trajectory toward normative roles of being, but also inspires the bride, Timas, to divert her own life.[69] However, Barney's work is not *just* queer in its ludic escape from normative roles; she employed music and dance to build this world.[70] Thinking about music from both queer and ludic positions allows us to explore music's potential to create temporal slippage. Tes Solminski, for example, has explored the queer pseudo-nostalgia in the women's music movement for performances never heard.[71] "Pseudonostalgia," Solminski writes, "emphasize[s] nonlinear temporality and questions of authenticity and normativity."[72] Sapphonics, as Wood reminds us, describes "a space of lesbian possibility, for a range of erotic and emotional relationships among women who sing and women who listen."[73] Barney's work shows how this space of lesbian possibility and the range of relationships exist among past women, future women, mythic women, and even imaginary women who sing and listen. Barney's revivified Lesbos in Paris bends our understanding of musical and historical authenticity toward a queer utopian nontime, nonplace: a future.[74] Lesbos became Paris, and Paris became Lesbos. For years Barney lived and performed an antiquity that was past, present, and future all at once. She drew other lesbian and bisexual women as well as scholars of antiquity into that "affective vortex [that pulls] audiences to a place they neither remember nor know through history."[75] She offered a historical play similar to the re-enactment play described by Rebecca Schneider in *Performing Remains: Art and War in Times of Theatrical Reenactment*. Re-enactment, she argues, is reperforming, redoing, or replaying an act or an artwork (the art museum, performance space, university, concert hall), but also closely tied to "living history" projects (history museums, theme parks, preservation societies). The desire, regardless of the venue, is to "try to bring that time—that prior moment—to the very fingertips of the present."[76] Sappho dies in Barney's *Équivoque* and so rejects lineage, but she still remains through citation both in performance and archived in the playscript, with its scholarly footnotes in ancient Greek. Her reappearance in the present is another example of Barney's crafting of a nonlinear temporality.

One could read Barney's theater through recent reparative works in queer theory (Elizabeth Freeman's "temporal drag" and David Román's "archival drag" leap to mind), but Barney's theater cannot really compare to the work of artists and writers imagining a queer future in and around the AIDS/HIV epidemic.[77] Her work is not that serious and not particularly political. Her queer temporal play is more about play. After all, music is often about play. The ludic, as William Cheng reminds us, is a critical part of "serious" musicological work, especially when concerned with queer topics: "[M]usicological forays into gender and sexuality," he writes, "rocked the boat not because they extended unthinkable claims per se, but rather because they aired out what had been known all along—that music is sensual, sexual, social; that it comforts, disrupts, coerces."[78] We know this to be true even when the music is missing. Cheng challenges us to test the boundaries between scholarship and leisure, to explode binaries of "musicology and non-musicology, work and pleasure, art and entertainment, scholarship and fandom, professional and popular, self and other, private and public, intellectual and sensual, and serious and playful."[79] An important part of doing that involves just these sorts of temporal games. It is just this type of play that fascinated Barney: she assembled lovers, ex-lovers, and future lovers to enact a queer drama all her own, to play in a historical fantasy world where queer relationships reigned.

Her theatrics also exhibit Carolyn Dinshaw's concept of "touch," a "queer historical impulse" that makes connections across time.[80] "Touch" is not far from "hearing." We *hear* the voices from the past just as we may *touch* the past. The distinction lies in hearing the past's absence of the artifact, or the archival totem of the past. When one hears the past, or listens queer, one is detached from the archive or disrupting it in favor of the repertoire.[81]

Other Performances: Love Stories

The unity of loss, desire, and Sappho's Greece becomes clear in tales from Barney's love life that mingled ancient Greece, music, Sappho, and erotics. A story retold by Barney's friend and biographer, Jean Chalon, illustrates the ways music functioned in her Sapphic play. Around 1900 Barney, upset over losing her lover Vivien to another woman, sent her good friend Calvé dressed as a street singer to serenade Vivien from beneath her window with "J'ai perdu mon Eurydice" from Gluck's *Orphée et Eurydice*. Chalon tells the rest of the story:

> Similarly disguised [as a street singer] Natalie collected the coins thrown to them. But Renée [Vivien]-Eurydice did not appear. Emma Calvé, who had dazzled American audiences in the role of Carmen, continued her concert with the famous: "Love is the child of Bohemia who has never known any law."[82] More susceptible to Bizet than to Gluck, Renée half-opened a window and Natalie threw up her poem [based on Sappho fragment 49],[83] attached to a bouquet. The passersby who stopped, recognized Emma Calvé, applauded as she and Natalie ran off.[84]

Barney employed her longtime friend Calvé to set a dramatic scene of seduction. In wooing Vivien, Barney often sent gifts attached to poetry in hopes of winning her heart and mind. According to one biographer, after their first sexual encounter, Barney had to sneak back home so her family would not know that she had spent the night in another woman's bedroom. The next day, Barney had an antique-looking flute delivered to Vivien, who replied by telegram: "How I love the silent music of this old flute. And thank you for the pretty thought that made you send this harmonious gift. I'll listen to the dormant memories that it contains. And I'll think tenderly of you. Until Tuesday evening."[85] Barney's gift and Vivien's reply invoke not only Greece, sexual desire, and silent voices, but most strikingly Sappho's own poetry. The encounter itself is a paraphrase of Sappho fragment 118: "Yes! Radiant lyre speak to me / become a voice."[86]

But all of these stories, and photos, and plays are not a musical performance, certainly not a repeatable one. All we have are photographs, with instruments being played—flutes and harps—or unplayed—the lyre cast aside on the periphery of the photo in Figure 3.2—but certainly unheard. The photos also reveal private scenes of antiquely flavored intimacy staged for future and most likely private consumption: with lovers, friends, and alone (see figures 3.6–3.8). Can we reperform these scraps of works and lives?

At Barney's home a different type of slippage occurred. There were not only private performances, but also semipublic ones. Like the Civil War reenactors described by Rebecca Schneider, participants were not only interested

FIGURE 3.6 Natalie Clifford Barney and Colette. Smithsonian Institute Archives, SIA2017-061363.

in reenacting the past, but also in preserving it for the archive—for history. Barney's performances were photographed, saved, and preserved. Sitting in a chilly reading room, perusing the photos of past musical performances of music long lost, reprising other long-lost Sapphonic performances, I feel like a visitor from the future. Concerning the presence of the audience in battle re-enactments, Schneider writes: "[T]here can arise at times a quasi and queasy sensation of cross-temporal slippage. At various and random moments amidst the myriad strangeness of anachronism at play, it can occasionally feel 'as if' the halfway dead came halfway to meet the halfway living, halfway."[87] The feeling of touching the past when alone in an archive touching century-old photos in your hand or reading private letters organized in plastic sheet protectors is strange. It reminds us of the importance of the body in the work of the historian. It is a tantalizing, magical time-traveling world just out of reach, just like Barney's own home.

Maps

Woody Allen's 2011 film *Midnight in Paris* captures some of that time-traveling magic as the protagonist (a twenty-first-century writer) finds his imagined Paris of the 1920s materializing before him at the stroke of midnight.

FIGURE 3.7 Natalie Clifford Barney and Liane de Pougy. Smithsonian Institute Archives, SIA2017-063167.

Each night he leaves the present to hang out with Barney's friends—among them Gertrude Stein and Djuna Barnes.

As historians, we map facts onto a historical narrative so that we can wander its long-silent alleyways. Like Barney's Lesbos in Paris or Woody Allen's fictional character, we too roam the streets of modern Paris, imagining what it was like when our musical heroes inhabited its streets. Recent digital humanities projects have developed new ways to explore the physical dimensions of past musical cultures. The website for the London Philharmonia Orchestra's "City of Light: Paris, 1900–1950" series opens with an interactive cartography of Paris past.[88] Just hover the mouse over the icons on the famous *Nouveau Paris Monumental Itinéraire Pratique de l'Étranger dans Paris* and bubbles pop out, revealing photos, videos, audio clips, and text on performance venues, musical personalities, and works from that period. Louis Epstein's *Musical*

FIGURE 3.8 Natalie Clifford Barney in Delphi, Greece. Smithsonian Institute Archives, SIA2014-03837.

Geography: Mapping the Sounds of Paris, 1924, another digital humanities project, offers a series of pages mapping the sounds of 1924 Paris in varied ways: follow the route of Langston Hughes on his first day in Paris in 1924 or click on another map to reveal every cinema in the city open that year; another map shows the homes of important composers, and another important venues, all laid upon a zoomable Google map.[89] These twenty-first-century projects provide a site to perform the imagined past of our scholarly interests, as Barney did for the past of her imagined scholarly interest: Sappho's Greece.

In 1929 Barney drew up a "map" of her friends (including Stein and Barnes) and other leading figures behind her salon (see figure 3.9). The map, like Woody Allen's Paris or Barney's *Équivoque*, represents yet another imagined landscape, a constructed geography. Her garden, with its temple to friendship at the top and the "Amazon" river weaving through it, represents a family

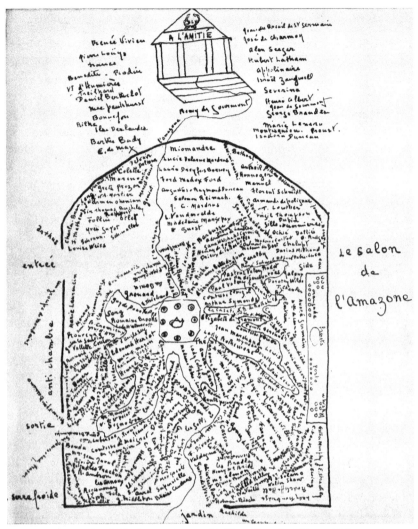

FIGURE 3.9 Natalie Clifford Barney's "map" of her "Temple à l'Amitié," frontispiece to *l'Aventures de l'esprit* (1929).

tree minus pedigree. This Amazon has no tributaries, and all present in the garden drink from its waters. Like Judy Chicago's *The Dinner Party* (1979)— in which Barney, famously, has a place setting—there is no head of the table, no patriarchal root to this genealogy of influence, no teleological chain from Jesse to Jesus, but rather multiple interconnected centers. At the top we find the temple of friendship, where the dead gather (Vivien, Alan Seeger, Marcel Proust, Isadora Duncan, Remy de Gourmont). Among the living, names are cloistered together: the musicians mingle in one corner (Jane Bathori, Calvé, Virgil Thomson, and Wanda Landowska); Dorothy Wilde hangs out near the bar (serving orangeade, whiskey, port, and punch) while André Gide, Élisabeth de Gramont, and Romaine Brooks sip tea at the center; and Carl Van Vechten and Sylvia Beach are wallflowers clinging to the periphery. Barney graphically transforms time into space. That is, in the absence of lineages and timelines leading from Sappho to Barney, Barney simply maps the past onto the present by flattening the historical sequence and making the vertical horizontal.

Le Salon d'amazone was not just for artists, but also for scholars, readers, watchers, and listeners. In her essay on the physical and literary landscapes of interwar expat lesbian writers, Amy Wells-Lynn identifies how Barney (along with Djuna Barnes and Radclyffe Hall) "construct[s] new Parisian geographic and literary female spaces in which their shared geographies evolve into a coded language used in their literary works." They also used "geographic codes to record their shared female Parisian experiences into their texts, [and create] a new Paris redrawn in their own terms."[90] Barney did not just reconfigure time and space in the cartography of her salon, but she also wedded music, ritual, and dance into a similar palimpsest of meanings, places, and periods. The 1929 map provides a different way of seeing, just as the project of queer musicology provides a different way of hearing.

For musicologists and performers, the repertoire, as defined by Diana Taylor, appears as a promising resource when we lack access to the archive or arrive to find what we need is missing. In those cases, the repertoire or the illusion of the repertoire is all we have. Especially in the case of queer performances, it is only natural to think that if the archive is barren, perhaps the repertoire (real or imagined) may yield its secrets. The archives I worked in contain photos of performance, but no script, no score, no plan. In the absence of a score, can we even talk about music? We certainly cannot reperform, but perhaps we can re-enact, or reimagine; that is, we can build something new, we can perform Barney as she performed Sappho, but not either of their works.

As we try to piece together the scraps from the archive and reconcile them with the repertoire, we as scholars must reconcile our desire to be part of the repertoire and the desire to be objective with the archive. The repertoire, as Taylor notes, "transmits live, embodied actions," and this means that it can reproduce the past in the present in ways that an archive cannot. Live bodies transmit the material, which they learned from other live bodies. For Taylor, "forms handed down from the past are experienced as present."[91] The key to our understanding lies in the transmission.

In many ways the performances chez Barney are a history of the loss of a repertoire and a fragmented and incomplete archive. Barney and her friends did not commune with the past in an unbroken line. Sappho was not a living tradition inherited from lesbian to lesbian to lesbian, and so forth. The imagined cartography of Barney's garden was a fantasy. She and her friends consulted the archive, which they then embodied. Taylor argues:

[The] efficacy [of performance], whether as art or as politics, stems from the way performances tap into public fantasies and leave a trace, reproducing and at times altering cultural repertoires. Performance, [. . .] constitutes a (quasi-magical) invocational practice. It provokes emotions it claims only to represent, evokes memories and grief that belong to some other body. It conjures up and makes visible not just the live, but the powerful army of the always already living. The power of seeing through performance is the recognition that we've seen it all before—the fantasies that shape our sense of self, of community, that organize our scenarios of interaction, conflict, and resolution.[92]

Thus we can view the project of historians as not only archival, but part of the repertoire; like other great discoverers, we too wish to peek into the long-dormant tomb, to hear the long-lost songs, to see and hear the past as it had never been seen and heard before, and who cares if that was *the* past, or merely *a* past?

The queer repertoire of Barney intersects, twists, and turns around the performed repertoire of antiquity; Barney and her friends manufacture, create, and improvise a history and repertoire so convincingly that as we will see in chapter 6, even the scholar can be fooled into believing that the reconstruction is the real thing. Barney's motivation for creating this repertoire is not deception, but absence. I'm not the first to lament the procreative impossibility of queer performance. Generation after generation of queer artists have been left to invent and/or dust off their queer history; the songs of Judy Garland, Barbra Streisand, Lady Gaga, and Sappho resurface and find reappropriation.[93]

A century ago scholars were unaware of the difference between these disparate ways of knowing or that special care may be required with performance. Today we can be reminded of the difficulties of the archive. As Diana Taylor argues, while they may be different, the archive and the repertoire form a network feed back into each other.

Fragments and Vampires: Conclusions

> Faire des fragments.
>
> —Natalie Clifford Barney, *Éparpillements*[94]

Barney seems to have been very aware of this feedback loop when she manipulated her own image to transform a photograph of a passive dancer into an act of Sapphic poetry—a photographic fragment. In the photo reproduced in figure 3.10, Barney truly re-enacted a Sapphic fragment by tearing and cutting away the other dancers in this image with scissors.

Like the lines of Sappho or the photos of an abandoned home, the image tells only a portion of the story, begging for its missing piece, inviting the viewer or the scholar to fill in the rest of the frame. Whose hand does she hold?

FIGURE 3.10 Natalie Clifford Barney as Sapphic fragment. Smithsonian Institute Archives, SIA2017-061361.

What else is there? A fragment of a fragment, Barney's image channels the desire for fragments through the willful manipulation of the remnants of the past.

So where do the Sapphonic voice and the voice of the ancient past meet? It seems that queer voices are almost always inherently fragmented or lost voices—muted and silenced voices—in the archival record like the missing sonic traces of antiquity. The scraps of Sappho's poetry exist in the archive. We can visit and reread them. However, they are voices without the cultural apparatus to record them as queer voices, as ancient voices lack the technical apparatus to be recorded at all. Sappho also exists independently in the repertoire: re-enacted, re-embodied, and reimagined century after century. As Sappho scholar Margaret Reynolds has written, "Sappho is always what we make of her. She may once have performed her, as I am performing her now."[95] The continual performance and re-enactment of Sappho, like the performance of Sapphonics, take place between performers but also scholars. In the project of history, we seek to embody the past through the tools of writing, not performance. That indeterminable Sapphonic voice seems only to be heard by the historian, never in the present, but always by some outsider eager to get in the ring—by listeners outside the system. Elizabeth Wood hears it in the voice of dead opera stars (e.g., Calvé), Peraino in Judy Garland. Gourmont, Louÿs, and Salomon Reinach heard it in Barney and Vivien, and Barney heard it in Sappho.[96] Performance requires an audience of scholars attuned to their song. An audience who demand, in the words of Sappho: "Yes! Radiant lyre speak to me / become a voice."[97]

––––––––––

Anna Livia [Julian Brawn]'s 1991 *Minimax*—a novel of contradictions—provides the scholar (Livia) with an opportunity to write Barney into her own queer time and space. A novelist, linguist, and translator, Livia taught in the French Department at the University of Illinois, Urbana-Champaign, and then at the University of California, Berkeley, before her unexpected death at the age of fifty-one in 2007.[98] While working on her doctorate in French linguistics at Berkeley, Livia took on a translation project of Barney's writings, *A Perilous Advantage* (1992), supported by Barney scholar Karla Jay. As she immersed herself in Barney's works as a scholar, Livia was finishing her novel *Minimax*, featuring Barney as an immortal vampire.

Set in Perth, London, San Francisco, and many places in between, *Minimax* is about lesbians, vampires, time, and letting go. Exemplifying many aspects of queer time and temporal drag, *Minimax* brings the elusive Barney to life in temporal and physical spaces she never could have imagined. The novel tells the story of Minnie, whom we meet alone in her London bathtub listening to a cassette tape of Mozart's *Die Zauberflöte*, singing " 'Pa pa pa; pa pa pa' in tune with the love-smitten bird-catcher [Papageno]."[99] Minnie, like Barney, has a fondness for opera. After reading the lyrics to Cherubino's aria "Voi, che sapete" ["You who knows"] from *Le Nozze di Figaro* in the frontispiece to Barney's first publication,[100] Minnie listened to the whole opera: "It was like discovering lesbianism after having resigned oneself to celibacy. Now Minnie would cry when certain arias were sung, like *Che farò senza Euridice?* (what *would* she do without Euridice?) and *Ardon gl'incensi* (the bathroom filled with the scent of burning incense)."[101] Opera and those Sapphonic voices of 1990s musicology play a critical role in the relationship between Minnie listening to cassette tapes in her bathtub and the mysterious response she receives from a fan letter she sent to the undead Barney that read, "Come, I must meet you." In Livia's novel "Pa pa pa," Papageno's nonsense lyrics to his beloved, mean "We are both strange birds seeking the one creature who can love us as we wish to be loved."[102] Minnie can't seem to find the love she desires on any continent (Europe, North America, or Australia), but only in the past, in Barney, whose words she has devoured. Minnie sings the first three notes of Papageno and Papagena's duet in the finale of act 2. In her global search for Barney, Minnie constantly hums the three notes, waiting to hear a response from the past. Mozart's aviary lovers complete each other's phrases: Papageno's antecedent followed by Papagena's consequent (see music example 3.1).

Minnie's call to her own Papagena, her letter to the past, invokes a response: "Come, I must meet you." Livia writes, "Didn't Minnie know what tremendous forces she summoned with those three notes? Well, the power was unleashed now; that'd teach her."[103] Minnie wanders the globe visiting family members and former lovers. Her sister Beryl has been house-sitting in Perth for the mysterious "R.V." (none other than Renée Vivien, and yes, she's a lesbian vampire, too), whose home is bedecked with statues of famed soprano opera singers and Barney's former lovers. Now in San Francisco, Minnie receives a fax from Barney that says, "*Hurry, hurry, hurry, hurry, hurry,*" and a letter from "R.V." containing the same message. Minnie is confused. She does not know either of these people, but they seem to know her. They communicate through Mozart, of course, and through Sapphonic voices. "She had never met Natalie [. . .], but she had read her books and owed to her every favourite opera. Secretly Minnie believed Mozart must have been a lesbian; nothing else explained that incredible music. A well-kept secret. '*Voi che sapete*,' indeed"[104] Minnie, like Livia herself perhaps, is constantly searching for the key to a life she desperately sought through scholarship but alas, could not find in the snippets of poetry. Livia, through her character, Minnie, may have wanted Barney to come to life, just as Barney needed her Psappha/Sappho to come to life.

When Minnie finally sees the vampires Barney and Vivien in the undead flesh for the first time, even her plastic grocery bag is affected. "For such is the power of the vampire," writes Livia, "that she appears all things to all creatures and holds sway even over the inanimate, so that each feels her to be the very thing their heart most desires."[105] For those of us who do this kind of scholarship, who hunt down snippets of music or photographs of performances, traces

of artistic lives that end up dominating our own, the idea of a subject as vampire doesn't seem so strange. Livia's description of Minnie's first encounter with Barney could be her own or my own, when I found myself standing in her bedroom. Sometimes that is all we get.

> Minnie knew, while gazing at the yacht from the black rock, that she had been waiting for it, and for she who sailed upon it, all her life; everything she had ever done had been leading inexorably to this moment (an allusion to the famous Leucadian leap?). Therefore she savored the moment. The sea spray blew in her face, unprotected by the rock; the exhilaration of the waves swirled at her feet; and from over the water sounded the five notes of *The Magic Flute*, which Minnie had mistaken for a bird hooting. She listened; one, two, three, four, five. "And now," she decided, "I will swim to that yacht and meet my destiny."[106]

Of course, upon meeting your obsession you begin to lose interest and see the fetishized object for what it really is; not an imaginary vampire, but a real human being. As Barney begins to seduce Minnie, she draws her a bath, but it isn't right; there is no Mozart playing. Something seems off. We soon learn Barney's motivations for hunting down Minnie. Barney believed that Minnie's fanaticism, her fandom for her books, could bring her back to life. "Something in Minnie's letter, the attention to her books, the glittering comprehension, had made Natalie believe that Minnie could bring her back to life, inspire her with desire to write again. This vampirehood was living death: Minnie would be her Lisbon *Traviata*, for like Maria Callas, Natalie would perform again more stupendous, more beloved than before."[107] Natalie and Minnie go on dates, they have sex, try to find a way together, but when Minnie asks, "Can a modern-day lesbian find happiness with a one-hundred-year-old vampire?,"[108] the answer is no. As Natalie takes her yacht and her magical past with her out to sea, leaving Minnie on the beach of Perth, for a second Minnie thinks she hears the Countess's act 2 aria, "Porgi amor," from Mozart's *Le Nozze di Figaro* specifically the lines "O mi rendi il mio tesoro, o mi lasci almen morir!" ("Either bring my darling back to me, or let me lie down and die!") Livia concludes her novel: "Minnie was struck with the bitter certainty that she could no longer find joy or solace in opera, for Natalie had written all the operas in the world, acted each one out in turn and many times. But the song which was playing was not music at all but a pop melody to which the only words were 'Woe woe woe' and 'Love love love'."[109] Barney isn't the salvation that Minnie sought. As we all know from Stephanie Meyer's *Twilight Saga* and HBO's *True Blood*, human-vampire sexual relationships rarely turn out well, queer or straight. It is difficult to live happily ever after with someone who is undead. Barney ultimately brought Minnie closer to the real people in her life, her family.

Throughout the novel, a Sapphonic voice calls out to Minnie. It arrives as both physical, archival material (letters from the vampire Barney), and as overheard songs, learned actions, and sexual encounters. Livia's novel, like the ludic aspects of queer musicology, provides yet another space for musical explorations for queer temporalities. The recreation of songs sung by long-dead opera singers, imagined arias, and singing birdpeople stands in for the erotic encounters Minnie/Livia seeks, just as the performances of Sappho's fragments in Barney's garden allow for a queer reperformance of Lesbos in a modern world. Music and performance have the power to truncate the distance between the past and the present and in so doing carve out new spaces immune to time. Barney's vampiric Sappho and Livia's vampiric Barney outlive both ancestor and progeny through their time-truncating songs.

To reperform Barney through scholarly work, archival journeys, experimental embodied theatrical practice, or the writing of fiction is to engage in the project of history. To examine Barney's own performances of Sappho challenges the ways we as scholars in the humanities write our histories and separate our own bodies from the archives where we sit and our own identities, loves, fears, and fantasies from the subjects we study. Barney reminds us how the embodied experience of being in the archive (or the bedroom) can itself become the object of study, rather than the secrets revealed therein. Archives yield few secrets; readers must excavate the buried past or make it up.

4 | Performing Scholarship for the Paris Opéra

MAURICE EMMANUEL'S *SALAMINE* (1929)

SINCE 2007 THE AMERICAN Association for the Advancement of Science has offered a "Dance Your Ph.D." competition in which PhDs and PhD candidates in the sciences are invited to create videos of themselves dancing interpretations of their dissertations, post them online, and perhaps win cash prizes and the chance to "achieve immortal geek fame on the Internet."[1] Examples on YouTube and Vimeo include dancers performing such dissertation titles as "Sperm Competition between Brothers and Female Choice"[2] and "Heterodyne Arrays for Terahertz Astronomy."[3] In a 2011 TED talk, John Bohannon—the founder of the competition—argues that dance is superior to traditional models of writing and mind-numbing PowerPoint slides to illustrate complex ideas in contemporary scientific research. The winning dances selected from each of the four categories (biology, chemistry, physics, and social science) are entertaining, informative, and certainly creative. But why aren't scholars in the arts and humanities allowed to participate?[4] Their ideas are plenty complex. Is it because the organizers assume that those working closer to the performing arts may have an unfair advantage? Does a Shakespeare scholar have a greater aptitude to translate their reading of *The Winter's Tale* into choreographic form? Can musicologists dance their dissertations better than their colleagues across campus? Perhaps the reason for their exclusion from this game is not their superior skills, but rather that many in the arts and humanities couldn't compete with the creativity of their colleagues in the sciences. Maybe musicology is just no good at transforming their theories into performance.

Musicologists have certainly tried to perform their scholarship throughout the twentieth century, as evidenced by the activities of the Historically Informed Performance (HIP) movement, but these examples are most often applications of scholarship to the performance of existing works, not the creation of new works based on musicological research per se.

This kind of marriage between scholarship and performance (of new work) is foundational to performance studies. Within that field one can very easily dance one's dissertation. Musicology has stayed away from such explorations in the past century. A notable handful of musicologists double as composers, librettists, and creative fiction writers, but as a field we have yet to fully interrogate their scholarly and creative works. Are they one and the same? Are they altogether separate and different? Should artistic interpretations of scholarly work be taken into consideration at all? Can performance clarify or even enliven scholarly ideas?

What happens when a musicologist composes an opera to illustrate their theories of music history?[5] Like his colleague Théodore Reinach, Maurice Emmanuel (1863–1938) studied the musical culture and theory of antiquity, and also like Reinach, his research led to performances that brought the art of the past to the present. Musicologist and composer Emmanuel's research on Greek dance and rhythm (*La Danse grecque antique d'après les monuments figures*, *Traité de la musique grecque antique*, and *Le Rythme d'Euripide à Debussy*) provided both inspiration and source material for musicians, artists, and choreographers alike. In *La Danse grecque antique* (based on his Sorbonne dissertation in musicology from 1895),[6] he provided a guide to help others perform ancient Greek dances through his detailed study of vases and statuary from antiquity and analysis of high-speed action photographs (this method is called *chronophotography*, a then-nascent cinematic technology) of modern classical ballet technique to reconstruct the movements from the distant past. Emmanuel's conclusions do not stand up to modern scholarly scrutiny. His writings on reconstructing ancient dance offer an imagined correlation among statuary, photography, and choreography. Nevertheless, in the first decades of the twentieth century his research on ancient Greek rhythm, dance, and music received widespread praise among the general public, placing him as the leading academic authority on ancient Greek dance and rhythm. While serving as a professor of music history at the Conservatoire de Paris for almost thirty years, Emmanuel found success in his academic positions as a pedagogue and scholar. In his true passion, composition, success was elusive.

Salamine (1929),[7] Emmanuel's second opera and his first premiered at l'Opéra, uniquely employs the scholar's own research on ancient Greek music and dance to produce a creative artistic work for a general audience. In essence, Emmanuel composed an opera based on his own dissertation (although *he* didn't actually dance his dissertation). The work illustrates the tensions between scholarship and performance, as well as between the study of antiquity and the crafting of modernity in the first decades of the twentieth century. Emmanuel collaborated with an eclectic group of scholars and artists on this opera: Théodore Reinach (see chapter 2) translated and adapted the libretto

based on Aeschylus's *The Persians*; a stalwart of conservative Italianate choreography, Nicola Guerra (1865–1942), the last choreographer at the Opéra before Serge Lifar took over in 1930, organized dances featuring the eurhythmic
dancer Yvonne Franck; and Emmanuel composed the opera's Debussyian,
neo-modal music. With the leading scholars of ancient music, drama, and
dance on board, *Salamine* performs antiquity like no other work from the period. Emmanuel's coup in bringing scholarship on ancient Greek arts to the
stage of the Opéra is unprecedented;[8] however, it was ultimately unsuccessful
as a staged work. Opera as a genre was created to reimagine and reinterpret
ancient Greek drama; thus it seems that opera *would* be the perfect genre for
Emmanuel's realization. But it never received a staged revival; the press did
not lavish attention on it; and it has been largely ignored by music, drama, and
dance scholars.[9]

In my examination of collaborations between scholars and artists in the performance of ancient Greece, *Salamine* should have been the crowning jewel,
the best example of the marriage of scholarship and performance. The scholar
created his own performance from his own research. Theoretically, this should
be the work truest to the style, aesthetics, performance practice, and feel of ancient Greek drama. Instead we find a work blending an early twentieth-century
modernist musical style with episodes of nineteenth-century ballet technique.
After taking stock of Emmanuel's writings on ancient Greek dance, I examine
the 1929 production of *Salamine* in order to outline and critique his scholarly
contributions to ancient Greek dance and music history and their performance.
I demonstrate how Emmanuel tried to bring his successful scholarly work into
his creative work by using his own theories about ancient and modern music and
dance as well as his aesthetic preferences for modern music (Claude Debussy
in particular) and classic ballet technique (as opposed to eurhythmic, barefoot,
or modern dance) within the opera. Exploring Emmanuel's methodologies
and aesthetics of music and dance—ancient and modern—affords us a unique
opportunity to see how these creative media were theorized and performed
in the tumultuous years after the Ballets Russes, while also illustrating some
of the conflicts between what Léandre Vaillat termed "the academic and
the eurhythmic" in dance and music.[10] Ultimately, examining Emmanuel's
methods for reconstructing ancient dance from *La Danse grecque antique*,
as well as his conclusions that ancient Greek music evolved into modernist
music and that ancient Greek dance evolved into *danse d'école*, highlights the
difficulty, then and now, in realizing history and theory in practice. The artistic
culmination of Emmanuel's scholarly theories, the opera *Salamine*, similarly
struggled to find a home. One would have thought that an artistic realization of
the leading scholar of ancient Greek music and dance theory and an acclaimed
professor and educator would be able to pull off a convincing performance, but
neither contemporary audiences nor history have found *Salamine*'s Debussy-
like music, staid libretto, and traditional choreography, all derived from the

decades of professional success of its principal creators, worthy of re-performance. That in itself is interesting.

The reasons for this non-success (I don't want to go so far as to call it a failure) seem to come from Emmanuel's own certainty in his historical conclusions. This ultimately dictates what the performance will be. Rather than engaging in dialogue between the archival and the repertoire, the scholarly and the embodied, the static and the dynamic, or the gnostic and the drastic, Emmanuel's theories demarcate the boundaries of performance. What is evident is that *Salamine* tries to fix the scholar's ideas into a vibrant performative event. It is a vibrancy muted by a successful career of scholarship backed by high-tech research but ultimately limited by the scholar's own aesthetic blinders. Emmanuel reminds us of the limits of our technologies and empirical methodologies in seeking truth and making art.

Maurice Emmanuel and the Music of Antiquity

From a young age Emmanuel had a diverse array of interests: science, ancient Greek culture, and music. As a student at the Conservatoire de Paris he studied music history under Louis-Albert Bourgault-Ducoudray (1840–1910) and took courses at the Sorbonne on classics and Greek. From his early student days, Emmanuel struggled to balance his dual role as artist/composer and researcher. In a letter to his father in 1882, Emmanuel explained why he was unable to just focus on one subject:

> But is it not strange to refuse artists the powers of thought and reflection? [. . .] I study philosophy because it is important to me as an artist to know who I am, where I came from; because my convictions will be reflected in my work, because I believe in the ideal. I study literature because it is important to me as an artist to know the soul in daily life and to know the heart of those whom I am referring. I study science because Nature dazzles me with its splendor and I find that in studying something of that ideal beauty it forces me to reflect on my own works and it matters to me as an artist to go seek out all the sources. And so I think [. . .] that one can be an artist, a philosopher, a scientist and that is indeed all the more necessary to be them all at once within certain limits since human nature is also limited, the artist often has to help the scientist, the philosopher and the scientist.[11]

His doctoral thesis shows the influence of Ernest Renan's *L'avenir de la science* (1890) as well as François-Auguste Gevaert's predictions in *Origines du chant liturgique de l'Église latine* (1890) about the future of science. These studies convinced Emmanuel that science could also aid art in uncovering the past through rigorous analysis of modern art and its ancient sources.[12] His novel approach to ancient Greek dance benefited from mentors at the Sorbonne and l'École du Louvre and friends at l'Opéra. Louis Havet's *Course de métrique latine et grecque* (1886) provided Emmanuel with a rhythmic analysis of the works of Pindar, Aeschylus, Sophocles, and Euripides, to be employed in Emmanuel's own reconstructions of ancient dance. Archaeologists Edmond Pottier and Maxime Collignon guided Emmanuel through ancient art history and helped him refine his artistic eye. Louis Mérante, maître de ballet at the Opéra, toured the Giampietro Campana collection at the Louvre museum with Emmanuel in the earliest days of the project. As they examined the statues and vases Mérante exclaimed, "That's us," and in front of the ancient models of dance he executed a perfect jeté, saut de chat, and pirouette![13]

The resulting scholarly work, Emmanuel's *La Danse grecque antique*, supplied inspiration and source material for artists, choreographers, and musicians. Containing more than six hundred illustrations of dancers reproduced from vases, bas-reliefs, and statuary from ancient Greece, the book resulting from his dissertation surveyed the range of gestures that survived in ancient Greek iconographic sources. Printed numerous times in French and translated into English twenty years after its first publication, this musicological document helped to solidify a concept and image vocabulary for ancient Greek movement, as well as a fashion for antique dances generally.[14] Comparing photographs of contemporary ballet dancers midstep to images from Grecian vases, Emmanuel matched ancient Greek gestures to what he interpreted as their modern equivalents (jeté, rond de jambe, etc.) and concluded that late nineteenth-century ballet movement vocabulary could be traced back to Greek origins. As shown here in figures 4.1a and 4.1b, Emmanuel demonstrated how the dancer's leg in his figure 219 will follow, executing a grand battement as in the photographs of the dancer in his plate II.[15]

10   11   12

FIGURE 4.1a Maurice Emmanuel, *La Danse grecque antique* (1896), plate II, figs 10–12.

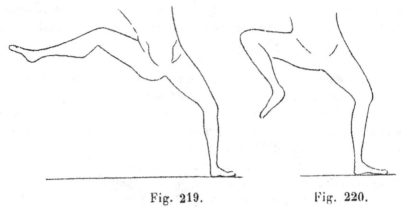

Fig. 219.   Fig. 220.

FIGURE 4.1b Maurice Emmanuel, *La Danse grecque antique* (1896), figs 219–220.

Emmanuel's method was grounded in that encounter at the Louvre with Mérante. The rhythmic philological practice of Havet, and to a lesser extent his musicological mentors, Bourgault-Ducoudray and Gevaert, provided new ways to abstractly theorize movement, to draw upon Eastern musical and movement vocabularies, and to seemingly objectively quantify and measure the object of study. Mérante and other living, breathing dancers offered an opportunity to study the object itself: an embodiment of the past brought back to life. In his biographical study of Emmanuel, Christophe Corbier remarks on the encounter: "Imagine Emmanuel's excitement seeing the still images of antiquity come alive before his eyes."[16] Emmanuel went on to assist Mérante (and then Joseph Hansen, director of the ballet at the Opéra from 1887 to 1907) at the Opéra, training and choreographing dances, all the time imagining the ancient figures in the modern steps of the dancers. All he needed to do was analyze these moving bodies and superimpose them on the still images captured by Greek artists millennia ago. Emmanuel's novel idea was to learn what ancient dance looked like (and did not look like) from living dancers and rigorous scientific methods.

Marey, Chronophotography, and the Analysis of the Moving Body

The photos for Emmanuel's book shown in figure 4.1a were taken by Étienne-Jules Marey (1830–1904) using his famous chronophotgraphic gun. As a researcher, Marey significantly added to the fields of cardiology, physiological instrumentation, aviation, cinematography, and the science of labor, as well as photography and cinematography. Aesthetics were of secondary or tertiary importance to Marey; his goal was to measure and quantify. Emmanuel and other researchers in the arts immediately saw the value in Marey's ability to render movements, like those of the dancers at the Opéra, into "raw scientific data." The aesthetic value of these proto-cinematic images remained secondary to the researchers.[17]

The early work of Marey was sparked by his desire to measure movement, and in the late 1850s he devised numerous machines that translated physiological functions of animals into graphs (respiration, circulation, muscle function). These led to explorations into more complex human movements (walking, running, jumping, etc.). Photography seemed the best way to record and measure the complex series of movements in a deceptively simple exercise such as walking, and chronophotography developed not to make art initially, but rather as a scientific endeavor, to measure the body's movement in time.

Marey invented a photographic gun (1882)—a device that looked like a sawed-off shotgun—that could capture twelve consecutive frames per second on one photographic plate (see figure 4.2). This greatly improved his ability to record, measure, and interpret data on movement in a variety of locations, not just in the studio. It also opened the door for others (including scholars working in the arts) to collect their own data using his process.[18]

Seeing his work as scientific, Marey did not discount the use of chronophotography for artistic purposes, but he wanted to stay away from aesthetic debates. In discussing some of his technology's possible artistic applications, he compared images of runners from antiquity with modern paintings of runners and noted that "the modern attitudes are quieter and better poised, so to speak, while in ancient works of art the figures sometimes appear in positions of unstable equilibrium."[19] Comparing them both to his chronophotographs of a man running, one would then see that both "attitudes" were present in the array of images. Marey concluded: "Instantaneous photography is an excellent means of showing the actual attitudes assumed."[20]

Emmanuel did not address his collaboration with the famous scientist within the body of his own treatise (except in the acknowledgments), and it is unclear how the two met. As a student at the Sorbonne and Collège de France after the Franco-Prussian War (1870–1871), Emmanuel surrounded himself with the German-influenced positivists of the "New Sorbonne," which included Gaston Paris, Alfred Croiset, Louis Havet, Paul Girard, and Henri Jolly.[21] Marey, another young positivist, fit right in with this circle of Latin Quarter intellectuals, and he proudly discussed his collaboration with Maurice Emmanuel in a chapter in his *Le Mouvement* dedicated to the artistic applications of chronophotography.[22] His remarks on collaborations with the musicologist fall under the section "The Fall of Drapery" (ancient Greek costume piqued Marey's interest as well):[23]

M. Maurice Emmanuel, who is bringing out an important work on the dances of antiquity, asked us to take instantaneous photographs of certain attitudes,

Fig. 1. Mode d'emploi du fusil photographique.

FIGURE 4.2 Étienne-Jules Marey with photographic gun. From Étienne-Jules Marey, "Le fusil photographique," *La Nature* 464 (April 1882): 326–330.

such as he noticed on some of his bas-reliefs and Greek vases. On looking at these photographs one cannot help recognizing a sort of general suggestiveness of the particular movement of the dance by the fall of the drapery.

Even the successive phases of a dance may be followed in a series of chronophotographs, but the narrow limits of this book only allow us to offer a few examples.[24]

Marey left the interpretation of the dancers' chronophotographic data for Emmanuel to discuss in his *La Danse grecque antique*, which came out the same year as *Le Mouvement*.

While Emmanuel did not try to argue that ancient dancers performed modern ballet, he did use this technique to argue that they were very closely related. With this new chronophotographic technology he believed that it was possible to reconstruct the dances in the way an architect might restore an ancient temple or palace based on the fallen remains.[25]

On the use of technology to illustrate tempos and steps of the ancient Greek dance, Emmanuel argues: "Their practiced eye knew how to see. With a bit of clay and a few theories they fixed the most elusive moments. Comparing their work with the photographs [of modern dancers], allows us to guarantee their accuracy."[26] Emmanuel's methodology demonstrates a very sophisticated use of modern technology to better understand the artistic practice of the past. Accepting photography as an unbiased technology to uncover empirical truth, he underestimated the trappings of his own analysis of the images.[27] Photography, like any technology, does not guarantee objectivity. As Susan Sontag wrote, "While a painting or a prose description can never be other than a narrowly selective interpretation, a photograph can be treated as a narrowly selective transparency."[28] To re-emphasize a claim made in chapter 1, the photograph and the subject it has captured appear to be one and the same: the photograph can appear to be a transparent window to the actual object under study. Following Emmanuel's logic, since the painted and sculpted images of ancient Greek dancers midstep resembled the photographic images of modern dancers midstep, they must be near equivalents. The media must be accurate tools with comparable fidelity to the dance itself. While the artists who painted and sculpted the images on the vases and bas-reliefs were limited in their ability to reproduce by their skill, for Emmanuel, photography allowed the scholar to avoid the biases and limitations of human artistry. The object being photographed exists, but its meaning (interpretation) is not clear. On the illusions of photography, Roland Barthes notes how while painting can "feign reality" and discourse is composed of signs that have referents, in photography one "can never deny that *the thing has been there*. There is a superimposition here: of reality and of the past."[29] This superimposition produced by the modern technology of fast-shutter photography allowed Emmanuel to read the movements of the ancient past in the still-wet photographs of the very recent past. Following the positivist trend of the Sorbonne, Emmanuel's use of photography seemed to bring scientific rigor to the emerging field of musicology. Science and its battery of technical apparatus propped up and made serious Emmanuel's subjective interpretations of dance aesthetics, past and present.

The camera as gun is a powerful image, not only created by Marey and employed by Emmanuel in their work, but also theorized by Susan Sontag in her *On Photography*: "Like guns and cars, cameras are fantasy-machines whose use is addictive. [. . .] The camera/gun does not kill, so the ominous metaphor seems to be all bluff—like a man's fantasy of having a gun, knife, or tool between his legs. Still, there is something predatory in the act of taking a picture. To photograph people is to violate them, by seeing them as they never see themselves, by having knowledge of them they can never have; it turns people into objects that can be symbolically possessed."[30]

Marey and Emmanuel's respective projects were indeed fantasy and indeed addictive. It would be great to be able to distill human movement into data that one can possess, manipulate, analyze, and codify; however, ephemeral movements are notoriously difficult not only to capture, but also to reproduce from static images. Performance exists in the present, in the spaces between the poses, the breath between the notes. But with new technologies come new opportunities to try to record the unrecordable and to quantify the unquantifiable. Photography's (and later cinema's) potential to help researchers systematize and taxonomize their subjects was a false promise. Already by 1927, Siegfried Kracauer urged caution about getting lost in the alluring qualities as modern society braved the "blizzard of photographs."[31] Technology does not diminish bias; technology's scientific certainty often creates it.

In the following analysis of Emmanuel's theoretical/historical and creative/compositional work, we should continually remind ourselves of his chosen position. We see the transformation of dynamic gestures to static images in Emmanuel's methodology, which he then reanimates through his scholarly writing into an imagined dynamic image of ancient dance (not *real* dance, at least not yet). Unlike scholars working in performance studies today, who navigate the gap between the live and the recorded, the performance and the traces of the performance, with an arsenal of theory and critical self-reflection, Emmanuel exhibited none of this sensitivity. Sontag's image of the camera as gun/phallus positions Emmanuel and Marey as the perpetrators of a crime, the crime of photography. While I doubt Emmanuel himself viewed his methods as predatory, dishonest, or biased, his certainty and reliance on the photographic evidence prop up his assertions about aesthetics of dance both old and new. That is to say, his conclusions about the relationship between ancient and modern dance are not supported by the chronophotographic images. The images are used to lend a touch of positivist credibility to his subjective discussion of dance aesthetics.

From Theory to Practice: *La Danse grecque antique* and the Modern Dancer

Emmanuel's dissertation based on his photographic analysis did not languish like so many others in the back of a dusty old university library. *La Danse grecque antique* became an incredibly popular work. In 1896 his dissertation was republished twice in France, followed by editions in Germany, Belgium, and Greece. He also published a series of articles for the *Gazette des Beaux-Arts* and *Ménestrel* that further promoted his theories on ancient dance to a broader public audience. Corbier also notes that the publications came out just in time to benefit from the hype surrounding Pierre de Coubertin's restoration of the Olympic Games in 1896 in Athens, Greece.[32] Emmanuel's treatise and his assertions served a larger audience outside of the academic community as well. With over six hundred images, *La Danse grecque antique* reached out to artists, musicians, dancers, and stage directors seeking an authoritative voice on ancient Greek dance and music, backed by cutting-edge scientific research on the movements of the past. Modern dancers studying Emmanuel's work were ultimately studying not just ancient images, but also Emmanuel's interpretation of them through the photographs of modern dancers.

The number of Emmanuel's images that correspond to the steps and poses of dancers from the first decades of the twentieth century who took an interest in ancient Greece is striking. Two notable examples are Isadora Duncan and the Opéra-Comique's Régina Badet, but the case could be made that Emmanuel's figures predate the many staple gestures in modern dance movement vocabulary. Figure 4.3a shows Emmanuel's sketch of the Greeks' mimetic "Praise Gesture," alongside images of Duncan in her *Ave Maria* from 1914 in figure 4.3b.

While it is very possible that dancers consulted Emmanuel's book instead of studying the original images in the museum, it is more likely that dancers and choreographers used both resources, since one can see similarities to ancient images housed in Paris (as well as other European museums) and to the dances themselves. While I could produce dozens of examples comparing images from Emmanuel's book and the gestures of modern dancers from the first decades of the twentieth century like the ones in figure 4.3, I would be just as guilty as Emmanuel in relying on static images to argue for a choreographic influence and genealogy. The similarities are certainly intriguing, and the

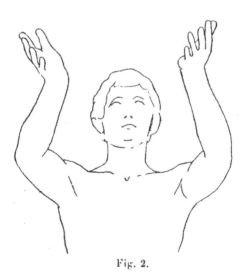

Fig. 2.

FIGURE 4.3a Maurice Emmanuel, *La Danse grecque antique* (1896), fig. 2 ["Praise Gesture"].

FIGURE 4.3b Isadora Duncan in *Ave Maria* (1914). Library of Congress, Prints & Photographs Division, Arnold Genthe Collection: Negatives and Transparencies, LC-G412-1476-D-030.

sheer number of correspondences between the images in Emmanuel's book and images of dancers like Duncan, Badet, Eva Palmer Sikelianos, and even Vaslav Nijinsky lend support to the argument that dancers used Emmanuel's book. However, it isn't just the correspondence of images of antiquity, but also the bold shared belief in the primacy of dance for a deeper understanding of music and drama and that ancient dance steps could be reconstructed from static images, that Emmanuel shared with this first wave of modern dancers.[33] These similarities are even more striking given that Emmanuel disapproved of much modern dance, eurhythmics, and barefoot dancers and used his treatise on the ancient Greek dance to argue for the primacy of classical ballet technique over the "corrupted" modern dance.

In her famous lecture "The Dance of the Future," Duncan explained: "If we seek the real source of the dance, if we go to nature, we find that the dance of the future is the dance of the past, the dance of eternity, and has been and will always be the same."[34] She followed this by noting that dance should recreate natural processes and beings, and she urged dancers to find "those primary movements for the human body from which shall evolve the movements of the future dance." She then provided an example of choreographic reconstruction from ancient statuary similar to Emmanuel's own methods:

As an example of this, we might take the pose of the Hermes of the Greeks. He is represented as flying on the wind. If the artist had pleased to pose his foot in a vertical position, he might have done so, as the God, flying on the wind, is not touching the earth; but realizing that no movement is true unless suggesting sequence of movements, the sculptor placed the Hermes with the ball of his foot resting on the wind, giving the movement an eternal quality.

In the same way I might make an example of each pose and gesture in the thousands of figures we have left to us on the Greek vases and bas-reliefs; there is not one which in its movement does not presuppose another movement.

This is because the Greeks were the greatest students of the laws of nature, wherein all is the expression of unending, ever-increasing evolution, wherein are no ends and no stops.[35]

While both Duncan and Emmanuel relied on images found in museums in dialogue with their own conceptions of natural movement, unlike Emmanuel, Duncan was not particularly interested in recreating the dances of the past as they might have been; she merely used these images as inspiration for her dance of the future. Emmanuel believed that the steps could be reconstructed. Duncan wrote: "[T]he dance of the future will be a new movement, a consequence of the entire evolution which mankind has passed through. . . . We are not Greeks and therefore cannot dance Greek dances."[36] Both Emmanuel and Duncan saw their contributions to dance as the inheritor of the ancient Greek traditions.

Madame Mariquita, Régina Badet's choreographer and mentor, took an approach similar to Duncan's and Emmanuel's. The costume designer, former dancer, "antiquarian,"[37] and choreographer at the Folies Bergère and the Opéra-Comique trained many dancers. Her obituary in the *New York Herald* described her as teaching "her students an appreciation of the beauty and grace of Grecian poses, which are now considered the basis of all ballet successes."[38]

Concerning the prospect of choreographing new divertissements for Gluck's *Orpheus* for Badet, Mariquita noted in an interview in 1908: "I immediately rushed to visit museums, I looked at antique vases, frescoes, statues . . . and in extensively examined documents, which I studied carefully, I found poses, attitudes, gestures, whereupon I based my entire dance. . . . What do you want, I'm only an interpreter. . . . I have not invented or created Greek art. . . . I just try to express beauty through dance inspired by masterpieces left to us, frozen in the splendor of the stones or marbles or in the magnificence of the frescoes!"[39] Although Mariquita, Duncan, and Emmanuel all used ancient Greek images to create their choreography, they produced extraordinarily different fantasies of the classical world.

Emmanuel used ancient Greek images to illustrate a teleological connection to classical ballet technique. Duncan used the forms as inspiration and appropriated the static exalted and extended poses seen on the vases, using them as momentary apparitions in a swirl, a brief pause in a hop, or perhaps the final extension of a grand gesture. Irma Duncan's directives for staging her mentor's "Tanagra Figures" describe a fluid dance involving the entire body reaching; shifting weight; and making use of the head, arms, and torso in sweeping gestures. The poses are fleeting, with images of Greek statuary and vases seen as fragmentary glimpses in larger modern gestures. Mariquita, on the other hand, often used twirling, lightly veiled dancers who variously held poses depicted on vases in a combination of pantomime and dance inserted into the narrative of operas.[40] Neither resembles Emmanuel's classical ideal.

Maurice Emmanuel's Aesthetics of Ancient Dance

What makes one realization of ancient imagery better than another? Retuning to *La Danse grecque antique*, Emmanuel's treatise on ancient Greek dance begins with a study of the sources in which he explains why images are best for reconstructing ancient dance by pointing out the faults of the other sources: the writings and the poetic rhythms.[41] But there is a problem that even he acknowledges: "If we can establish—and this study has no other purpose— that, apart from the fantasy or the inexperience of artists, dance movements set on vases and reliefs are faithfully translated, we willingly accept that these accurate representations of dancing scenes are the most precious that we can consult."[42] While images may be the most precious, their value in no way reflects their ability to accurately translate ancient Greek movement into an array of data for scientific reconstruction. And so to animate the dance, Emmanuel relied on contemporary aesthetics to create his own formulations for reproducing ancient aesthetics.

Emmanuel looked around at what "ancient Greek dance" looked like in fin-de-siècle Paris and did not like what he saw. In an open letter to Jacques Dalcroze, Emmanuel wrote that he regretted putting off reading the latter's book on rhythm and music for so long. His excuse was that "alongside fervent and faithful disciples, you have left imitators in Paris, and some impudent 'knock-offs,' which divert attention or hinder sympathy."[43] Emmanuel did not fault Dalcroze's theory; it was just the (mostly) women in Paris, the "eurhythmic dancer[s]," who put it into practice. The dances of Loïe Fuller, the students of Madame Mariquita and later Isadora Duncan, with their free movements, uncorseted bodies and bare feet, translated to Emmanuel's eye as a Dalcroze "knock-off," artistic "fantasy" and/or "inexperience." His return to the archival sources and comparing them to the rigid formalism of classical ballet technique contrasts with the embodied experience (not inexperience) of Duncan and her peers, who placed their own bodies in the poses depicted on ancient vases to enact their own fantasy of ancient movement.

Emmanuel's comment from the 1890s predates the familiar controversial dances of Duncan, but nonetheless points to a similarly sinister set of sylphs.

The desire for wild bacchanals and other scenes of ancient excess flourished in the last few decades of the nineteenth century. The Bacchanale scenes from Saint-Saëns's *Samson et Delilah* (1877), Delibes's *Sylvia* (1876), more popular performances like Phryné's lascivious dances shown in music hall programs on classical themes and of popular intrigue, Loïe Fuller's dances, or dances from any of the other popular operas and ballets set in biblio-Greek antiquity would surely have irked Emmanuel's aesthetic of ancient Greek dance.[44]

For Emmanuel, American barefoot dancers and eurhythmic dancers found their source in the bacchic excesses of debased Orientalist dances. Emmanuel's critical stance toward modern movement was blended into descriptions of the poses of ancient statues in order to maintain the familiar historical narrative. After all, he did not wish to supplant classical ballet technique with ancient choreography, nor did he envision a new dance vocabulary for the future.

Ancient images that he found obscene, grotesque, or just inconsistent with modern practice were dutifully cataloged and then quickly dismissed. When confronted with images of rigid hands, flat palms, and pointed thumbs, he categorized them as "purely grotesque." Describing images of the body bending back, Emmanuel rejected these "contortions" as the result of "orgiastic delirium" and concluded that such "deformation" should be referred to pathologists, not dance and music scholars.[45] His connections to Marey and other French scientists interested in kinesiology and psychology place him firmly in a camp of scholars whose theories of antiquity (specifically of orgiastic dances) drew upon the scientific analysis of hysterics.[46] These scholars sought to diagnose nervous disorders not only in ancient bodies, but also in modern ones, and even theorized about their effects upon their viewers. As part of a larger anti-Wagnerian and anti-Nietzschian discourse, these scientists described Dionysian gestures as invoking hysterical fits in not only the dancing worshippers, but also the viewing subjects. As discussed by Jonathan Marshall, in his dramatic descriptions of ancient scenes of Dionysian ritual Dr. Henry Meige "indicated how such hysterical manifestations were brought on by a specific type of performative environment. It was the gaudy richness of the décor within the Temple, [. . .] the exaggeration of the priestess's performance [. . .], and the musical accompaniment, that enabled a truly hysterical and implicitly contagious performance to become manifest."[47] What we see here is not necessarily a tension between scientific method and imagination, but between hubristic certainty of "knowing" something—writing it in stone, capturing it on film—and using bits of knowledge as mere inspiration, with the perfunctory acknowledgment that the ancient world cannot be captured. Emmanuel did not try to capture ancient Greek dance; rather, he captured traditional French ballet with the chronophotographic gun in order to reanimate the static ancient images he captured (in line drawings) in his thesis. His scholarship lays out the blueprint for executing these rediscovered dances for a modern audience.

Contemporary dance aesthetics weighed heavily on Emmanuel's own formulations for reproducing ancient aesthetics. He advocated drawing upon our own understanding of what makes the dance great in the absence of any ancient treatise on methodology: "But without a methodical treatise—which appears to never have been written—it is permitted to learn for oneself the Greek idea of dancing and to delineate the domain of that art. It is for us to point out that which is singularly great and beautiful in it, and it is for us to teach, however badly, the process of the gymnastics of the dance; it is for us to learn that it is a divine art, and that it plays a considerable role in the education of man."[48] Emmanuel dismisses Lucian's *Dialogue of the Dance*, calling it "inconsequential, replete with gaiety" that only relates to Roman customs. In fact, Emmanuel dispatches with all of the writers on dance and only occasionally looks for clues in the actions and words of the characters in the tragedies and comedies.[49] After dismissing all other forms of analysis, Emmanuel warns his readers to be on the lookout for fakes and to use caution when reading archaeological and other writings on antiques.[50] Reconstructing the past should be done with care, and the few remnants of the cultures of antiquity require preservation and careful stewardship. This position, popular among scholars, found its way to practitioners of the arts as well.

As a necropolis, the museum protects and preserves the relics of the past from other nations, from scholars, and from itself. Like other cultural institutions, the museum forms a site of community memory, and perhaps it is more than coincidental that a short stroll down L'Avenue de l'Opéra connects the Louvre to the Palais Garnier. As a musicologist, Emmanuel had little control over the cultural guardianship of the plastic arts, but he could remove the "falsifications" and "restorations" at the Opéra and resurrect the neglected statues from the necropolis on the stage.[51] "Fantasy" and "inexperience" of artists could then be "corrected" through a public performance of Emmanuel's vision for *Salamine*: ancient Greek music and dance reconstructed for modern audiences free of "orgiastic delirium." Emmanuel trained as a musicologist as well as a composer, and like most composers he had always kept his eye on the Opéra.[52] If *La Danse grecque antique* spoke to the practitioners of dance, an opera based on these ideas could speak to a much larger audience. Seen in light of his scholarly writing and its audience, the opera *Salamine* illustrates how Emmanuel adapted these concerns for the Parisian public. If the dances of the past could be reconstructed through modern technology, why couldn't a Greek tragedy?

The Persians and the French: Atossa's Dream

In the first act of Emmanuel's opera *Salamine*, we are introduced to Atossa, the Persian queen, wife of the deceased leader, Darius, and mother of

Xerxes. She relates a dream in which her son falls from a chariot pulled by a Greek woman and an Asian woman yoked together. In Aeschylus's drama, Atossa's dream foretells her son's fall; Xerxes tries to unite two opposing forces by attempting to harness the futures of the Occident and the Orient. The dream allegorizes the difficulties in wielding power, that is, Xerxes's ultimately failed attempt to build a military bridge between Asia and Europe. The ghost of Darius looks down in disappointment at his son's failure, and the young Persian king tears at his robes in anguish. The metaphor aptly characterizes the forces at work in *Salamine*: a blend of Debussyian harmony, ancient Greek melody and mode, reconstructions of ancient Greek dance, Cecchetti ballet technique, and eurhythmics. For Emmanuel, yoking modern and ancient musical and dance techniques in this Cerberean opera proved to be a Herculean labor.

In shaping the libretto, Reinach divided the earliest surviving Greek drama into three acts. The first mainly features the chorus as well as the Persian queen Atossa's dream. She retells the dream of her son's fall; a messenger then arrives to bring the news of Xerxes's defeat at Salamis. The second act is set outside the tomb of Darius, where Atossa summons the ghost of the former king, who admonishes his son, Xerxes, for defying the oracles. The last act rounds out this extended funeral dirge with the antiphonal cries of Xerxes and the chorus. Reinach and Emmanuel took the text for *Salamine* directly from Aeschylus's drama with the intention of representing the ancient Greek verse as closely as possible in a French translation. In his scholarship Emmanuel often criticized those who tried to update, falsify, and restore works of antiquity, constantly warning his readers to use caution when reading archaeological and other writings on antiques.[53] Reconstructing the past should be done with care, and the few remnants of the cultures of antiquity required preservation and careful stewardship. *Salamine* was far from the first modern musical work to use an ancient text; however, Emmanuel and Reinach did this in a new way. Instead of writing "simple" music, like Gabriel Fauré, to clothe an ancient melody (see chapter 2), Emmanuel sought to compose "authentic" yet challenging music for a contemporary audience (based on his understanding of ancient Greek rhythm and mode and his aesthetic preferences for modern music) to bring the past to the audiences of the Opéra.

Modern Music in *Salamine*

The scene from the opera described here illustrates Emmanuel's modern musical setting for this ancient text. In Aeschylus's drama, Atossa's dream, a premonition of impending doom, comes early in the play; the queen is the first character we meet after an initial chorus. Clarinets play a whole-tone gesture (Debussyesque and Stravinskian) in thirds before the coryphée introduces the

queen (see music example 4.1). The dream warns about the dangers of bringing disparate peoples and ideas together. Atossa's act 1 soliloquy also illustrates the fusion of modern, Debussy-esque parallel chords with Emmanuel's chromatic modality, which creates a sense of harmonic stasis: a chromatic and twisting recitative punctuated by octave leaps as the prophecy turns more ominous, runs on the flutes, and chromatic triplet rhythms in the orchestra end the sequence.

Similarly, the entrance of the messenger in act 1, scene 3 is heralded by a flutter of chromaticism, while Darius's monologue begins as a simple ode uttered on a reciting tone and accompanied by diatonic root-position triads and shimmering ninth chords in a stately ³₂. Modern musical inflections are best demonstrated in Darius's monologue in act 2. This soliloquy ends with stately seventh and ninth chords over a sustained D♭ pedal (see music example 4.2). Contemporary reviews in 1929 immediately noted similarities in Emmanuel's score to the style of Debussy.[54]

Although the work appropriates the past, Emmanuel acknowledged that in this project it would have been impossible to write a work for the Opéra that remained faithful to the practices of ancient Greek music theory. "It would be absurd and nearly impossible to attempt an imitation of ancient Greek music," he wrote in the introduction to *Salamine*.[55] Not surprisingly, the text setting remains the most "authentic" Greek element of the production, but as Emmanuel noted, even here compromise proved necessary. Reinach initially hoped to keep the entire text declaimed rather than sung for performance at the Comédie Française, but Emmanuel's decision to keep the text sung pushed the premier to the Opéra. Even though the two Hellenists supported each other's scholarly work, they fought bitterly over the creation of their artistic collaboration, *Salamine*. Compromises were not easy. They fought over whether it should be spoken with only sung choruses or sung throughout, but Emmanuel found Reinach's translation so flat that he figured he should set it all to music. Reinach preferred a more Orientalist decor; Emmanuel wanted something more stark. It was only Reinach's death in 1928 that allowed Emmanuel to go ahead with the work as he saw fit.[56] Ultimately, only one spoken role remained: the coryphée declaimed his words, which Emmanuel notated rhythmically above the staff, accompanied by the orchestra to "ensure continuity of the music."[57] The rest of the characters sing their lines, but they flow in an

MUSIC EXAMPLE 4.2 Maurice Emmanuel, *Salamine* (1929), act 2, scene 2 (VS, pp. 116–117).

almost Pelléasian recitative. The rhythm of Darius's warning in example 4.2, for example, stresses the natural delivery of the text emphasizing key words, similar to Debussy's treatment in *Pelléas et Mélisande* (1902).[58] Emmanuel communicates the sense of mythic time that Debussy captured and formed into the mysterious erotic languor of *Pelléas*.[59] Aeschylus's characters walk around lost in a world of ghosts and despair; like Maeterlinck's characters, they are similarly bound by fate, doomed from the beginning. In both operas the characters are fully aware that they are headed for catastrophe. Mélisande's fate is clear from the beginning, as is that of Xerxes, and they drift through their respective worlds with impending warnings of a dark conclusion.

Debussy and Emmanuel

Although the similarities in plot between *Pelléas* and *Salamine* may end with their fatalist sensibilities, their significant kinship and Emmanuel's own strong affinity for Debussy's music indicate a tacit approval of a modern Debussyian musical vocabulary to evoke ancient Greece, which seems in conflict with Emmanuel's belief that ancient Greek dance evolved into classical ballet technique but not modern dance. Whereas Debussy's "Greek" works often leaned toward the erotic—*Prélude à l'après-midi d'un faune*, *Syrinx*, and *Les Chansons de Bilitis*—Emmanuel made use of this musical language to frame the strophes and antistrophes of Aeschylus divorced from their sensual sources.[60]

Emmanuel's appreciation of Debussy was far-reaching. In 1926 he penned an essay titled "Le Rythme d'Euripide à Debussy" as well as a landmark study of Debussy's *Pelléas et Mélisande*. In the treatise on rhythm, Emmanuel built an argument that Euripides's ultimate liberation of rhythm from Aeschylus was analogous to Debussy's from the work of Richard Wagner: "Euripides had turned his back on Aeschylus. By passing through the grid of bars, that are not for him signals of percussive time, of rhythms constantly undulating, Debussy turned his back on Wagner, who, innovative in design and length of periods (not square), remains, by persistence and the insistence of these rhythmic formulas, a disciple of the great German classics."[61] Emmanuel praised Debussy for turning his back on Wagner, but this is not praise for a modern turn or a break with tradition. Emmanuel extolled the composer's break with the recent past. Emmanuel's theory of art centered on a Darwinian belief in artistic evolution, that the best art of the modern world had its roots in ancient Greek models.[62] New generations added to it, bringing new innovations, but it remained essentially the same. This is a teleological model of historiography, but also a compositional tool in Emmanuel's hands. He writes in his *L'Histoire de la langue musicale* that the ancients lay at the heart of modern music, inspiring new works based on ancient ideals, "[a]nd in the eternal turning of time they return, discretely, without imposing to our vanity the yoke of old things. They let us create the old new."[63] Emmanuel sees this best realized in *Pelléas*, and in his analysis of the work he concludes: "Ancient history will be repeated as long as original artists emerge, and that art will know, thanks to them, the required renewal."[64] Emmanuel's reading of Debussy's opera highlighted the work's engagement with the past and its resonance with timelessness. He labeled the opening motif "Les temps lointains," yet this became a cipher for his ultimate claim that the opera is indeed timeless.[65]

It is telling that Emmanuel paid so much attention to *Pelléas*, a work that thwarts conventions of time both musically and dramatically. *Salamine* attempts a similar timelessness. Dramatically, it presupposes that the first surviving drama (Aeschylus's politically relevant *Persians*) is indeed a classic. Musically, Emmanuel used a combination of measured speech and free, *Pelléas*-esque vocal lines in *Salamine* to create a simultaneously modern and ancient feel, yet every attempt was made to retain the rhythms of the Greek.[66] Emmanuel wrote in his introduction to the published score that the "rhythms reflect those of Aeschylus, but they claim nothing more."[67] For its authors, since the setting of the text is "natural" it thus adheres to ancient practice. Emmanuel takes the idea that poetic rhythm fuels the three musical arts and argues in *La Danse grecque antique* that if one understands the rhythms of poetic verse, one can then reconstruct the rhythms of music and accordingly those of dance.[68] Of course there are some obstacles, according to Emmanuel. For example, "the true poetry of the dance has movements much more free from restraint of the set metrical type than the poetry of the choruses of Aeschylus, Aristophanes, or Pindar so that we cannot make an exact analysis of it. [. . .] But, despite the gaps that remain (and it may be difficult to fill them) the Greek Rhythm which we find in poetry is a direct source of information and fruitful to which the historian of dance must draw."[69] Thus, based on Emanuel's own assertions, the funeral dance at the opening of act 2 of *Salamine* might be imagined from the score based on the rhythms, stage directions, and reviews, despite the lacunae of more detailed information.

(Re)creating the Funeral Dance in *La Danse grecque antique*

In *Salamine*'s dance sequence from act 2, Emmanuel opts for restraint and solemnity versus Orientalist vibrancy. In a letter to the choreographer, Guerra, Emmanuel expressed his initial hope that the act 2 funeral dance would be performed en pointe, but he later realized that it was not appropriate for such a solemn scene.[70] Instead, Emmanuel requested a dance comprising "slow attitudes, on the theme of elongated index and middle fingers [and] small, only moving the torso and arms."[71]

These initial instructions closely resemble steps outlined in Emmanuel's own research on reconstructing ancient Greek dance. For the act 2 funeral dance of *Salamine*, Emmanuel's music bespeaks a stoic calm with a lilting allegro tempo in quadruple meter whispered by the orchestra. A restrained funeral dance as outlined in *La Danse grecque antique* might reasonably follow. As a scholar of ancient Greek dance, Emmanuel was eager to use the dance sequences to test out his theories; however, unlike other examples of "Greek" dance in early twentieth-century France, such as Michel Fokine's *Narcisse* (1911) and *Daphnis et Chloé* (1912), the dances created for *Salamine* seem to have been performed devoid of eroticism and harken back to a sober classical style (see music example 4.3).

In *La Danse grecque antique* Emmanuel discussed the evolution of ancient Greek funeral dances, which had origins in an ancient tradition of hired female mourners pulling their hair, but the gesture had evolved into a more symbolic expression, seen in the placement of one hand on the head and the other directed toward the dead body. In Emmanuel's figure 543 one can see the earlier depictions of the ritual, which were later replaced by the stylized gesture in figures 551 and 553 (see figures 4.4a and 4.4b).

Emmanuel described these latter poses as "prototypical" funeral gestures and stated that although the ritual of tearing the hair had been lost, the gesture had been retained; moreover, Emmanuel described the dance for these funeral rites as "full of calm" versus the violence of the threnodic hair pulling.[72]

Emmanuel very likely had his own choreographic instructions for recreating ancient dance in mind when writing the music for this scene. If this is indeed true, then that is an extraordinarily rare example of a scholar of dance history composing the music for his own reconstructed dances.

That Emmanuel and Guerra used restrained stoicism as the predominant aesthetic for the funeral dance was reported in reviews of the performance. In an article for *Candide* titled "Grecs et Barbares," André Levinson praised Emmanuel's opera and specifically drew contrasts with other "Greek" dancers.[73] After noting the quality of the "Asian mourners" who "accomplish a brief example of a funeral mime," he lauded Emmanuel for his treatise on ancient Greek dance. Emmanuel, he noted, brilliantly proved his thesis and even anticipated the later writhing of the "Anglo-Saxon gymnasts, personified by the barefoot Isadora Duncan."[74] Pitting the funeral dances from *Salamine* against the American barefoot "Greek" dancers such as Duncan (who often felt the brunt of the press against her "free" movements) illustrates the intention of the reviewer to establish an enterprise like *Salamine* as chaste, calm, stoic, academic, and ancient, versus the free, dynamic, and modern American dancer of the future. While Levinson's appraisal of Duncan had always been lukewarm, he repeatedly complimented Emmanuel and Guerra's work. In

Fig. 543.

FIGURE 4.4a Maurice Emmanuel, *La Danse grecque antique* (1896), fig 543.

Fig. 551.

Fig. 553.

FIGURE 4.4b Maurice Emmanuel, *La Danse grecque antique* (1896), figs. 551 and 553.

admiration of Emmanuel's *La Danse grecque antique* he wrote that it was "high time that the prejudices which range the antique Hellede upon the side of the Duncans and Dalcrozes in the combat against the art of the ballet, be eliminated, for it is a presumption founded upon a misconception."[75]

Like Levinson, Emmanuel preferred to couple a modern musical style (the music of Igor Stravinsky and Debussy) with a more conservative classical ballet technique. It is thus unsurprising that the Opéra assigned Guerra to create the choreography for *Salamine*. Guerra was never known as a modernizer in Hungary (where he failed to update the Hungarian Opera Ballet's repertoire), Paris, or Milan.[76] As Giannandrea Poesio has shown, Guerra's Italian version of Sergei Diaghilev's Ballets Russes "proposed a repertory lacking in innovation [and perpetuating] a lifeless tradition."[77] As an unwavering representative and supporter of the nineteenth-century Italian school, Guerra's short-lived 1915 Balli Italiani di Nicola Guerra helped cement the reputation of the choreographer and pedagogue as decidedly old-fashioned.[78] For a "classical" choreographer, adapting to the styles of the modern "Greek" dancers was not easy. His frustrations with Jacques Rouché and the Opéra's flock of eurhythmic dancers are legendary.[79] As Lynn Garafola has noted, Guerra routinely argued with the director of the Opéra for forcing him to share the stage with Dalcroze choreographers. In one interview, Guerra was particularly dismissive of the "new dance," noting: "Classical dance has its roots in Olympus, and we have been taught by the gods. Modern dance is not even bacchic, it is at best lunacy."[80] Yvonne Franck, the lead dancer in *Salamine*, was a crossover dancer who trained in both the classical ballet tradition and eurhythmics. Like her colleague, Yvonne Daunt, Franck's technique blended the "Greek" barefoot style with traditional pointe and demi-pointe work.[81] In addition to her role as a Mariandyne dancer in *Salamine*, Franck led the ballet in the 1926 and 1928 revivals of Gluck's *Alceste* (choreographed by Nijinska),[82] appeared in Philippe Gaubert's opera *Naïla* (1927), and choreographed *L'Eventail de Jeanne* (1927) with Alice Bourgat.[83] These events, however, marked the end of the Opera's eurhythmic experiment, followed by Levinson's gleeful obituary for the canceled eurhythmic class at the opera.[84]

While Levinson sung the praises of *Salamine*'s dances, no other reviewer seemed to care about the dance sequences, or for the rest of the opera, for that matter. Most critics found the music cold and intellectual. Emmanuel, discouraged as usual by the relative failure of his compositional works compared to his scholarly successes, blamed the lukewarm reviews on his collaborator, Reinach.[85] The scholar-composer's students and friends jumped to his defense, including Paul Dukas and Olivier Messiaen, but the work never received another staged performance after its initial run. Emmanuel's biographer, Corbier, attributes this to chronic "bad luck," but perhaps it wasn't just fate that thwarted

Emmanuel's compositional works. Perhaps the scholar-composer could not perform his own scholarship.

Dissonance between the musical and the choreographic in a work like *Salamine* was not uncommon. The parallels and counterpoints that occur within the remaining sources of *Salamine* reside at the broader interpretive level. In the act 2 funeral dance we cannot say with any certitude how the positions of the hand interact with Emmanuel's sinuous music; the evidence is insufficient to reconstruct the choreography. The counterpoints become manifest when we explore what this music and what these dances might have meant to Emmanuel, Guerra, and their audiences. In his scholarship on ancient Greek dance, Emmanuel contended that the mechanisms of dance remain the same: the classical ballet dancer essentially descended from the ancient Greek dancer. Modern dance was pathologized out of the narrative.

Levinson was pleased with the turn to the past, the dismissal of modern barefoot technique, and the reawakening of the *danse d'école* and saw it as "a deliberate return to French tradition. [. . .] Embracing the beautiful cadences of classicism, the Opéra rejects the idioms of Geneva and pidgin-French exoticism."[86] As Lynn Garafola has argued, the "death [of the eurhythmic experiment at the Opera] marked a turning point in the 'reclassicization' of ballet, a call to order."[87] In her telling, it was "the end of the experimentalist dance movement born in France in the first decade of the twentieth century from the combined influences of Duncanism, aestheticism, exoticism, eurhythmics, and the Ballets russes."[88] The fact that its run at the Opéra was a nonevent praised by Levinson but all but ignored by history shows Emmanuel's challenges in realizing his own research.

Emmanuel's scholarship on ancient Greek dance and modern music had a limited impact on performance, but a successful opera could reach a far wider audience than scholarly treatises or university hall lectures. *Salamine* was an opportunity to put Emmanuel's empirical study of antiquity into practice. In so doing, he allied himself with contemporary scientists and art critics, not only by following the paradigmatic Western tropes of representations of the East and Oriental Greece, but more important, by placing these within a discourse of musical and choreographic relationships to the modern and ancient body. To Emmanuel, the body signified an instrument as integral as music to bringing the past into the present. Debussy's "timeless" music and Guerra's classical technique had roots in the most timeless art of all—that of antiquity. Nevertheless, while generally condemning erotic and "pathologically" affected modern representations of ancient Greek music and dance, Emmanuel found no problem with eroticism in ancient Greek music when practiced by his friend Debussy. Yoked together—like the Greek and the Barbarian of Atossa's dream—the Dionysian and Apollonian forces break free of each other, and Emmanuel's musical representations of antiquity tended toward the Apollonian and the scholarly rather than the bacchic or the sensual. Based on archival materials (vases, bas-reliefs, treatises, texts), Emmanuel saw the embodied working through of ancient dance as only useful in realizing his own conclusions. While figuring out how to yoke the past to the present in these two media, Emmanuel did not seek unity. Wedding modern music with conservative choreography made sense to a scholar who argued that modern music and classical ballet were the true inheritors of the Greek tradition, while modern dance was the result of perversions, pathologies, and Americans.

When we take stock of which collaborations left a lasting impression and which have dissolved into history, it does seem surprising that the academic credentials and bona fides of Emmanuel and Reinach would end up on history's cutting-room floor. Greek dance and music lives in the legacies of Duncan, Nijinsky, Debussy, Stravinsky, and Palmer Sikelianos (in Greece, at least). "Greek" dance and music was popular, as Emmanuel so noted, but his attempts to have his own scholarship performed on the stage of the Opéra fizzled. While his scholarly publications impressed and inspired dancers, his own creative mediation of that research lacked dynamism. The complexities of influence—classical ballet and modernist music's shared ancient Greek legacy (as argued by Emmanuel)—muddled the work so hopelessly that only fellow scholars could make sense of his argument through performance.

In balancing the message with the medium of performance, Emmanuel may have failed. That said, I have found it an engaging piece to listen to and to think about. Meanwhile, over 1,750 miles away in Delphi, Greece, Palmer Sikelianos was planning her own experiments in reconstructing ancient Greek music, drama, and dance, not based exclusively on models found on vases and statuary, but rather through embodied experience, living history, and ethnography (see chapter 5).

Conclusions: Scholarship and/versus Performance

Emmanuel's *Salamine* serves as a particularly bad example of how to translate one's scholarship into performance. Unlike contemporaries like Palmer Sikelianos and Natalie Clifford Barney, Emmanuel's resulting performance avoided self-reflection, communication, process, and embodied traditions. The work captures (like the photographic technology employed in his own research) his academic prose but does not "perform" it in the modern meaning of the term. It is almost as if the opera "realizes" his theories, even if they don't really work out on stage because Emmanuel is blind to his own biases.

Scholarship and performance of scholarship *are* different. As Richard Schechner writes in the preface to the third edition of *Performance Studies: An Introduction*: "Performance studies is unsettled, open, discursive, and multiple in its methods, themes, objects of study, and persons. It is a field without fences. It is 'inter' [. . .]. Being 'inter' is exploring the liminal—participating in an ongoing workshop."[89] Emmanuel (after the death of his collaborator Reinach) presented the opera not as part of some ongoing collaborative workshop, but rather as a fait accompli, a done deal. As such, it existed as a novelty, but does not resonate. It speaks only to what the composer had already written, his own collection of treatises and lectures: a Wagnerian *Gesamtkunstwerk*. As such it is irreproducible, because not only is it far easier to read Emmanuel's writings than to try to reconstruct and restage the work, but who would want to besides the scholar/composer himself, who is long dead?

We never really know what the future will hold for any work, but operas like *Salamine* show that performing one's research does not always work. The project of re-enacting ancient Greek music and dance took place both in print and on stage, and success in one does not guarantee success in the other. Emmanuel's determination to put forth his version of ancient Greek dance and music in the face of the myriad eurhythmic, free, and modern dance versions of ancient Greek movement as danced by Duncan, Fuller, Badet, and the like aimed to rewrite the narrative, to bring into performance his theories to combat the embodied traditions of Duncan and those other dancers, whose work was far more popular on the stages of Paris and around the globe. The power of performance, after all, is not to perform what could just as easily be read, but rather to translate an idea into a new medium. Emmanuel may have known ancient Greece as a scholar, but as a creative artist (the creator of an opera), he did not know his subject or his audience. Nonetheless, failure is an important part of scholarship and performance. We should never stop at least trying to perform our scholarship or dance our dissertations.

5 | "To Give Greece Back to the Greeks"

ARCHAEOLOGY, ETHNOGRAPHY, AND EVA
PALMER SIKELIANOS'S *PROMETHEUS BOUND*

U NLIKE MAURICE EMMANUEL'S PARISIAN experiments in the reperformance of ancient Greek drama for the stage of the Opéra, Eva Palmer Sikelianos's experiments in ancient Greek performance took place seventeen hundred miles away at the archaeological site of ancient Delphi. In 1927 and 1930 Natalie Clifford Barney's childhood friend Eva Palmer Sikelianos, along with her husband, the poet Angelos Sikelianos (1884–1951), founded the first modern Delphic Festival in an effort to revive the ancient Greek rites that took place on that spot over twenty-five hundred years before. Through a combination of sport, music, theater, dance, and handicrafts, the Sikelianoses sought to rekindle the collaborative pacifist spirit of the Panhellenic movement in the interwar period.

There is something almost magical and definitely theatrical about the archaeological site of Delphi where the Sikelianoses staged their festival. Winding your way on a mountain road, you arrive at the bottom of the site and then climb up. Unlike other archaeological sites where the theater is on the periphery or in the back, the theater in Delphi sits in the center of the site. The path snakes around a mix of ruins and reconstructions (e.g., the Athenian Treasury reconstructed by the French school in Athens between 1903 and 1906, where the musical notations for the hymns to Apollo discussed in chapter 2 were found). David Roessels writes that there is a uniquely American presence in Delphi today due to the legacies of Palmer Sikelianos and the playwright George Cram Cook.[1] Their graves are now part of the reconstructed archaeological site. Palmer Sieklianos's body is literally part of the site itself. Her remains lie at the omphalos—the mythical navel of the world at Delphi—the spot where Zeus's two eagles met. The navel is not only the center, but also the soft spot, the vulnerable core, the link to the womb and to other wombs (mother to daughter). At the heart of the Delphic omphalos, of course, you find the theater. This is the virtual meeting place of the American dancer Palmer

Sikelianos and the French archaeologist Théodore Reinach. Delphi is the fraught meeting place of the past and the ongoing reproductions of that past.

Far from Paris, the Greek performance of ancient drama, music, and dance stands apart from the performances on the other side of Europe. Palmer Sikelianos's project shared notable similarities in gesture with performances she participated in at Barney's home (see chapter 3), as well as a movement vocabulary found in the Ballets Russes's pre–World War I work. However, her work's genesis and enacting in Delphi, Greece, make it different than the Western European staged performances in her blend of archaeology, ethnography, re-enactment, and site-specific performance.

This chapter explores Palmer Sikelianos's choreography, rituals, and music for her reconstructed *Prometheus Bound* in light of her research on ancient Greek culture, conducted in both Paris and modern Greece. Thinking of Delphi as omphalos, this chapter relocates ancient re-enactment from Paris to Delphi and in so doing forces us to reconsider what happens when modern Greece is no longer on the periphery of an imagined ancient Greece. What does it mean when modern Greece and ancient Greece meet, when the temporal, geographical, and ideological all align at the omphalos? How do we come to know ancient Greece in the modern world? How do we arrive at its center? Is the center a place, an idea, a set of documents, a lived experience, a thought, a feeling, a performance? In this chapter I discuss re-enactment as a knowledge-seeking process and talk about the archive and the body as epistemological instruments.

Based on silent film records of Palmer Sikelianos's 1930 festival, her own autobiography, her collaborations with Barney on Greek-themed theatricals in the early 1900s, and comparisons to the movement vocabulary and other contemporary stagings of ancient Greek music and dance (by Michel Fokine, Vaslav Nijinsky and Bronislava Nijinska), I demonstrate how Palmer Sikelianos navigated between the needs and methods of the archaeologist and those of the performer. She blended the oldest sources on ancient Greek ritual music and dance that she could find with what she saw as an authentic "spirit" of Greek culture that she observed in the space of performance, its environs, and modern Greek society. Her performances drew from archival/archaeological sources (ancient treatises, dance iconography) and lived practices (folk song, modern dance, Byzantine chant traditions). To delve deeper into the archaeological tendencies of Palmer Sikelianos's productions, I compare them to the Ballets Russes's re-enactment of ancient Greece in *Daphnis et Chloé* and *Faune* (1912), and to pagan Rus' in *Le Sacre du printemps* [*The Rite of Spring*] (1913). Like the Fokine and Nijinsky models, Palmer Sikelianos's staging redefines ancient dance through the prisms of ancient sources and modern concerns, but also through an engagement with place: the archaeological sites in Delphi. In addition, her project of returning the spirit of antiquity back to the Greek people is examined in relation to postcolonial theory.

Despite her upbringing and training, Palmer Sikelianos refused to blindly apply Western concepts of antiquity to the lived experiences of the modern Greeks with whom she worked. That is not to say she staunchly resisted colonialist tendencies; she struggled, and it is that frustration that helped her reshape modern Greek arts and culture. Still heralded as a founder of modern Greek dance, her work is continually evoked as foundational by contemporary Greek scholars of dance despite her sometimes complex relationship as both an insider and an outsider.[2] Ultimately, this chapter forces us to look at the role of place and what happens when archaeology, ethnography, performance, and the archive meet. In conclusion, it is only fitting to expand the temporal frame of the study to the near present: my own trip to Athens in the summer of 2015 during one of the most serious economic crises in the country's history. I address some issues of contemporary performance of Greek heritage in the wake of the Greek debt crisis of the 2010s and the vulnerability of exploring the omphalos in a time of uncertainty.

Traveling to Greece

In 1903 Barney and her lover Renée Vivien took the Orient Express to Constantinople and from there took a steamer to Lesbos. Early on the morning of their arrival, Vivien and Barney stood on the bow of the ship eager for their first glance of the island where Sappho's sandals had tread. The serene quiet of the sea was rudely interrupted by a "nasal" phonograph blaring the popular French song, "Viens, Poupoule, viens poupoule, viens!"[3] Barney did not make it clear where the jarring popular song came from. Was it on board, or was it blaring from the place that she had idealized? Either way, the lyrics of the jaunty polka had little to do with the Lesbos of Sappho or the Lesbos imagined by Barney and Vivien: "Come little chickies, come little chickies, come! / When I hear songs that make me naughty / Come little chickies, come little chickies come! / Remember that's how I became a papa!" (see music example 5.1).[4]

Safely ashore and out of earshot of the offending music, they set foot on the dust (most likely the pier at the Port of Mytilene) "consecrated by the sandals of Sappho and her poets" and "resumed [their] pilgrimage despite modern intrusions."[5] They spent the rest of their time on the island happily walled off from the population of Mytilene. Barney writes that none of the inhabitants of Lesbos were dignified enough to be considered followers of the poet. They saw lovely boatmen, fishermen, and shepherds, but alas, no poets. "The rest of the people," she writes, "possessed mongrel traits like that of their language [Le reste de la population avait les traits abâtardis comme leur langage]." Nonetheless, they enjoyed themselves in the charming, rustic "ancient simplicity [simplicité ancienne]" of their hotel with terra cotta water jugs and food

MUSIC EXAMPLE 5.1 Adolf Spahn, "Viens poupoule!" (1903).

cooked in olive oil and served by an old lady with a dog.[6] The initial arrival was a shock to the pair, but they soon found the Lesbos they were looking for, but only populated by Lesbians, not lesbians.

Barney was not alone in feeling discomfort with the reality of a place that differed from the one constructed in her imagination. Countless travelers have found their arrival in modern Greece unsettling. They expect to see Plato orating from the Agora or Socrates strolling the streets of the Plaka. Our sense of space and time of these sites is influenced more by literary sources than the spaces themselves. "Lesbians do not come from Lesbos," writes Kate Gilhuly in her study of the Athenian and Roman comic plays that established Lesbos as a site of promiscuity and same-sex desire. "Lesbians come from literature."[7]

Western literary tropes not only colored Barney's view of Lesbos as oriental and foreign but have inspired colonialist assaults on the Greek people. Pernicious and racist attacks on the modern Greeks as not "Greek" but Slavic, Byzantine, or Albanian infiltrators in the land of Pericles and Socrates persisted throughout the nineteenth century, even bubbling into the press amid the political fallout of the Greek debt defaults in the summer of 2015.[8] Barney, like many, may have held similar views. Her lifelong friend Palmer Sikelianos, however, ultimately adopted modern Greece as her home. In her autobiography, Palmer Sikelianos expressed frustration with her friends' and family's misconceptions about her adopted homeland: "I had gone to Spain alone, and nobody cared. But when I said I was going to Greece, they all took on as if I had been headed for an African jungle."[9] To understand Palmer Sikelianos's ancient Greece, one needs to understand her modern Greece, for she, unlike Barney, saw them as inextricably linked.

Barney revealed her feelings about the ancient and modern Greeks in a letter to Palmer Sikelianos that praised her work in the Delphic Festivals of 1927 and 1930. Barney's short letter, dated October 21, 1930, concludes with the following words about Palmer Sikelianos's Delphic Festivals: "I may at last applaud your magnificent effort to give Greece back to the Greeks by those productions of plays that live ever in the minds of men but that you have brought to life again before their eyes."[10] What did she mean? How does one give Greece back to the Greeks? Read in light of Barney's memories of Lesbos, I see this as a dismissal of the modern Greeks. Barney did not just praise her friend for her work on these festivals; she also signaled that she viewed these projects as part of a colonialist mission to repatriate a "true" Greek identity back to a land and a people who had lost it. Due to the many years of collaboration and friendship between Palmer Sikelianos and Barney centered on neo-Sapphic performance, Barney's line also seems to confirm that these festivals had some root in their youthful plays from the early 1900s. In essence, Barney may be hinting that Palmer Sikelianos was able to restore their youthful fantasies of Greece to the place from whence they came, from where it all began. Palmer Sikelianos did not choose the eastern island of Lesbos, but rather the central Grecian location of Delphi. She was not interested in reperforming Barney's Greece, but rather had envisioned a new model of Greek music and theater for the Delphic Festivals. While Barney, Emmanuel, and the Reinach brothers all saw Western European institutions and models as inheritors of the ancient Greek spirit, Palmer Sikelianos was not immune to Western visions of antiquity but nonetheless believed that ancient Greek music and dance could best find life within southeastern Europe. In holding this belief, Palmer Sikelianos journeyed from a colonialist toward a postcolonialist relationship with the Greeks, both ancient and modern.

Eva Palmer Sikelianos's Musical Training: Early Wagnerian Influences

As Artemis Leontis has shown, despite Palmer Sikelianos's claims that her move to Greece in 1906 wiped clean her previous Western influences, her production of *Prometheus Bound* "drew on a lifetime of learning."[11] She collaborated with Barney and her mother on amateur ancient Greek-inspired theatricals in Bar Harbor around 1900, studied Greek at Bryn Mawr College in the 1890s, and took formal drama and music lessons as well. Best known for her drama, she displayed impressive musical skills as well (see chapter 3).

In Paris she had numerous theatrical opportunities: an offer from Sarah Bernhardt to play Mélisande to her Pelléas, performances for Barney, and other professional acting work in Scotland and with the famous actress Mrs. Patrick Campbell.[12] Palmer took voice lessons in 1902 with the goal of performing Isolde's "Liebestod" from Richard Wagner's *Tristan und Isolde*. She wrote to Barney about her desire to sing Isolde's transfiguration to be closer to her brother, Courtland Palmer, a well-known pianist and composer.[13] She explained that Courtland did not approve of her and Barney's romantic relationship, and the siblings had not spoken or written much for two years. She hoped that music, and specifically singing the "Liebestod" for him, would bring them closer together again.[14] Music played a large role in the Palmer family. Musicians regularly stopped by their home, including Fritz Kreisler, Emma Eames, Marcella Sembrich, and Emma Calvé (a mutual friend of Barney).[15] As Artemis Leontis has discussed, part of Palmer's early artistic inspiration came from being an artist for someone. She wanted to sing the Liebestod *for* her brother. Her early romantic habit of equating performance (and singing in particular) to love and friendship created a mini-crisis, as Barney's letters voiced disapproval of Eva's Liebestod studies for Courtland, and Palmer ceased her voice lessons only a few months later to follow Barney to Paris in 1902.[16]

After abandoning her Wagnerian vocal studies, Palmer tried her hand at directing Swinburne's Greek tragedy, *Atalanta of Calydon*, in Bar Harbor during the summer of 1905, featuring "Greek dances" and "Greek music." She next took a prominent role in creating Barney's *Équivoque*, wherein she discovered the music of Penelope Duncan. After meeting Penelope's brother Angelos in 1905, she left with him for his homeland of Greece the next year. Thus she arrived in Greece with a repertoire of Western "Greek" performance styles at her disposal.

Palmer Sikelianos in Greece: Weaving a Lifestyle Antiquity

In her own telling, moving to Greece facilitated a clean break with Palmer Sikelianos's past. As Leontis writes, "All of Greece became her garden, its open air her stage, and performing a living Greekness her daily care."[17] At the home of Raymond and Penelope Duncan in Kopanos, Palmer Sikelianos wove her own Greek tunics and wore them daily. She studied Greek art, music, and language. She carried herself differently in Greece and adopted a Greek "pitch" to her voice.

While Barney and Théodore Reinach both exhibited traits of performing a "lifestyle antiquity," Palmer Sikelianos's experimental process, which she refined in Greece, *became* the creative magnum opus of her life. Barney's Greek performances more or less ceased with her exile from Neuilly and the death of Vivien in 1909. Reinach performed antiquity as long as he could still enjoy modern comforts: his ancient Greek villa on the French Riviera had modern plumbing and a modern piano. Barney's performance of antiquity only suited herself, in that her work was not for the public. Palmer Sikelianos, on the other hand, modeled her quotidian and professional creative work on Greece, past and present. Ethnography on modern Greece was an important window into the past. It could not be done in Paris or America; it had to be done in Greece itself. Palmer Sikelianos came to realize that archaeological knowledge and archival materials only made sense when reanimated in the living world of modern Greece.

Weaving was central to both Palmer Sikelianos's daily experiences and her stage work. Just like living history interpreters and historical re-enactors, her work began with the quotidian and the experimental. This is typical even today for re-enactors, as explained by Vanessa Agnew; "[Re-enactment's] mode is agglomerative—discrete pieces of information are gleaned and corroborated through firsthand experience. Reenactment thus emerges as a body-based discourse in which the past is reanimated through physical and psychological experience."[18] Palmer Sikelianos experimented at the loom with her future sister-in-law, Penelope Duncan. Visiting Greek peasants' homes inspired her exploration. She noted that the villagers were always very welcoming, reminding her of Zeus, "the Protector of strangers."[19] At almost every home there was a loom, on which the eldest daughter wove her dowry. Palmer Sikelianos soon became obsessed; she ordered a loom of walnut and started making her own clothes so she wouldn't have to wear the constricting factory-made garments she had brought from Paris. "At first this was chiefly a matter of personal taste" she writes, but soon she found immense joy in shearing the sheep, washing wool, preparing the materials, weaving the cloth, and stitching her own clothes. It was more than just a hobby. Weaving was reparative:

> It took on, for me at least, the proportion of a solution to certain social evils, such for instance as the problem of unemployment, where hand work, all along the lines, seems so much pleasanter than either starving or being fed on a pittance by public charity. . . . What are we in the world for at all, unless it be for each human being to enlarge his consciousness though the development of

his own creative capacity: and how can this be done when in the bare process of living man himself is turned into a machine?[20]

Palmer Sikelianos's trope on weaving shows that for her, to weave was not only a means of reaching some sort of historically authentic costume or something comfortable, but also a process that in itself would repair the world. That is, to participate in the ancient handcrafts of Greek villagers was reparative. It was a way to avoid the mechanization of modernism. Weaving requires focus, and the world is full of distractions, as Sappho wrote in Fragment 102: "Sweet mother, I cannot weave–/slender Aphrodite has overcome me/with longing for a girl [child]."[21] And while Aphrodite may not have lured her from her work, other forces tried to break Palmer Sikelianos's resolve.

Greek village life was far from the distractions of Paris, or of Athens, for that matter. It is important to remember that Palmer Sikelianos had just come from the busy Parisian metropolis, where the engineers of the new metro had torn up the streets to make way for more machines. After spending years in Greece Palmer Sikelianos found the textile factories of Athens equally disgusting.[22] By the 1930s it was not that difficult for her to imagine that men were turning into machine-like insects: "Their airplanes are like dragonflies, their automobiles are like beetles or like cockroaches, their steam-lined trains are like processional caterpillars, their gas-masks are probably like themselves when the ultimate metamorphosis will have been perfected."[23] The Greeks ("natural craftsmen") were the only ones who could resist "mechanized gestures."[24]

By 1938, when she began writing her autobiography, Palmer Sikelianos's vision of antiquity had become fraught with artistic anxiety and a turn away from the mechanized world. In explaining the music and dance of antiquity and her own past, she wrote a manuscript professing great fear of the future. A technophobia looms over her writing, like many authors interested in cults of antiquity.[25] John Anton discusses Palmer Sikelianos's technophobia: "The onslaught of the machine age, obliterating every traditional value it met on its ominous march, was introducing in its wake new ways to oppress the spirit of its own makers."[26] Dismissing trends, material goods, and fashion, she retreated: "The more clearly she perceived the threats of the approaching storm, the more determinately she became to exchange personal comforts for the imperative of a universal vision."[27]

This universal vision was also a vision of the past, but more than a vision; it was a process. Palmer Sikelianos began to perform a living Greekness by adopting a lifestyle antiquity. *Lifestyle antiquity* shouldn't be confused with Lynn Garafola's "lifestyle modernism." Garafola identifies lifestyle modernism as one of three trends in the Ballets Russes's repertoire of the 1920s, which "was associated with Jean Cocteau's art of the sophisticated commonplace."[28] It embraced the popular, the modern, the fast-paced, the consumerist, the machine, and a look toward the technological future. A lifestyle antiquity is not an aesthetic of stage dance, but rather a way of life, a rejection of the technologies of modernism, traditional stages, in favor of an embodied practice that adopts activities and gestures of antiquity. That is, it is the antidote to life-style modernism. Like other modernists, Palmer Sikelianos imagined creating her own transformative theater: "The kind of theater I was dreaming about is the thing, if greatly used, which can liberate simultaneously all the faculties of man, and also direct them to noble uses. It is essentially beyond local barriers and boundaries, and can lift us, if anything can, into that Panic of insight and love which alone can make man sane."[29] However, it was not merely theatrical, but permeated every aspect of Eva Palmer Sikelianos's daily life.

Lifestyle modernism, in contrast to lifestyle antiquity, was after all coined to describe the work of the Ballets Russes, starting with *Parade* (1918) and culminating in Cocteau's last contributions for Sergei Diaghilev, *Les Biches* (1924) and *Le Train Bleu* (1924). These works do not share aesthetic or methodological ties with Palmer Sikelianos's *Prometheus Bound* (1927). Earlier Ballets Russes's projects that took inspiration from archaeological sources, like *L'Après-midi d'un faune* (1912) and *Le Sacre du printemps* (1913), resonated more with her process and motivations.

Reconstructioning Other Ancient Dances: Nijinsky, Roerich, and Hodson

The re-enacted performances of *Prometheus Bound* were central to the Delphic Festival. Like her studies of music, Palmer Sikelianos relied on a variety of sources (archaeology, ethnography, and embodied knowledge through performance) to help realize the ancient drama for the Delphic theater. I liken her project to that of other dance re-enactors, namely Millicent Hodson and Kenneth Archer, who famously reconstructed the Ballets Russes's *Le Sacre du printemps* (1913) in 1987. To be clear, the comparison is not ideological but concerns the technical means employed. Hodson and Archer were not working with nearly as ancient materials as was Palmer Sikelianos. Their process, described in the 1996 edition of their reconstructed choreographic score, relied on a combination of anecdotes, photographs, drawings made in a darkened theater, notes on a piano score, and memories. The rest was taken from the scholar's imagination through embodied practice. To borrow terminology from Diana Taylor, how much is owed to the archive, and how much to the repertoire?[30] How much did Hodson and Archer take from musical, choreographic, iconographic, written, and material sources, and how much was reconstructed with embodied knowledge, lived experience, experimentation, and tradition? Both the seriousness with which Hodson treats her fragmented evidence and her imaginative dance reconstruction are reminiscent of Nicholas

Roerich's (1874–1947) own methods, used in the conception of *Le Sacre du printemps*. Hodson spins creative and vibrant colors out of a few threads of surviving relics. In other ways, her work mirrors that of Palmer Sikelianos. Both *Le Sacre du printemps* and *Prometheus Bound* are excellent examples of this type of collaboration between archaeology and performance. They were not the first, nor are they the last, but placing them in conversation with each other allows us to view *Prometheus Bound* as part of a larger project to re-enact the past as a work of archaeology and performance.

Le Sacre owes much to Roerich's archaeological passions. He discovered the excitement of archaeology at an early age, helping to excavate burial mounds outside his hometown as a boy.[31] As Lynn Garafola has written, "From his earliest years, he used the fragments of the real past to supply details of a legendary one."[32] Archaeological study went hand in hand with art. Roerich's earliest drawings include academic studies of ancient Greek statues (Aeschylus and Sophocles). Within a few years his paintings turned to more Slavophile subjects, namely the ancient civilizations of the Bronze Age inhabitants of what would eventually be part of the Russian Empire. Many years later Roerich described how these early childhood experiences of unearthing rusted swords and axes coincided with his "beloved history lessons, but in my memory lie close to geography and to Gogol's fantastical historical fiction as well."[33] His methods were similar to those of other wealthy scholars at the time. Roerich established a familiar process: archaeological research, often conducted without the newly popular scientific methods of the West (photography, grids, stratigraphy, etc.), rendered into a work of art, in this case a painting. For the *Le Sacre*, the source material—the scholarship—is another work of art, rather than a more scholarly exegesis. Millicent Hodson describes the transfer as such: "When Nijinsky set the solo for the Chosen Maiden on his sister, Bronislava, he asked her to visualize certain Roerich paintings and told her that 'the beauty of the tinted stones and the wall paintings of the cave dwellers have inspired Roerich's own art.' . . . Among the canvases he asked her to visualize was *The Idols of Ancient Russia*."[34] Kenneth Archer has suggested that Roerich's paintings were indeed the "archaeological sources" relied upon by Nijinsky in devising his choreography.[35] According to Nijinska, her brother had much to gain from his collaboration with Roerich. She recalled, "Vaslav often told me how much he liked to listen to Roerich talking about his studies of the origin of man, describing the pagan rites and prehistory of the tribes 'that roamed the land we now call Russia.' "[36]

Part archaeology, part ethnography, *Le Sacre* blends Russian folk tunes with the magical realism of Roerich's imagined past. The vibrant peasant costumes worn by the dancers incorporate iconography of the old Slavonic deities along with rural folk costumes, which Hodson has argued appear in the choreography as well. If Hodson's reconstruction is correct, the motifs on Roerich's costumes inspired Nijinsky's ground designs.

The result—the harsh angular modernism of Stravinsky's music and Nijinsky's choreography against the bright colors and "fusty romanticism,"[37] to quote Roger Fry, of Roerich's design—seems incongruous. We can, however, view the scene and costumes along with Roerich's paintings as the archaeological source material for the other two collaborators' ritual sacrifice. Palmer Sikelianos's intellectual and ideological task is much more like Roerich's than like Hodson's and Archer's, although her techniques of reconstruction are more like the latter's.

While Palmer Sikelianos's approach to re-enacting ancient Greek musical material differed from those of her contemporaries, her techniques for staging "Greek" dance closely resembled those of other scholars and artists of the time. She wrote: "I made a great quantity of sketches in the Museum with a friend who was a sculptor and then, phrase by phrase, I tried to fit the highlights, as it were, or the principal accents in means and music, with what seemed to me appropriate gestures from the vases."[38] She then taught the music to the chorus from *Prometheus Bound* orally, as they were not interested in learning the Byzantine music notation in which it was composed, and Palmer Sikelianos then encouraged the dancers to act like a real chorus and improvise some of their movements based on the vocabulary she taught them.[39] Thus, it should be no surprise that her methodology shares similarities to that of Madame Mariquita, Isadora Duncan, and the early choreographers for Diaghilev's Ballets Russes (see chapter 4).

Léon Bakst, Diaghilev, and Fokine employed historical and ethnographic research in their earlier "Greek" ballets. As Lynn Garafola writes, Bakst "decided against 'accessorizing' contemporary attire with Greek touches—the usual solution to theatrical costume then—in favor of reconstructions of classical dress."[40] Fokine, in his libretto for *Daphnis* (1907), argued that in "producing a Greek ballet in the spirit of the [Hellenic] age. . . . No balletmaster could commit the [. . .] mistake [of having] Greeks dance the French way?"[41] As part of his larger concerns for realism in ballet, Fokine was an ethnographer, writes Garafola, "bringing the methods of the naturalist to the study of living peoples." That also meant that "[w]hen dealing with the past, he adopted an equally empirical course, rummaging libraries and museums for the shards of lost civilizations."[42] Fokine, of course, stressed the academic roots of his Hellenic subjects and minimized any influence the American Isadora Duncan may have had on him. Fokine took liberties with facts in his memoirs in attempts to distance himself from Duncan's reputation. While claiming originality, he nonetheless still praised her.[43] For his part, Maurice Ravel was less interested in academic fealty to the real ancient Greece. Rather, he famously described his score as "a vast musical fresco, less concerned with archaism than with faithfulness to the Greece of my dreams, which is similar to that imagined and painted by French artists at the end of the eighteenth century."[44]

Similar to *Daphnis*, in the creation of *L'Après-midi d'un faune* (1912) Bakst, Diaghilev, and Nijinsky all spent time studying ancient Greek statues and vases in the Louvre while preparing the dance; however, this may provide us with only part of the story. Each has variously claimed to have originated the idea of modeling a dance from ancient Greek vases. For the purposes of argument, I think it is safe to say that all three played an active role in the conception and execution of *Faune*.[45]

The Greek images in question span centuries and pay homage to multiple museum collections. As critic Henri Gautier-Villars (a.k.a. Willy) wrote concerning *Faune*: "These visions are a comprehensive review of Greek art galleries in the museums of Europe. They are the result of a scholarly archaeological compilation: herewith the bent-knee comes from a German museum, this decline of the shoulder was noted at the Louvre and, in the National Gallery has been observed the gesture of forearms."[46] Certainly Willy was right—there was no one vase, no one museum's collection—but perhaps there was one book—Emmanuel's 1896 *La Danse grecque antique*—that supplied both inspiration and source material for artist and choreographer alike. This is further evidenced by Emmanuel's decision in his treatise to organize his material not chronologically, but rather by gesture, thus placing preclassical next to late Hellenist images, just as Nijinsky did in *Faune*. In all likelihood the three creators of the ballet used more readily available sources such as lithographs, photographs, and other collections of images in addition to the arsenal of sources at the Louvre. Emmanuel's treatise, with over six hundred illustrations of dancers reproduced from vases, bas-reliefs, and statuary from ancient Greece, remains the most likely candidate. The correspondences between the scholar's descriptions of the Greek walk in dance and the extraordinary way Nijinsky had his dancers move across the stage prove illustrative. The photographs taken for Willy's review for *Comœdia Illustré* highlight the work's adherence to classical poses, particularly ones mentioned in Emmanuel (see figures 5.1a–5.1c).

Re-enacting *Prometheus Bound*

Just as Nijinsky, Nijinska, and Roerich helped create an unknown Russia for Parisian audiences in *Le Sacre*, Palmer Sikelianos brought an unknown Greece back to the Greeks (as Barney said). Her work touched modern Greece in powerful ways. Her chorus leader, Koula Pratsika, said of the process of creating *Prometheus Bound*: "We followed Eva's lead to discover an unknown Greece, the existence of which we hadn't imagined, a Greece of our own and for ourselves."[47]

In the first decade of the twentieth century, Palmer Sikelianos developed an immersive, embodied process blending ethnography and archaeology to bring

FIGURE 5.1a Photographs in review of *L'Après-midi d'un faune* in *Le Comœdia Illustré* 4e année, no. 18 (June 15, 1912): 6–7.

FIGURE 5.1b Maurice Emmanuel, *La Danse grecque antique* (1896), fig.139.

FIGURE 5.1c Maurice Emmanuel, *La Danse grecque antique* (1896), fig. 154.

back the lost dance of the ancient Greeks to modern Paris. Through Barney, she met the Duncans—Isadora, Raymond, and his Greek wife, Penelope. Their love of Greek antiquity inspired Palmer Sikelianos to adopt the eccentric dress of Raymond and his wife.

She married Penelope Duncan's brother, the poet Angelos Sikelianos, during the summer of 1907 in Bar Harbor, Maine, and the couple resettled in Greece. With her husband, Palmer Sikelianos founded the first modern Delphic Festival in 1927, which included a performance of *Prometheus Bound* by Aeschylus in the amphitheater, an Olympic-style athletic contest, and an exhibition of Greek "peasant handicraft."[48] Palmer Sikelianos explained her theories of how to reproduce ancient Greek drama and music as seen in the Delphic Festivals throughout her posthumously published memoirs; after viewing other's recreations of antique music and dance, she vowed to do better. The Greek government ultimately supported her efforts because it saw how re-enactment could become a draw for tourists. As Vanessa Agnew describes, "With its vivid spectacles and straightforward narratives, reenactment apparently fulfills the failed promise of academic history—knowledge entertainingly and authoritatively presented."[49] Re-enactment sells.

As Artemis Leontis has argued, Palmer Sikelianos did not seek the same kind of authenticity as might a Civil War re-enactor. When praised by an archaeologist for her ability to solve "archaeological problems which [the scholar] had been working fruitlessly on for years," Palmer Sikelianos responded:

> I have read archaeological books only to forget them, and I have never thought of your problems. And besides . . . the performance was bristling with archaeological mistakes, but even you did not detect them, and you are not even conscious of them now. And that is because the place was moving around its own pivot; it was emotionally true, or almost true—and that was sufficient to make you feel that it was correct archaeologically. There is no such thing as archaeological correctness. There is nothing in Greek drama except the emotional truth and consistency of the performers, and the immense responding emotion of those who are present.[50]

Leontis calls Palmer Sikelianos's process an "alternative archaeology," borrowing Bruce Trigger's term.[51] Leontis argues: "Calling modern dance's extensive engagement with relics of Greece's past an 'alternative archaeology' brings into view the role artists play in speculating on the lost performing arts using their peculiar talents, experience, and knowledge, and asking interesting questions about ancient space and the human activities that distributed themselves within it from an alternative perspective."[52]

However, Palmer Sikelianos discounted archaeological fealty in one breath and basked in the accolades of professional scholars in the next. While she took pride in convincing the scholar that she performed a "real" ancient Greek drama when she knew there were inaccuracies, that does not mean that archaeological correctness was not a concern. Her method was not to merely discover what ancient Greece was or to reproduce a performance for the archive, but rather to discover how to re-embody it in the present: to bring the ancient Greek past from the archive and into the repertoire.[53] Her adoption of a lifestyle antiquity dovetails with her stage performances as well. Whether it is an alternative archaeology or lived antiquity, Palmer Sikelianos's knowledge of Greece (past, present, and future) was mediated by the Greece she observed and performed on a daily basis.

That is to say, while Leontis may view Palmer Sikelianos's work as distinct from living-history interpreters, such as American Civil War re-enactors, Rebecca Schneider's work helps us see the dancer, choreographer, actress, and weaver as a performer cum historian. It was the daily practices, the citational, repetitive, and "twice-behaved" behavior (to use Richard Schechner's term),[54] that gave Palmer Sikelianos the authority to know the past. Schneider explains how this authority works with battle re-enactors: "Battle reenactors can reenact the US Civil War because they can place their bodies in the gestic compositions—the sedimented sets of acts—that US Civil War soldiers composed when those soldiers were themselves behaving as they had been trained to behave, or as they emulated other to behave, behaviors likewise *and at the time* based on prior practices and precedent notions of what it means and what it might mean to fight."[55] The gestic, the embodied, and the lived experiences of Greece (past and present) formed the center of Palmer Sikelianos's appeal and authority. Like battle re-enactors, finding authenticity in costume and other quotidian material tools became critical in achieving an authenticity in gesture and performance. Instead of going to the archaeological record, Palmer Sikelianos engaged in an experimental practice.

In her memoirs, Palmer Sikelianos wrote about the first time she had Raymond and Penelope Duncan over to her home in Neuilly outside of Paris at the turn of the century. She described their "Greek" attire and their shared experimental method: "For many years, I had made ever renewed efforts to imitate the Greek clothes we see on statues, bas-reliefs and vases. [. . .] I had made a number of dresses [. . .] I had also worked in leather, and had copied some of the complicated sandals on Greek statues. Penelope and Raymond had made attempts to solve this same problem."[56] The Duncans' and Palmer Sikelianos's conversations in these early days in Greece centered around their various attempts to solve the same problems, to recreate archaic Greek dress to wear and live in, but not to hang in a museum. At the same time archaeologists such as the Sorbonne professor Léon Heuzey sought to reproduce ancient garments for the archaeologist to study.[57] These problems were solved when Raymond Duncan arrived at the idea of making a loom so that they could weave a cloth that would hold the folds they desired. The Duncan couple soon moved in with the single young American woman, and Raymond began testing his skills at ancient Greek handiwork around her home: painting ancient Greek-style friezes, making chlamyses, etc.:

> During all these first days in my house, Raymond had been very busy. From about the first moment, he had started to paint a little frieze in one of the rooms just under a low ceiling. He put in a terra cotta background, and silhouettes of athletes, in various postures, running all round, and looking somewhat like a black-figured vase. He had also acquired a sheet of copper, out of which he produced clasps for our chlamyses, with archaic animals chasing each other round the edge. He was evidently an excellent craftsman.[58]

Palmer Sikelianos's focus on archaeological authenticity in production of a "Greek" lifestyle led to the building of a loom to create her own fabric. In her autobiography, she interrupted her discussions of weaving and dressmaking experiments with notes on archaeological discoveries made later that validated her experimental process:

> While writing this chapter, I received a letter from Mrs. Eugene Vanderpool, of the American School of Classical Studies in Athens, which says: "We have just been to a lecture by the director of the American School, who said: 'While excavating a Geometric tomb we came upon evidence bearing out the theory of Eva Sikelianou'." It seems that they found an iron object which had lain against the shroud of the body buried in the tomb; and which, during the process of rusting, had picked up the imprint of the cloth. It clearly showed the pattern of the weave: a heavy warp, and an almost imperceptible weft. Mr. Morgan said that it not only proved your theory, as shown in the weaving of the Delphic Festival, but it showed that ten centuries earlier in Geometric times, this method was used for the same reason: to produce the richness of folds seen through Greek and pre-Greek vase painting.[59]

With the archaeologists' validation that her fabrics were indeed the same warp and weft as those made by the ancient Greeks, Palmer Sikelianos felt confident in her process. So despite her disavowal of archaeological correctness, answering archaeological questions with modern experimental or embodied practice became a dominant theme in Palmer Sikelianos's writings. These questions are most evident in her discussions of music, dance, and the staging of the first two modern Delphic Festivals with her husband in 1927 and 1930.

As Artemis Leontis explains, Palmer Sikelianos used "modern Greek forms to convey ancient drama."[60] In resurrecting the rituals of Aeschylus's *Prometheus Bound*, she restaged the ancient tragedy at the theater of Delphi in modern Greek, with a cast and chorus of amateur Greek actors and dancers. As in *Le Sacre*, the tensions between the historical sources and the requirements of a contemporary performance are evidenced in Palmer Sikelianos's writings.

Reconstructing Music and Dance
in *Prometheus Bound*

Palmer Sikelianos balanced archaeological correctness with ethnographic knowledge in the costumes for *Prometheus*. For the music, however, she dismissed archaeological sources in favor of ethnographic ones. Thus, to fill in the music of *Prometheus Bound* she did not turn to Théodore Reinach or to the ancient musical notation found a few yards downhill from the ancient theater of Delphi that he deciphered and edited (see chapter 2). She found little use in trying to work with the ancient systems of notating music. Comparing the reading of ancient musical notations to Egyptian hieroglyphics, Palmer Sikelianos wrote: "[T]he use of this same anadromic method will lead musicians, not to a recovery of exact tunes, but to the recovery of a musical theory different from that familiar today, and closely resembling what the Greeks themselves wrote about music."[61] Dismissing the work of archaeologists, she doubted that excavations would ever turn up the actual melodies of Aeschylus and Sophocles, but as long as performers knew "the manner, or approximately the manner in which they composed, we can enhance their words, or any words of our own, in melody suggesting motion, and so recover the emotion, or an analogous emotion to the one they experience in their theatres and festivals."[62] Rejecting the scholarly apparatus and more or less stable documents of Emmanuel, Reinach, and others, she turned to living traditions to re-enact these emotions. The goal of reconstruction was not to make things exactly as they were then, but rather to make them using the same methods anew, in the present. Thus, to make the new music she drew musical inspiration from her friend Penelope Duncan and Byzantine liturgical chant.

Palmer Sikelianos shared a detailed discussion of Penelope's singing in her autobiography:

Occasionally, during intermissions in our weaving, Penelope would sing to me. It seemed another world: one that took me back to that summer in Bar Harbour when I first looked into Jowett's Plato. I was about eighteen. It was an incredible experience which had no breaks, no contrast. From the first Dialogue to the last my feet did not seem to touch the ground, and wherever I went I had the sensation of flying.

"Then felt I like some watcher of the skies,
When a new planet swims into his ken."[63]

I was absorbed in the many problems which Plato always evokes, [. . .] But one problem evoked no response from me. It left me dull and sad, so that only through the will to forget it could I regain the strange equilibrium which the rest of the work gave me. What did music mean to Plato? What was he talking about when he exiled one mode from his *Republic*, and preserved another? What was the Dorian mode which he retained, and what was the Lydian mode he rejected? Whatever is a musical mode, anyway? Of course I had learned the school-boy stuff about the Dorian mode beginning on D, and going straight up the white keys of the piano, and the Phrygian mode beginning on E, and so forth; and I had heard some rather silly compositions which were supposed to represent these modes. I had also heard in Paris a whole opera which claimed to be written in a purely Greek manner, which was nevertheless insufferably dull.[64]

It is remarkable that the section begins with the women weaving and singing, a perfectly quotidian activity in keeping with Palmer Sikelianos's emerging lifestyle antiquity aesthetic. The singing, however, transports her out of Greece, back to Bar Harbor, Maine, and her first experiences with Barney reading Plato and making love. She then turns to a discussion of Plato. She dismisses the "school-boy stuff" about the Greek modes and the scholarly attempts at recomposition or reconstruction of ancient Greek music, which she found "insufferably dull." It is entirely possible that Palmer Sikelianos may be referring to Emmanuel's *Salamine*, which she could have seen in Paris. She was there at the time, but since she doesn't mention any work by name this is pure speculation.

So what would make her work better than those of the men she doesn't mention (Reinach and Emmanuel)? Instead of pouring over the ancient sources in the archive, like Emmanuel and Reinach, and then filling in gaps with embodied or modern practice, Palmer Sikelianos wove together the modern folk and liturgical repertoires of Greek performance, which she then draped over archival sources.

Before focusing on Penelope Duncan and Byzantine chant, Palmer Sikelianos probably drew inspiration from Isadora and Raymond Duncan's Greek journey in 1902 (organized by Penelope and Angelos Sikelianos). Not only did Isadora famously dance in the open air atop the Acropolis, but like her brother, she also saw connections between modern Greek singing and ancient Greek song upon hearing a group of boys singing in the theater of Dionysus:

> We were of the opinion, as are many distinguished Hellenists, that the hymns of Apollo, Aphrodite, and all the pagan gods had found their way through transformations into the Greek Church. Then was born in us the idea of forming once more the original Greek Chorus from these Greek boys. We held competitions each night in the Theater of Dionysus and gave prizes to those who could present the most ancient Greek songs. We also enlisted the services of a Professor of Byzantine music. In this way we formed a chorus of ten boys who had the most beautiful voices in all Athens. The young Seminarist, who was also a student of Ancient Greek, helped us set this chorus to *The Supplicants* of Aeschylus. These choruses are probably the most beautiful that have ever been written.[65]

Palmer Sikelianos dismissed Isadora's efforts as "barbaric and completely unGreek" in that they made the boys sing unfamiliar music devised by some "Professor of Byzantine music."[66] In Vienna, Munich, and Berlin, where Isadora toured her chorus, critics received them coldly. "If, instead of these rather pitiful performances, Isadora had let Aeschylus alone, if she had allowed her ten Greek boys to sing the songs they knew, and had taught them to express what they were singing in movement, [. . .] she would have had a true beginning for a Greek chorus."[67] Isadora Duncan's fateful error, according to Palmer Sikelianos, was shoddily patching together ancient tragedy with peasant tunes (too thin a warp to hold the weft). Instead of contrafactum, Palmer Sikelianos suggests studying the Greek musical system (the warp) and then composing new songs (the weft) to fit the text. This became the process she herself would use for the music of the Delphic Festivals.

Originally wishing to perform the work intoned monophonically, she conceded (as did Théodore Reinach in his editions of the Delphic Hymn) that modern audiences needed harmony. That is to say, archaeological correctness would not work for her own body and the bodies and minds of her collaborators and audiences:

> The Greeks knew nothing about what is now called harmony; *ergo*, although they were fine architects, fine sculptors, probably fine painters, and certainly great philosophers, great poets, and the rest of it, in music they were morons. This conclusion seemed final. There was no getting around it; no fooling oneself into believing that they did know anything about harmony; no escaping the fact that, today, music without harmony is pure nonsense, a contradiction in terms. [. . .] With this, my state of levitation was in decided danger. But I succeeded in steering my mind away from it; in pretending that I did not care. There were so many other things in which they excelled. What matter if the Greeks were not musicians?[68]

Palmer Sikelianos based her imagined ancient monophonic Greek music on a combination of Greek Orthodox Church modes and her friend Penelope Duncan's own folk singing (about which we know little), and she employed this music in numerous venues. These ideas developed when Palmer Sikelianos moved outside of Athens to Kopanas with Raymond and his wife, and they ultimately formed the basis of the choruses she created for the Delphic Festivals. Palmer Sikelianos and Penelope Duncan took up studies with Professor Konstantinos Psachos (1866–1949), a scholar of Byzantine music at the National Conservatory in Athens who was also named "Master Teacher of Music of the Great Church of Christ" by the patriarch of Constantinople, and with his assistance, she attempted to create a modal organ, to properly accompany the melodies and ancient temperaments she believed were authentic. Ultimately Psachos composed the choruses in Byzantine notation, which he then sent to Palmer Sikelianos to teach to the performers.

After two summers of work with the chorus, Palmer Sikelianos had completed weaving all of the costumes and felt her work was nearly ready for performance. She was surprised to then receive Psachos's orchestral accompaniment for the choruses to *Prometheus Bound*. Horrified, she wondered, "What was the point in adding the very thing which I had been striving to avoid; why must the greatest expert on the Greek musical tradition bow to the prevailing fashion?"[69] Reluctantly, Palmer Sikelianos engaged an orchestra led by Filoktitis Oikonomidis (director of the Pireaus Conservatory), which "did not sound very badly."[70]

Ultimately, *Prometheus Bound* was performed in modern Greek in a translation by Ionnis Gryparis[71] outdoors, with costumes woven by Palmer Sikelianos herself. She thought it best in the end to use modern Greek so that peasants could understand it, to avoid problems in pronunciation, and to prove Greek was indeed a "living" language.[72] She took the musical instruction of the chorus upon herself as well, giving lessons in "Byzantine music, alternating with gymnastic exercises [. . .] and [visits to] the national Museum to study, and [. . .] to make copies of the [. . .] ancient vases."[73] Palmer Sikelianos viewed the process of teaching the material as critical, almost more important than the final project. We see the importance of this in her discussions of a trip to America after the staging of the first Delphic Festival.

Between the first and second Delphic Festivals, Palmer Sikelianos returned to America for the first time in twenty years to help spread the gospel of the Delphic idea and inspire interest in Angelos's plans for a Delphic University.[74] She wrote that George Pierce Baker, a cofounder of the Yale School of Drama, begged her to teach his students the choruses of *Prometheus Bound* exactly the way she had taught the women in Delphi. Her rejection of his proposal, which she later rather regretted, emphasized her commitment to a lived experience, fundamental to the creation of the art: "I would be teaching in a language which no student would understand, and in a kind of music which, perhaps, no musician in Yale would understand. The best I could do would be to produce a good class of parrots."[75] She feared the parrots would then teach a next generation of student parrots, and without the theoretical underpinnings or the language and vocabulary of Greek music, "they would have only a caricature of one part of one Greek play"[76]—a legacy of bastardized performances.

Second Delphic Festival

The Sikelianoses were able to correct some of the mistakes from the first festival as they began preparations for the second festival. They mounted a new production of Aeschylus's *The Supplicants*. She trained the chorus in Athens as before and asked Psachos to compose the music again, but this time without the orchestral accompaniment. He acquiesced and wrote music for chorus and single flute or oboe to introduce or play interludes. They decided to offer a new version of *Prometheus Bound* as well, and again, at the last moment Palmer Sikelianos found out that Psachos had composed a full orchestral score for the play and requested a hidden orchestra à la Richard Wagner's hidden orchestra in Bayreuth. The rehearsals in Delphi were a disaster. The conductor (Oikonomidis again) could not hear, and while *Prometheus* was passable, the more complicated movements for *The Supplicants* resulted in "pandemonium."[77] Palmer Sikelianos then arranged for Oikonomidis to reduce the instrumental forces to "two harps and a few wood-winds" and place them under the parapet of the auditorium in the center so that only the first few rows of the audience could see them. Palmer Sikelianos was pleased, but she wrote that she would still prefer to have both plays accompanied only by a "single flute, on the stage, as part of the chorus."[78] This of course is almost identical to the instrumental forces of Barney's *Équivoque* (1906), which featured a flute-playing member of the chorus discussed in chapter 3.

In a 1930 film of Palmer Sikelianos's staging of *Prometheus Bound* from the Delphic Festival one can see a plastic choreography in which the chorus moves in unison, akin to the frozen nymphs of Nijinsky's *Faune*: angled, heads in profile. Dancers strike poses (i.e., arms extended in front of the face with palms turned out) while moving slowly in metered time.[79] A photograph of the 1930 production reproduced in color in *National Geographic* captured the author's impression of the dance: "like figures on a Grecian urn." These filmic clips, however, do not share the lyricism of the Duncan style. Their rigidity aligns more closely with a later modernist aesthetic (see figures 5.2a–5.2b).[80] The film is more reminiscent at times of Bronislava Nijinska's *Les Noces* (1923) than of her brother's *Faune*, minus the pointe work and athleticism. Palmer Sikelianos's Greek folk-inspired costumes for *Prometheus Bound* share similar lines and materials with Natalia Gonchorova's Russian peasant tunics for *Les Noces*.[81]

Palmer Sikelianos believed that authentic performance was crucial to the athletic contest as well. Taking place just up the hill, an archaeologically correct performance of ancient Greek sport embodied by modern Greeks reinforced the theatrical performance as well. For the Pyrrhic Dance, she had thirty suits of armor copied from sources in the National Museum, hammered out by hand, which soldiers from the First Army Corps of Greece wore to perform her heavy steps. They danced in a similar plastic manner, making strong forceful gestures to hold static poses. They slowly bent down on one knee and then rose up quickly, and they moved back and forth alternately in plastic poses with their swords up and then with their swords pointed down in cross movements. They would hop, stand sentry, and then march. In the next sequence, they lifted their arms up with their swords and shields while squatting, made a little hop, and then raised their arms as they turned in profile and knelt down, oddly reminiscent of the Dance of the Chosen One in the finale of

FIGURE 5.2a Photograph of the Oceanids from Eva Palmer Sikelianos's *Prometheus Bound*, Delphi (1927). Eva Palmer Sikelianos Archive, Benaki Museum, Kifisia, Delta House, 189.4.377.

FIGURE 5.2b Photograph of the Oceanids by Nelly's from Eva Palmer Sikelianos's *Prometheus Bound*, Delphi (1930). Eva Palmer Sikelianos Archive, Benaki Museum, Kifisia, Delta House, 189.4.462.

Le Sacre or the hops of the bridegroom in Nijinska's *Les Noces*.[82] All of this was documented, filmed, photographed, and written about. It was performed and dutifully archived.

Documenting *Prometheus Bound*: Archival Experiences

Palmer Sikelianos laid out her theories of Greek music, movement, and theater in her unpublished autobiography, but also documented her stagings of Aeschylus both in Greece and later in America. She took photos or arranged for photographers to capture the works; she saved musical scores in both Byzantine chant and Western notations; and as mentioned above, she even arranged for a silent film of the festival. The bulk of her papers, now at the Benaki Museum Archives in Kifisia, Greece, include music, lots and lots of music, drafts of musical ideas, and completed musical scores for a possible future version of *Prometheus Bound* to be performed in the United States, based on translations by Edith Hamilton for chorus and with oboe or flute interludes.

The extant pieces of music in Palmer Sikelianos's own hand are not copies of Professor Konstantinos Psachos's original music for the 1927 and 1930 festivals, but rather were written in America, where she moved after her marriage with Angelos Sikelianos fell apart and she exhausted her inheritance. They most likely represent the ideal version Palmer Sikelianos describes in *Upward Panic* and which she hoped to mount in America with dancer and choreographer, Ted Shawn. In the absence of the Psachos materials, Palmer Sikelianos's own compositions are the best archival evidence we have. As musical compositions, however, they are quite simple, almost rudimentary. The opening flute music for the entrance of the Oceanids, for example, has a limited range of an octave (d to d') and centers around a; it often includes a lowered second, adding a modal flavor to the mostly stepwise melody (see music example 5.2).

The following choruses are not much different. They move mostly stepwise and are mostly set syllabically. Melismas paint the text on the words "wings" and "flying" in familiar ways. The music doesn't seem particularly special except for the fact that the text is quite awkwardly set. For someone who cared so much about the rhythm of words, it was odd to elongate the end of the first line "friends are here" and place a particularly awkward run on the word *fly-y-i-i-i-ing* (see music example 5.3).

These examples come from just the first page of the score. All twenty pages reveal a weakness in setting English text (melismas on weak vowels, etc.) and awkward writing for the flute (unless the part is to be played an octave higher, it would sound particularly weak on a modern flute). The notated rhythms

MUSIC EXAMPLE 5.2 Eva Palmer Sikelianos, entrance of Oceanids, *Prometheus Bound.* Eva Palmer Sikelianos Archive, Benaki Museum, Kifisia, Delta House, 189.18.

MUSIC EXAMPLE 5.3 Eva Palmer Sikelianos, first chorus, *Prometheus Bound.* Eva Palmer Sikelianos Archive, Benaki Museum, Kifisia, Delta House, 189.18.

feel too metrical for the English prose, which seems antithetical to Palmer Sikelianos's urgings for music to follow the natural rhythms of the text.

In addition to the disappointing musical material, Palmer Sikelianos's archive included photographs from the 1927 and 1930 performances of *Prometheus Bound* and *The Supplicants* depicting dancers moving alone and in ensemble, wearing costumes Palmer Sikelianos wove herself. We also have the film versions of *Prometheus Bound.* Despite her rejection of a modern mechanized society, Palmer Sikelianos was apparently not averse to using film and photographic technologies to archive her work.

The most familiar and frequently reproduced photographs of the Delphic Festivals by Nelly's [Elli Sougioultzoglou-Seraidari] feature the dancers or athletes in their costumes (handmade ancient garments and armor) (see figures 5.3 and 5.4).[83] They are meant to index, archive, and preserve for future generations Palmer Sikelianos's work. They do not appear to be designed to help execute a faithful reproduction; they are not a blueprint, nor a choreographic score.

Palmer Sikelianos firmly believed in the process and lived experiences that came together to make *Prometheus Bound* a success in the 1920s and 1930s. The photos and film, shot in a newsreel fashion, document her triumphs.[84] The careful editing and multiple camera angles, postproduction shots, extreme close-ups of the actors, and title cards signal to Pantelis Michelakis that "the film is preoccupied with authenticity."[85] Michelakis further argues that her interest in "authenticity" and "material remains from Ancient Greece" resonates with the power of photography to seemingly index reality and modernist "assumptions about movement as a quantifiable and linear concept that can

FIGURE 5.3 Photograph by Nelly's of Eva Palmer Sikelianos's *Prometheus Bound*, Delphi (1930). Eva Palmer Sikelianos Archive, Benaki Museum, Kifisia, Delta House, 189.4.460.

FIGURE 5.4 Photograph by Nelly's of Eva Palmer Sikelianos's Delphic Festival (1930). Eva Palmer Sikelianos Archive, Benaki Museum, Kifisia, Delta House, 189.4.475.

be broken down to its constituent parts for analysis, storage, and retrieval," traits shared with Loïe Fuller.[86] While Michelakis's understanding of Palmer Sikelianos's authenticity may differ from the one argued here, his reading of her film allows us to see her seemingly contradictory reliance on mechanical technological tools to archive her works born out of a rejection of a modern mechanized life.

These tools of archivation, however, do not just capture what Palmer Sikelianos wished us to see, but more important, they also reveal what she didn't want us to see. Photography, and cinematography for that matter, indiscriminately records the details of the frame, which, as Christopher Pinney writes, "will ensure a substrate or margin of excess, a subversive code present in every photographic image that makes it open and available to other readings and uses. [. . .] however hard the photographer tries to *exclude*, the camera lens always *includes*. The photographer can never fully control the resulting photograph, and it is that lack of control and the resulting *excess* that permits recoding, 'resurfacing,' and 'looking past'."[87] Photographs are art-historical texts; they are indexical, but they are also moments in time, controlled by people, nature, and chance. The music is also outside the frame and in formats not readily accessible to dance or classics scholars, let alone musicologists unschooled in the details of Byzantine chant notation.

The photographs in the Benaki archive offer another way to "look past" (to borrow Pinney's term) Palmer Sikelianos's indexical motivations. Snapshots, not taken by Nelly's, challenge the narrative of a complete and unpolluted ancient experience on the side of Mount Parnassus. The following two images, for example, center on Palmer Sikelianos's dancers, but in the corners of the frame modern musicians lurk (see figures 5.5 and 5.6).

Figure 5.5 clearly shows a pair of timpani, music stands, and male musicians wearing modern neckties and jackets rather than the handmade costumes Palmer Sikelianos designed for the stage performers. In figure 5.6, only the music stands and musicians' legs are visible in the photograph. I am struck by the contrast between the attitudes held by the chorus and what we can see of the musicians. The female chorus members hold out their right arms, some with their palms rigidly turned downward, others with their palms open, and all with their heads turned sharply over their shoulders. One musician appears to have his right leg crossed over his left—a stance of repose—passing time awaiting more structured movements.

Of course Palmer Sikelianos did not want the modern orchestral instruments and musicians within the frame of her Greek drama. Not only did she disapprove of their inclusion and feel pressured to accept Psachos's accompaniments, she also saw them as a corrupting foreign influence on the authentically produced melodies, costumes, and gestures of the production. It must have been difficult for her to reconcile these impulses: fealty to a mentor and one's own artistic

FIGURE 5.5 Photograph of Eva Palmer Sikelianos's *Prometheus Bound* (1927). Eva Palmer Sikelianos Archive, Benaki Museum, Kifisia, Delta House, 189.4.380.

FIGURE 5.6 Photograph of Eva Palmer Sikelianos's *Prometheus Bound* (1927), Eva Palmer Sikelianos Archive, Benaki Museum, Kifisia, Delta House, 189.4.383.

integrity. We try not to include things we are ashamed of in our archival work, but the camera does not lie; it captures the good, the bad, and the inauthentic.

The Archaeologists Respond

Despite the modern intrusions, the verisimilitude of the amateur performers' *Prometheus Bound* captivated audiences. Historian Robert Payne said of Palmer Sikelianos in the 1960s: "She had a strange power of entering the mind of ancients and bringing them to life again. She knew everything about them—how they walked and talked [. . .] how they latched their shoes [. . .] what songs they sang, and how they danced, and how they went to bed."[88] I don't think the offhand "went to bed" comment refers to the ways Greeks said their prayers and laid out their clothes for the morning. Payne hints at the lure of antiquity and those with special access to it. Palmer Sikelianos didn't just figure out how the Greeks lived and made art; her bodily knowledge of Greece was carnal. She made love to men and women, Americans and Greeks. Others noted the "archaeological correctness" of the Delphic Festivals. Ernst Buschor, the director of the German School of Archeology, wrote to Palmer Sikelianos praising this correctness, to which she responded (as discussed earlier) that it was *not* correct; he was just too blind to notice. It was the play, in the outdoor theater (with the mostly hidden orchestra) that galvanized the archaeologist's imagination.

Ann Cooper Albright argues that the only archaeologically correct element of the Delphic Festival was the costumes, made with Palmer Sikelianos's hand-woven fabrics. She asserts that authenticity in costume (Palmer Sikelianos used silk, which was not available to ancient Greeks), music, and dance was sacrificed for the drama,[89] but it is clear from Palmer Sikelianos's writings that all modern concessions in archaeological correctness were judiciously made. It is not that archaeological correctness should not be sought; it is just that it is impossible in a modern world: the main problem was the modern world. The tensions between archaeology and ethnography, the past and the present, the archive and the repertoire continued to haunt Palmer Sikelianos throughout her project.

Within a generation, archaeology had adopted a strictly positivist methodology, leaving the engagement with performance behind: scholars dug, performers performed. The engagements discussed in this chapter between modernism and modern science not only capture the evolving ways we perform antiquity, but also provide models for how performance can lead to a more vibrant scholarship for disciplines outside of dance and performance studies (such as musicology).

From our current historical and disciplinary perspectives, it is easy to point out Palmer Sikelianos's compositional weakness and the archaeological inaccuracies and dismiss these projects outright. Dispelling their myths of fidelity and accuracy, however, does not preclude the enjoyment of these works. Despite the laborious scholarly preparations to capture the ancient world, perhaps the true value of these collaborations lies in the visceral act on stage, when logic is momentarily abandoned to capture the primal, ineffable magic of a fleeting artistic moment, which transports both the performer and the audience out of time, beyond history and into mythical eternity. When Barney praised her friend for giving Greece back to the Greeks, it was despite all of this, despite the colonialist tendencies and archaeological inaccuracies. The Delphic Festivals provided an escape from the West's archival fascination and celebrated the here and now of what modern Greece could do. It was a return of agency back to Greece at a time when the country needed it, much like today.

When I worked in the archives in Greece it was difficult for me to separate my archival mission from the current political and economic situation in the country. It must have been difficult for Palmer Sikelianos, too. In the 1920s refugees from Turkey and Russia flooded into Greece. The government struggled to house them all, and many found shelter in temporary housing on Athenian archaeological sites. To help raise awareness of the interconnected problems of refugee housing and archaeological preservation, Palmer Sikelianos staged a performance of Angelos Sikelianos's *The Dithyramb of the Rose*, the proceeds of which would fund the preservation of the archaeological sites.[90] Is it strange that the proceeds were not set aside to help refugees (potential new Greeks), but rather the remains of long-dead ones?

The Delphic Festivals and Dance Advocacy: Past and Present

The Delphic Festivals of 1927 and 1930 remain a well-deserved point of artistic pride within Greek dance history narratives.[91] Their choreographic and archaeological importance overshadows Psachos's lost music. While Artemis Leontis and others have previously explored Palmer Sikelianos's career before arriving in Greece, this chapter places her in a much wider context of ancient Greek performance. Returning to Barney's praise of her friend's work, Palmer Sieklianos had returned Greece to the Greeks after "Greek" had taken a brief holiday in Paris. Once Barney had moved away from ancient Greek performance in favor of a more austere interwar salon for literature, it was then okay for "Greece" to go back home. Barney was done. This was a gesture of kindness: we can't use it all up, we need to return them (lovers or a culture) to their home after making love all night long, after an evening of mutually joyful corruption.

Like the Elgin Marbles, "Greece" has been taken, but like the marbles, Barney and Palmer Sikelianos's Greece can be returned. This is the beauty of performance. The treasures in the archives may get weighed down by politics, tied up in red tape, and held hostage; they are objects and their value is fixed. A post-Brexit United Kingdom does not seem poised to repatriate the Elgin Marbles to a teetering postcrisis Greece.

Palmer Sikelianos "learned" and "discovered" Greece in Bar Harbor, Maine, and in the Parisian suburb of Neuilly. At the time, those places were the center of ancient Greek culture for her. She fostered it, let it grow and mature, developed it, nursed it—gave herself to it and then brought it home. Palmer Sikelianos may have seen herself as a teacher, fostering Greece's development before returning it to its home. Now that Greece is "home," what traces of Paris does it keep? Does it function like Marta Savigliano's idea of cultural economies of the tango: Buenos Aires to Paris and then back?[92] Palmer Sikelianos's Greece grew *su vitro*: under the glass of Parisian American performers-scholars. It was a cultural life that she felt needed protection but shouldn't. That's the tragedy. Maybe that is why Palmer Sikelianos's projects never planted roots in Delphi. After her death the festivals were abandoned. There was no American-Hellenist-Parisian scholar/performer to lead the enterprise, no one to tend the garden.

At the end of the day, Greece has never been fully returned. I carried out my research trip to Athens in the summer of 2015 under the threat of yet another debt default and other threats to Greek independence and autonomy. The loss and the fear of loss are mounting, and at the time I am writing this, Greece remains on the precipice of defaulting to its creditors—the same ones who stole its culture a century and two centuries ago. While Palmer Sikelianos was fascinated by the reperformance of antiquity in modern Greece, I couldn't help thinking of the reperformance of early twentieth-century Greece in an age-of-austerity Greece in the summer of 2015.

In the winter of 2012 dancer and scholar Ann Cooper Albright spent seven weeks teaching physical mindfulness, contact improvisation, and dance theory to academics, dance professionals, and nonprofessionals in Athens, Corfu, Thessaloniki, and Nafpoli. Albright came to Greece in the midst of political unrest, riots, and financial uncertainty to "encourage people to keep dancing even in the midst of uncertain support or government funding." She described her model as "dancing triage, a movement-based parallel to Doctors Without Borders (Médecins Sans Frontières)."[93] She taught workshops that emphasized playful exercises and improvisation, falling, and gravity's pull on the body. These experiences were designed to work against the more formal movement training. Albright recalls: "I think that one of my more useful contributions [. . .] was to model an approach to dancing that does not separate theory and practice, moving and thinking. As we all know, there is an important intelligence located in the body that we come to understand only through dancing. It is crucial to realize, however, that this kind of physical mindfulness can also help us respond to the world outside of a dance studio."[94]

Barney was wrong: Palmer Sikelianos's work in Greece was not part of some colonialist project. Albright, like Palmer Sikelianos before her, came to return Greece to the Greeks, but not in some Western-savior, I-know-what's-best-for-you way. Both women came to Greece to help Greece find its own strength, its own identity, amid the burned and vandalized ruins of the past to reconnect to the vulnerable center, the omphalos. Recently, archaeologists have suggested that the physical omphalos stone purportedly thrown by Zeus from heaven that landed in Delphi originally stood precariously atop the great thirteen-meter Akanthos column at the top of which stand the three Delphic dancers (of Claude Debussy's *Préludes* fame).[95] If that theory is correct, the center of the world rests on the hands of dancers. As many Greeks feel their country slip from the safety of Europe, as the center of Europe seems to shift farther and farther north and west, and as refugees from Asia and the Middle East wash up on the shores of Lesbos, contemporary Greek dancers use their bodies to regain control of a world seemingly spinning out of control.[96] Unlike Barney's experiences in Lesbos, Palmer Sikelianos accepted Greece as it was. She took the time to learn the past through the fears and hopes of people in the present.

6 | Scholars and Their Objects of Study; or, Loving Your Subject

Devotion to the past [is] one of the more disastrous forms of
unrequited love.

—*Susan Sontag, "Unguided Tour"*[1]

I T IS DIFFICULT TO love someone or something that doesn't love you back. This chapter returns to Natalie Clifford Barney decades after she stopped dancing her Sapphic dramas, to explore the complexities in relationships between scholars and their objects of study, musical and human, who cannot reciprocate a scholar's love. Elsewhere in this book I have discussed how the love of Greek antiquity has inspired new performances of ancient works and texts. The stories told in this final chapter produced no issue. The scholar's love of his subject and the subject's love of her scholar left everyone disappointed. I revisit musicology's problem with the past, the discipline's love of the dead, its erotic tendencies, and its reperformance in the present. Musicology's kinship with photography and voyeurism presents an opportunity to discuss music's love for the dead and the dead's inability to love back. These scholarly tendencies and methods have the potential to lead to an unhealthy relationship with music: a hopelessly tangled web of relationships, erotic affinities that are either not reciprocated or are exploited. However, despite the risks inherent in the methodologies of performing antiquity and the methodologies of *loving* antiquity, this book hopefully has demonstrated that regardless of intent, performing is love.

The conclusion is in two parts. The first section uses Jeremy Denk's and Steven Stucky's opera *The Classical Style: An Opera (of Sorts)* (2013–2014) to probe the eroticization and de-eroticization of scholarship, the objects of scholarship, and the scholars themselves. I then turn back to Barney and look at the Parisian archaeologist and art historian Salomon Reinach's obsession with her,[2] Barney's own infatuation with the scholars who studied her, and how twentieth- and twenty-first-century scholars love and perform their archives when they can't love back. To love antiquity so much that one performs it allows a way out of the endless critical loops when the subject can't love back. Performance allows for reparative readings of the beloved musics and dances of the distant past and the critics of the more recent past.

What If Musicology *Is* Sex?

Musicology's problem with performing the past was recently parodied in an opera. Stucky and Denk's comedic *The Classical Style: An Opera (of Sorts)* is based on Charles Rosen's musicological tome *The Classical Style* (1971).[3] While Stucky and Denk would not consider themselves musicologists— Denk calls himself "a huge musicology nerd, and fanboy"[4]—the treatment of Rosen's work is a performance of a scholarly text. The comic opera (of sorts) opens with Mozart, Haydn, and Beethoven in heaven lamenting the "death of classical music as announced by *The New York Times*." They soon discover Rosen's *The Classical Style*, a work that unapologetically studies great works by great men in great analytical detail, avoiding their reception and social histories at all costs. The trio of composers seek out the famed author, who may help them reinvigorate their legacies. They crash a musicological symposium, stumble into a bar where Tonic, Dominant, and subdominant hang out, and end up in Charles Rosen's own dining room. In the end, their beloved classical style is safe, but their celebrations are not complete without punishing those responsible for the style's near obliteration. And who in this opera is to blame for the near death of classical music? Musicology, of course, as personified by the character of the young and nerdy PhD candidate, Henry Snibblesworth (student at the University of California, Berkeley, studying with Richard Taruskin—one of Rosen's favorite musicological supervillains).[5] Unlike Rosen, who was a scholar-performer, the PhD candidate doesn't make music; he merely talks about it, a lot. In the opera, Snibblesworth's nasal tenor whine and nerdy analysis of Mozart's music render Don Giovanni impotent. He gives up attacking Donna Anna, and the usually virile Don walks away, shocked that he is no longer "in the mood." The musicologist is the annoying, quasi-hysterical fly buzzing in the ear of Mozart, Haydn, and Beethoven. And of course it is the musicologist who gets dragged down to hell at the end. As Kristi Brown-Montesano wrote on the American Musicological Society's blog, *Musicology Now*, Denk's libretto mercilessly parodies the humanist trend in musicology, naming names (Richard Taruskin), and mocking (albeit Denk claims it was not intentional) "new" musicology's critiques of the gendered meanings of the classical repertoire.[6] In the last scene Mozart, Haydn, and Beethoven interrupt Charles Rosen's dinner. They have been looking all over for him because of his great book, and they know he can help them be loved, be relevant, and be understood today so that classical music will not really die, but be reborn. Because, as Mozart, Haydn, and Beethoven sing: "A style, when it is no longer the natural mode of expression, gains a new life—a shadowy life in death. We imagine ourselves able to revive the past through its art. For this illusion of reliving history, the style must be prevented from becoming truly alive again."[7] It is ultimately good to be dead. The "death of classical music" lamented at the opening of the opera becomes a cause for celebration. The past needs to be past in order for it to be worshipped. At the end of his review of a performance of Denk and Stucky's opera at Zankel Hall in 2014, *New York Times* critic Anthony Tommasini wrote, "It's hard to say what the future holds for *The Classical Style*. But even those who lack understanding of the rudiments of harmony would surely enjoy it, while also learning something in the most entertaining way."[8] Denk and Stucky are not against the scholarship of music; they use their opera to promote their own views on how musicologists should do musicology.

Denk and Stucky, like Barney, Théodore Reinach, Maurice Emmanuel, Salomon Reinach, Eva Palmer Sikelianos, and the other scholars in this study, use performance to ensure that their ideas about the music of the past (in Denk and Stucky's case, the genius of "classical music") do not die, by re-enacting scholarly ideas in singing and dancing living bodies. While Emmanuel, the Reinach brothers, Barney, and Palmer Sikelianos were more interested in an older classicism than Denk and Stucky are, the project of making an opera to advocate for a specific way of reading history remains the same. The irony, of course, is that performances are less durable than books and articles. The parting image of *The Classical Style: An Opera (of Sorts)* paints the musicologist as Don Giovanni himself: a haughty youth arrogant enough to invite a stone guest to dinner. But here the musicologist's sins are not sexual; Henry Snibblesworth is no libertine. He's more like a cross between the short-statured and sloped-shouldered musicologist played by Austin Pendleton and the high-strung fiancée played by Madeline Kahn in Peter Bogdanovich's *What's Up Doc?* (1972): high-pitched, nasal, sniveling, and decidedly unsexy. We tend not to sexualize our scholars, despite the enduring problem of sexual harassment and abuse in academia.[9] When we do, it can be unsettling. What if, for example, Henry Snibblesworth's meddling in the *Classical Style* actually enflamed Don Giovanni's libido? What if he got as excited about musicology as he did about the subjects of his musicological research (Mozart, Haydn, and Beethoven)? For Denk, that was impossible: musicologists who concern themselves with social history and reception studies rather than the music itself are the ultimate anaphrodisiac. This brand of musicology doesn't give new life for Rosen and Denk; it kills permanently. Snibblesworth's version of the catalog aria from *Don Giovanni* doesn't fetishize sexual conquests, but rather "new" musicological contributions: "But in Berkeley, 3000 essays on gender constructs,

3000 essays on gender constructs and Beethoven alone!"[10] Apparently, musicology isn't sexy.

Suzanne Cusick begs to differ when she famously asks: "What if music IS sex?"[11] Musicology's answer over the past few decades has been a resounding, "Yes, music can be sex." I want to go a step further (and perhaps further anger the ghost of Charles Rosen). What if, in stark contrast to Stucky and Denk's opera *The Classical Style*, musicology (and other disciplines across the humanities) can be sex? It's an idea flirted with throughout this book: Reinach's private immersive antiquity verges on sexual role play, Emmanuel's scholarly posture echoes Denk's rejection of a "sexy" musicology, and Palmer Sikelianos and Barney at various points integrated scholarship and performances of ancient Greek music with sexual and relational identities. Cusick herself flirts with the idea in an essay about the power of love in musicology. "Increasingly," she writes, "we think, talk, and write as if music were not a thing, not an autonomous entity, but a relationship."[12] Musicology, Cusick argues, is sustained by musicologists' adherents' love of music. They come to annual meetings, engage in the discipline, and suffer its humiliations because "we are here to talk, think, make, write, be in the glorious presence of a medium and a relation and sometimes even, yes, a thing that we call 'music' and that we just love, often with embarrassing and unaccountable passion."[13] Elsewhere, Cusick has eloquently described the relationship between the musicologist and music as relational: "I mean that we who are musicians and scholars of music have chosen by years (even decades) of practice, playing, listening, writing, to make 'music'—whatever we understand by that word—intrinsic to our very selves (to our subjectivities, self-images and social identities). The effect of that choice over time is that we have mutually constitutive relations with 'music,' relations that we renew with our every musical act."[14]

If musicology is in a "relationship" with music, who is to say it is always a healthy one? I argue that it is not always healthy. Maybe those "embarrassing and unaccountable passions" are the byproducts of a toxic relationship, a parasitic blood sucking of the thing we love so much: music and the people who make it. Unlike in Denk and Stucky's *The Classical Style*, which allows music to die so that it can be reborn, this parasitic love prevents death: it sucks out life without allowing for renewal, rebirth, reproduction, redemption, resurrection, or reperformance. Parasitic love of one's subject is not unique to musicology, but the unique position musicology is in with past musical works and music makers and the performance of those pasts in the present creates untold traps and obstacles. William Cheng asked if the fostering of knowledge, the raison d'être of the academic's life, is really a harmless act. "Do paths to truths ever come with unforeseen tolls?"[15] That is to say, maybe Denk's operatic portrait of the musicologist is spot on?

Musicology, Love, and the Archive

One way to have an unhealthy relationship with music is to abuse the privilege and access musicologists have to the sources of music. Musicology comes with privilege. For many musicologists the *real* privilege of their vocation is getting a front-row seat to the musical (and musicological) past. Musicologists get to touch the artifacts of music history—the scores, the instruments, the diaries, the concert programs—and get to have a hand in the writing of history. To be a musicologist is to be not just a time traveler, but a world traveler as well. Many of us have the privilege to crisscross the globe (on someone else's dime) and to gain special access to the world's musical heritage. Archival work remains critical, and much of musicological training still involves the development of skills for the successful navigation of these archives and their many musical secrets. There is no shortage of writings on music historiography, from Guido Adler to Carl Dahlhaus and beyond, but there are fewer field guides to navigating the spaces where the musicologists begin their craft.[16] While there is a lot of talk about music and texts, and sources, and binding and paper sizes, and paleography, and types of notation and types of print, one thing all of these handbooks fail to mention is the dangers of the archives. I don't mean to imply that the job of a musicologist is fraught with peril. Paper cuts aside, physical injury, even with really big books, is rare. So what is so dangerous about musicology? It is the danger we all face in our lives: falling in love. Love is something rarely talked about in musicology. What does it mean to love music, your object of study?

In *Loving Literature*, Dierdre Shauna Lynch explores the love-hate relationship the field of literary studies has had with the "love" of literature, versus the "work" or "duty" of reading literature. She outlines the complex forms of love that eighteenth- and nineteenth-century readers felt toward their texts: grateful love, possessive love, quotidian love, love and loss, and the gothic love for dead forebears.[17] Lynch reminds us that professors of literature can still work on things they love, albeit with a detached professionalism. The scholars may try to conceal or mask their love, but that doesn't mean it isn't there. It is always there.

Scholars are trained to be objective, or at least to perform objectivity in accordance with disciplinary and institutional "scripts": to approach musical sources divorced from personal attachments, to probe and interrogate the musical texts, looking for clues that other scholars may have missed to tell the story of music. As Richard Taruskin puts it in the introduction to his behemoth, six-volume *Oxford History of Western Music* (criticized by Charles Rosen):[18] "Espousing a particular position in the debate is no business of the historian [. . .] But to report the debate in its full range, and draw relevant implications from it, is the historian's ineluctable duty. That report includes the designation of what elements within the sounding composition have triggered the associations – a properly historical sort of analysis."[19] He warns of the risks and urges all to separate their authorial voices from their advocacy for "great works"—something Charles Rosen was never afraid to do. Taruskin gleefully responded to Rosen's criticism of his methods: "Advocacy is not a historian's task, and a historian who indulges in it is in fact a propagandist. As one who regards Rosen's literary output—all of it—as Cold War propaganda, I am heartened that he perceives the distinction between our objectives and our methods the same way I do."[20] When it comes to history we want the facts, just the facts. Since the 1990s musicology has recognized that the discipline is unavoidably political.[21] Taruskin doesn't offer any advice to the scholar whose politics, personal affiliations, opinions, views, and loves want to be heard within the history. Rosen, of course, is a proponent of advocacy, of standing up for genius (he doesn't use the word *love*): "Taruskin's claim neither to advocate nor to denigrate the music he discusses is a hollow one: you cannot make sense of music without advocacy, and not to make sense of it is to condemn."[22] *Advocacy*, though, seems like a way to avoid saying love. Rosen loves the music he writes about.

What if musicology *is* sex? What if scholarship *is* sex? Just as we may develop bonds as players of music to long-dead musical creators and performers, so can we develop similar bonds as scholars. Of course not all scholarly relationships have to be sexual, but exploring the erotics of musicology offers new ways to examine the relational aspects of scholars to their objects of study.

Elizabeth Le Guin's "carnal musicology" places the body of the performer on equal footing with the work performed, creating a relationship that is "revelatory, voyeuristic; at its best and sweetest we might call it intimate, implying that it is somehow reciprocal."[23] The carnal intimacy Le Guin describes verges on the erotic. Not only does Le Guin provide a rather traditional analysis of Boccherini's String Quartet in E Major, op. 15, no. 3, G. 179, but she follows this with a conversation among the members of her quartet and later the recording producer in which those intimate with the music discuss their own intimacy with the long-dead composer, and how their shared musical experiences with the quartet provided connection, intimacy, power, and both bodily pleasure and displeasure.[24] Elizabeth Freeman similarly identifies an "erotohistoriography": the erotics of the work of history. Unlike the proper historical re-enactors who perform to remake the present as the past, erotohistoriography treats the present and the past as a hybrid by using "the body as a tool to effect, figure, or perform that encounter."[25] Musicologists might be familiar with this (although we tend not to talk about it much), as are other scholar-practitioners. Freeman describes how historical materials "can be precipitated by particular bodily dispositions, and that these connections may elicit bodily responses"; among these is of course sexual pleasure.[26] How many musicologists have sat in an archive's reading room humming quietly to themselves or silently fingering a passage to "hear" it? But we aren't actually hearing when there is no sound; instead we are "feeling" the music. Those of us working in dance studies do this all the time. We look at photos and try to feel what it meant for that dancer to strike that pose, to execute that turn, to lift that other dancer in that unique way. For Freeman, queerness unbinds time and space from history's ream of fabric. Like Carolyn Dinshaw's work, Freeman imagines a dialectic between past and present sexualities. And while it is fairly common for those of us working in queer history to ask how we go about accessing and constructing long-dead queer bodies, the job of historicizing them does not prohibit us from also desiring them.[27]

It is not just queerness that does this; archives themselves also do this. Freeman's discussions of erotohistoriographies emphasize the ways eighteenth- and nineteenth-century historians theorized the physical sensations of those doing history. Even at that time the fear of the "carnal" haunted the relationships "between the historian and his object."[28] Arlette Farge's love letter to the archives offers another recognizable and intimate portrait of the importance, the carnality, the feel, the desires, and the allure of archives. Farge describes the feel of the cloth ribbon holding together packets of documents not touched in centuries, the power of unbinding that ribbon, and letting the past mingle with the present in the cold reading room. "As if, in unfolding the document, you gained the privilege of 'touching the real.'" These feelings of ecstasy in the archive do not last. "The physical pleasure of finding a trace of the past is succeeded by doubt mixed with the powerless feeling of not knowing what to do with it."[29] Each page of her lyrical essay could just as easily be about the encounter with a past lover rather than a stack of dirty, insect-eaten judicial documents. The ribbon could just as easily bind a bosom rather than a packet of letters stuck to each other with petrified rodent droppings. One can develop a relationship with one's object of study, but when scholars merge their hobbies of collection with scholarship or move from advocacy to fetish, they cross ethical boundaries. The methods used by Reinach (unscrupulous editing), Barney (eliding the scholarly and the erotic), Emmanuel (forcing scholarly theories onto the stage). and Palmer Sikelianos (reconciling the archaeological and the ethnographic) all have the potential for ethical abuse. The story of Salomon Reinach and Barney illustrates the unreciprocated scholarly desire to touch the past and the sexual obsession that accompanies that desire. It acknowledges that the past is unable to give consent. Telling this final chapter in Barney's story (for now, at least) brings us full circle back to her dreams of the past and others' dreams of her past, the risks of obsession and dangers lurking in the archives.

Salomon Reinach and Natalie Clifford Barney: A Love Story (of Sorts)

πέρροχος, ὡς ὅτ' ἄοιδος ὁ Λέσβιος ἀλλοδάποισιν

Superior as a singer from Lesbos to those of other lands.

—Sappho, *Sappho: A New Translation*, frag. 106[30]

Théodore Reinach's older brother Salomon studied archaeology, but his academic interests in the ancient world also focused on Greek art and philology. Aside from his academic credentials, lists of publications, and awards and honors, he took a keen interest in the private salon of Barney and the belle époque courtesans who passed through her garden. In Barney's map from her 1929 *L'Aventures d'Esprit* (see figure 3.9), Salomon's name appears among those closest to the temple, alongside such notables as Renée Vivien, Marcel Proust, Isadora Duncan, and Pierre Louÿs. When describing the "map," Palmer Sikelianos also mentioned the Reinach brothers in her list of Barney's circle, noting: "Some of these [people] were already her friends in Neuilly, enough of them to show the trend and to make my mother's fear for my future isolation appear in an unexpected light."[31] Salomon's prominent positioning on the map did not seem to trouble the respected scholar and museum director. When not in the National Museum of Antiquities at Saint-Germain-en-Laye or in the field, Salomon seemed to spend much of his free time corresponding and socializing with the courtesans and lesbian lovers of Barney's salon, Liane de Pougy in particular.[32]

In 1914, five years after the death of Vivien, Salomon Reinach abandoned his archaeological research to compile a history (never completed) of her love affair with Barney. Vivien and Barney's love affair did not end with Vivien's tragic death in 1909, but continued for decades in the imagination of fans and followers like Reinach. The search for Sappho's lost voice infused Barney and Vivien's liaison with added mystery and eroticism, but their historically informed "Sapphic" affair in turn became Reinach's sought-after "archeological treasure." It was the worst kind of unrequited love.

Salomon Reinach followed Vivien's and Pougy's careers, and years after their famous affairs with Barney he encouraged Pougy to write a memoir of her life as Barney's lover; Pougy found that his attention made her uncomfortable. Reinach's interest became an obsession, and his two passions—ancient Greek culture and its contemporary imitations—blurred. In one of his first letters to Pougy he wrote:

> You should not write anything about her [Pauline Tarn/Renée Vivien] that I would be distressed to read. First, my worship of her is not idolatry: I criticize her severely when I consider her ruined health, her wasted life. After

Flossie [Natalie Clifford Barney] left her, she had to remain a *widow* or get married; her *passing* years are dreadful. Second, no part of such a great genius is a matter of indifference, even its inevitable humiliations. And don't pretend that you don't desire to empty the cornucopia of your memories into my hands. Therefore, write, about her too, several pages that I will not read. Describe your quarrel and the reasons for it, search your memory; tell all. But only tell that of which you are certain; fair judges do not give weight to *hearsay*.[33]

Already he seemed to have realized the dangers of finding out too much about the women he had taken an interest in. He warned her not to write anything he wouldn't want to read and to keep certain details private, but at the same time he warned his chronicler to write what she knew to be true. He came in with a preconceived image of Vivien and Barney's shared life that he did not want sullied ("Vous ne voulez pas écrire sur elle ce que je serais affligé de lire"). To complicate matters further, much of Salomon Reinach's archaeological research focused on the Asiatic traditions of Greek art, namely terra cottas from Lesbos.[34] With Vivien and Barney he may have sought out the modern embodied performance of his ancient objects of study.

Reinach first began corresponding with Barney around 1914, when he began to accumulate materials on Vivien. His first letter requested materials related to Vivien.[35] We only have his letters to Barney, and none of her replies, but the tone of his correspondence to her indicates that their friendship lacked the intimacy he desired. He copyedited her French prose, sent her copies of his scholarly articles on Sappho in English and French, and made requests. He asked for materials relating to Vivien, he asked for information on Pougy, and he inquired about Barney's personal life.

It appears that Barney was not as forthcoming as Reinach would have liked. In a letter from the fall of 1926 he wrote, in English, "I will come on Friday, and send beforehand a long kiss to a beautiful hand"; he concluded by chiding Barney for her lack of letters, "But you have been very stingy with letters, so has Liane [de Pougy]."[36] In another letter from 1930 after a long absence of correspondence, Reinach wrote that he would gladly come to her home, remarking, "I have almost forgotten the flavour of your hands. It will be quite a new lease, after much prolonged absence."[37] After that meeting Reinach penned a letter that evening in response to a question Barney had asked him about Sappho. He identified a Sapphic fragment for her and offered a translation of the Greek, as well as a detailed analysis that wove Barney's own identity into his scholarly discussions of Sappho's biography. Regarding the translation of Sappho fragment 134 ("I conversed with you in a dream Kyprogenia [Cyprus-born]"),[38] he plays on the ways Barney saw herself as a modern Sappho. He explains, "She is only styled the Cyprus born, as you could be styled the Cincinnati born [*sic*]."[39] Musing on Sappho's relationship with Atthis, a woman mentioned in

Sappho fragment 49 (a favorite of Barney's),[40] Reinach noted how ancient scholars dismissed Atthis as merely a friend, not a lover of Sappho, reasoning that the church fathers would never accept a woman of dubious morals as "the tenth muse." Weighing in on contemporary debates over Sappho's sexuality, he sides with Barney and those who argued for her queerness. He concludes, "Of course we cannot know what happened or did not happen; but in the actual state of our knowledge, it seemed that Sappho and Atthis may have been just like Pauline Tarn [Renée Vivien] and Violet Shillito [i.e., a never consummated love affair] / My thoughts go straight to the dearest hands /S."[41] And so, when Barney needed a scholar of Greek antiquity to help prove that Sappho loved women, Reinach stepped up, and when he wanted to kiss the dearest hands of Sappho, Barney was the next best thing.

Once all of the Vivien materials were collected, Reinach deposited them along with Vivien's own manuscripts in the Bibliothèque Nationale, with the stipulation that they would remain sealed until January 2, 2000. Barney, in her writings on this relationship between a living scholar and his deceased object of desire, noted: "A scholar's heart is a dark well in which are buried many aborted feelings that rise to the surface as arguments. These concepts that he believes he is reaching by reasoning testify to instincts, awakened through the same mind that intended to condemn them to oblivion. And certainly, I have not resisted all faiths to believe in the infallibility of the human mind, however learned it be."[42] She then moved to a more biting criticism of the academic's personality: "He hides his ardor as badly as he satisfies it through the peccadillo of kissing women's hands. And isn't it with a lover's jealousy that he attempts to amass relics and defend them with so much ferocity, until the moment when he is sure that he will no longer suffer from their exploitation, until the year '2000'?" [43]

She cites a selection from a letter he wrote to her explaining his decision to keep Vivien's correspondence secret until the next century. Nothing about her life will add to their love of her poetry. He claims everything else will be a distraction. Barney then continues:

> And it is also to the year 2000 that he bequeaths the love letters that her female contemporaries will want to entrust to her secret museum. If I now felt able to write my own book about Renée Vivien, would he only lend me the notes and documents he has collected on her? Certain letters that René Vivien wrote me and which I allowed Salomon Reinach to take were returned to me, but on their front engraved with a garland of violets he had written, in small letters it is true, but discernible, in the corner of each page, "copied." Nothing leaved the hands of science unscathed![44]

While clamoring for access to the distant past, Reinach simultaneously tried to gain access to a closed-off world in the present. All he could really do was copy and cordon off their archival traces. Both realms held their secrets and were similarly unattainable. There is a comparable appeal in both the elite social worlds and ancient social worlds; their rarefied nature endows them with a sense of authenticity. The private settings themselves—the Sapphic rituals, the backstage world of the Opéra, the private dances and performances—become artifacts as well. They are artifacts of the present just as valuable as the artifacts of antiquity, and Salomon Reinach the scholar only had limited access.

Voyeurism, for Reinach, *was* scholarship. In his odd behavior, covetous nature, and collecting frenzy, Reinach was indeed listening for the kinds of Sapphonic voices discussed in chapter 3 (although he might not have known it). But these voices were *not* singing for him. Despite his best efforts, Reinach remained on the periphery of Barney's private world and simultaneously near the center of a more public space. As demonstrated through his letters to her, and despite his—and let's just call it what it is—creepiness, Barney kept him around because he validated and authenticated both her historical lesbianism and her "ancient Greekness." After all, it is flattering to have a scholar call on you and study you. Barney was adept at navigating Reinach and later used her own position as the object of study to manipulate scholars looking to tell her story.[45] She rightly bristled at Reinach's fetishistic attempts to chronicle and collect the Nachlass of the erotic lives of his favorite courtesans and their lovers. She resisted his attempts to biograph her and offered up only what was necessary for her to keep his scholarly attention.[46] Reinach and Barney used each other to help meet their scholarly and private needs. Barney decried those who used her, the men she let kiss her hands, but she was just as adept at manipulating them. These relationships between living scholars and living subjects are naturally complicated. Musicologists (unlike ethnomusicologists) are generally insulated against such encounters, but as Barney and Reinach show, archives can also become sites where the living scholar and the living archivist may also try to contest the ownership and presentation of history. For historians, subjects are more often than not dead. Suzanne Cusick, though, reminds us that while the people are dead, the subject itself is music, and that is alive. Musicologists come to musicology out of love.[47] If we are to have a relationship with our subjects, as Cusick suggests, how do we have a healthy one, when archival voyeurism has become normalized as acceptable scholarship?

Scholarly Voyeurism: Photography and Tourism

In my work I see that many scholars working in the archive become jealous of those embodying the repertoire (the living traditions of what the archival scholar studies), and vice versa. The scholar holds knowledge that the practitioner rarely can claim, and the artist possesses a different kind of bodily knowledge that cannot be known through documents—Reinach knew ancient Greek art, music, dance, poetry, sex, and culture through archival documents, and Barney *knew* ancient Greek art, music, dance, poetry, sex, and culture though her lived repertoire of experiences. Examples (both musical and nonmusical) of these relationships run throughout this book.

Salomon Reinach knew this struggle first-hand. While he could not perform the past he wanted, he could capture it in photographs. His work allowed him to take many pictures of the things he wanted: mostly women, living ones, representations of long-dead ones, and imagined ones. Reinach sought to capture the present the way he had captured the past in his archaeological work. Like his German American counterpart Heinrich Schliemann, Reinach often single-mindedly dug to discover his intended object and tended to ignore all other remains.[48] As was the practice at the time, Reinach saw no problem manipulating artifacts from dig sites when presenting them in his scholarly works, and he encouraged others to do the same.[49] He viewed artifacts primarily as things to be manipulated. His methods are similar to the ways his brother, Théodore Reinach, treated the *Hymne à Apollon* as an object to modify and tweak. Where more meticulous contemporary scholars, such as Alexander Conze, William Matthew Flinders Petrie, and Hermann Hilprecht, carefully sifted through levels of earth, adventurer-archaeologists like Reinach and Schliemann were often more concerned with unearthing treasure and finding evidence to support theories they devised from literature and the Bible than with systematically uncovering the past.[50] In Reinach's *Conseils aux Voyageurs archéologues en Grèce et dans l'Orient hellénique*, a guide written more for the adventurous traveler than for the academic, Reinach urges the tourist to bring a camera (or purchase one there) and photograph the numerous antiquities that have yet to be published: "Searching out these inscriptions and carefully photographing them would be an attractive task for a traveler of good will. Unlike the epigraphist, one would not need even a cursory knowledge of classical languages nor tedious preparation. Just the habit of photographing on sensitive paper would put him in a position to make the greatest service and to fill a real gap in our knowledge, still so incomplete, of the monument figures of antiquity."[51]

With the best of intentions, Reinach unwittingly inspired tourists to contaminate potential dig sites by seeking out antiquities and photographing them. Seemingly harmless, the tourists most likely followed procedures in documenting the artifacts similar to those Reinach used.[52] In a collection of essays published in 1888, he presented a group of sculpture fragments in a staged tableau placed in an arrangement that seems to have suited him. He arranged the child's hand and the adult's arm around the head as if they belonged together, when they clearly do not (see figure 6.1).

Such manipulation of artifacts muddies archaeological sites and makes stratigraphic dating (a methodology that was becoming more popular at that

FIGURE 6.1 Photograph from Salomon Reinach's research in Tunisia. From Reinach, *Esquisses Archéologiques* (Paris: Ernest Leroux, 1888).

time) impossible.[53] The emphasis here is not on the works' historical relevance, but rather on their worth as aesthetic or commercial, or even as fetish objects (e.g., Théodore Reinach's *Hymne à Apollon* or Villa Kérylos).

Later in his travel guide to the archaeologically curious, Salomon Reinach warns tourists about smuggling antiquities, but his condemnation of the practice is not very forceful: "The export of works of ancient art is prohibited by Greek and Turkish law, and we do not recommend buying antiques that are offered. But if the traveler has the chance to find a *Venus de Milo*, and the courage and ability to carry it in a safe place, we will send our compliments, but these tips do not claim to teach or encourage smuggling."[54] Reinach then devoted the next few chapters to helping the tourist discern what types of artifacts were worth "finding," where to "find" them, and how to avoid being cheated by locals when "finding" them.[55]

Through his short guide, Reinach hoped to allow others the opportunity to own a little piece of history just like him: to not just be a voyeur, but to touch the past, to hold it up against their cheeks, to smell it, to breathe in its history as it was cradled in their hands. If one can't find artifacts, one can always build them, as Théodore Reinach did with his Villa Kérylos, or stage them like Barney, Palmer Sikelianos, or Emmanuel. But a few artifacts or a fabricated ancient palace are just pieces of an entire irretrievable but desired world. The Reinach brothers, despite their efforts, could not own a living antiquity, only portions of it, and they were lucky to have the artifacts they had.

Salomon's infatuation with Barney and her group can then be compared to his brother's infatuation with creating an ancient Greek villa. Both of these scholars sought a world where their fantasies of the past would come alive. However, while Théodore owned Villa Kérylos, Salomon was only a visitor in Barney's Sapphic circle; the women held the privileged position of owning this "antiquity" through embodied practices, unlike the archaeologist, who was merely a beggar at the doorsteps of the "Greek" lesbians.

Throughout this book we have seen that while men often controlled the archives of Greek performance, it was women who controlled the repertoire. Barney and her friends realized a fantasy, and in this way they inflamed the imagination of other seekers, just as the past incited a desire for knowledge and encouraged fantasy to fill in the space occupied by the unknown.

One could be a voyeur in the archives, but also in a box at the Opéra. Images of antiquity came alive not only in Emmanuel's *Salamine*, but also in countless other productions that exhibited a flavor of ancient Greek music and dance. Concerning the prospect of creating new "Greek" divertissements for Gluck's *Orphée et Eurydice* for her protégée Régina Badet to dance, Madame Mariquita professed, "I am just the interpreter! . . . I neither invented nor created Greek art."[56] Neither Mariquita nor Badet claimed to have reconstructed real Greek dances, and most of Badet's fellow dancers had no interest in archaeological authenticity, either.[57] In an article for *Musica*, Badet playfully recreates a scene for her readers between the maître de ballet and the less studious members of the corps de ballet. After the teacher announces the new "Greek" dance, some of the more studious "girls bury themselves in difficult texts, 'bone up on' the engravings that explain them, 'cram' mythology." However, the result of this studying is not really Greek, even though everyone believes it to be.[58] Badet references not only the dancers' interest in studying, but also the complex bonds formed between the dancers and the scholars. After first reproving the childish dancers, she explains how the different dancers responded to the "Greek" dances they often performed: "And, once the first rehearsal is over, while the dancer who laughed at it from the beginning exclaims: 'How do you say "boring' in Greek?' the conscientious, ambitious dancer who did not make fun of it keeps buying informative books. Thus we see a very Parisian scene: the pretty silhouette of a small woman hurrying past on the boulevard, clinging tightly to M. Salomon Reinach—the printed version, that is."[59] Yes, even scholars of antiquity were attracted to the exotic world of the dancers and courtesans who "performed antiquity" on the stages of Paris. Salomon Reinach's peccadillo of kissing women's hands and clinging to young dancers may not seem like a major distraction from his scholarly work, but that ignores the fact that the hands he kissed and clung to were the very hands that also embodied the past he studied.

Reinach's potentially erotic fantasies of the past and present, while personal to him and perhaps distasteful to some, were a critical element in his understanding of ancient Greek culture. While the courtesans, musicians, and dancers should have been coming to the scholars for advice and counsel in creating authentic performances of the past, it was very often the other way around: musicologists and classicists sought out Gabriel Fauré, Palmer Sikelianos, and Barney and her friends, and this interplay among scholar, artist, and history fueled the creativity of all parties. Scholars jumped at the opportunity to see the past come alive before their eyes and ears via the talents of the leading artists of the time, and artists gained respectability by clinging to the validating protection of scholarship (or, as Badet writes, the arms of scholars).[60]

For Barney, Reinach crossed an ethical line. At the very least, his behavior would raise red flags for scholars today.[61] But I wonder if it is that unusual. Archives are as seductive as they are addictive. (Can I afford one more trip?) There's never enough time; there is always something left behind. Much like the photographer's ability to capture the past and the present, the power of the scholar in the archive is intoxicating. Sontag writes about photography's power—as a weapon, a gun like Étienne-Jules Marey's chronophotographic gun (see chapter 4):

> Like guns and cars, cameras are fantasy-machines whose use is addictive. However, despite the extravagances of ordinary language and advertising, they are not lethal. In the hyperbole that markets cars like guns, there is at least this much truth: except in wartime, cars kill more people than guns do. The camera/gun does not kill, so the ominous metaphor seems to be all bluff—like a man's fantasy of having a gun, knife, or tool between his legs. Still, there is something predatory in the act of taking a picture. To photograph people is to violate them, by seeing them as they never see themselves, by having knowledge of them they can never have; it turns people into objects that can be symbolically possessed.[62]

It is not enough to photograph; it is important to touch, to make the physical contact with the past. That is why we go to the archives. That is why scholars perform antiquity: to engage, to touch.

Toccata: The Scholar in the Archive

Toccata (It., past participle of *toccare*, "to touch").[63]

For many, to perform musicology is to touch the thing one cannot touch: to experience the materiality of music, its presence and all that music means, the love it holds, musics bound to time and history. It is a toccata: associations flit about; it is experimental, sectional; we touch the instrument and flirt with keys.[64] We also touch the archives where we play. We play them like an organ (musical/sexual). Only later, when we are home, do we fugue (if we are Bach, for example). We chase ourselves, we play imitative games, we worry if our answers are "real," we make sense and prescribe order and structure to the things we played within the archive. But why do we need to stop playing and get serious at all?

"Touch" puts the scholar in contact with the object of scholarship. I argue that it is just as powerful to touch the past as the present. Carolyn Abbate cites Vladimir Jankélévitch's discussion of how the technologies of music making "shock" the body into action: "Instruments impact the hand; they 'shock' the body,"[65] but it does not have to be a *new* invention. Abbate continues: "Tools, instruments, technological artifacts, all shock our hands (or, moving across the sensorial hierarchy, our eyes or ears), with backdrafts issuing from the seat of consciousness, and it is this messy sloshing around, unknowable alchemies between body and imagination, that captures Jankélévitch's attention."[66]

Modernity need not be privileged over antiquity; the past can concoct a similar alchemy. I have had my share of uncanny moments in the archive, moments when I touched the past, experienced its presence, and touched the private and personal objects of the past I studied.

Is there a responsibility for those of us who have this access aside from protection of sources for future generations? What else must we do? Should there be an additional obligation to heal, to perform scholarship responsibly in a way that honors and values past and present? Maybe it is time to think twice about the things we touch in the archive and to reconsider the ways we touch the past with love and care, to engage in a reparative encounter with our archives. To touch music may be another way to pursue reparative strategies in musicology. Eve Kosofsky Sedgwick (borrowing terms of Melanie Klein) positions the reparative against a paranoid mode of reading "to realize that the future may be different from the present [. . .] that the past, in turn, could have happened differently from the way it actually did."[67] Paranoid reading values the revelation of hidden meanings, the belief that the exposure of the hidden will itself solve problems, and the belief that the audience of the criticism would be unable to discover this on their own.[68] Criticism (the product of the paranoid reading) offers privilege to the critic, it proudly states what the thing is, whereas those pursuing a reparative reading "seek new environments of sensation for the objects they study by displacing critical attachments once forged by correction, rejection, and anger with those crafted by affection, gratitude, solidarity and love."[69] Performing antiquity has the power to do just that: it can provide new environments for meaning to flourish that are not necessarily predicated on authenticity or truth but rather desire, play, and, yes, love. A reparative reading suits the reader and the object being read. For Sedgwick, a reparative mode of reading was "[n]o less acute than a paranoid position, no less realistic, no less attached to a project of survival, and neither less nor more delusional or fantasmatic."[70] The paranoid and reparative are impulses toward objects of study and the ways the reader situates their own authority. The concepts are not antithetical; Sedgwick never argued that one should throw out the paranoid, and similarly, literary scholar Robyn Wiegman doesn't see the reparative turn as a replacement for the paranoid critique, but rather as a "means to compensate for its increasingly damaged authority."[71] A reparative reading values an intimacy with the object of study but not necessarily an erotics with it. It is a step away from judgment.

A reparative reading can be one of love.[72] To echo calls to turn toward a reparative musicology by both Suzanne Cusick and William Cheng, an archival examination of the early twentieth-century lovers of antiquity tries not to nitpick who got what wrong, but rather celebrates the performative impulse of the scholar. Cusick struggles to imagine a reparative musicology that is a "reconstruction of shattered objects" (i.e., Sapphic fragments?) that restores love for music and reconstructs "musical experiences so that we could love them (which is more than to appreciate them, more than to understand their functions, more than to feel their performative power or their saturation, with social, political, economic forces)."[73] Cheng takes up where Cusick left off and adds: "[A] reparative musicology would simultaneously restore love for people and reconstruct the opportunities for care among them. It means reflecting on our incentives to do good work; dissolving all objections over whether a graduate student's well-being is a scholarly concern; asking how we can make it better for people of all persuasions; and keeping the music—the conversations—going."[74] It is that last bit, the "just-keep-going" part, that most resonates with the work of the scholars and performers profiled in this book. Since we always bring ourselves to our work (How can we not?), why not just roll with it? It is foolish to bring music into being without being in it, so go all in. This is the challenge of a reparative musicology, to surrender to the subject *as* a scholar. You can't just half love something; you either love music or you don't.

Shattered objects like Sappho's poetry, broken tablets with Greek music notation on them, and the archival traces of long-lost performances of Greek music and dance demand a reperformance only because they are loved, and loved so much. Maybe some loved them too much (Salomon Reinach, for example), and let that be a lesson to all scholars and performers. Embracing the role of musicologist-as-performer in scholarship opens up scholarship *to* performance and may help us come closer to reparative ideals.

Like the other characters in this book, the closer I came to my subject, the more I became involved with it. It has been at times a frightening adventure. Standing in Barney's bedroom in the summer of 2007, I could not help but think of Salomon Reinach, who so desperately dedicated his free time between academic appointments and digs to greedily documenting and hoarding the relics of the liaisons between Barney and her friends. As I handled private, intimate photos of Barney and her lovers naked and engaged in love making, I felt like an intruder. These were not meant for me, but there I was in a reading room in Washington, D.C., wearing little white protective gloves, surrounded by piles of nude and otherwise intimate, private photos of Natalie Clifford Barney and her friends.

Salomon Reinach was right; any tourist can help write history with the aid of a camera. However, when looking at the digital photographs of photographs I took in the archives, I am reminded of the limits of these images. They are merely fragments of an experience, much like the ruins of the house are fragments of a life. In the summer of 2015, for example, I found myself in the archives on Eva Palmer Sikelianos in Kifissia, Greece, outside of Athens. To sit in this house and sift through Palmer Sikelianos's music and photos, one also has to sift through the rest of her life. I read personal letters to her husband and from her former female lovers, and a pink slip from when she was fired from the Works Progress Administration in the 1930s. I held photos of Palmer Sikelianos with friends and a photo taken by her son moments after she died. Being alone in a mansion in a suburb of Athens with her life spread before me felt exhilarating and weird, like reading your lover's diary. I was doing my job, but I felt guilty. I am supposed to love my subject, but I was also acutely aware that my subject can't love me back. I was always going to be an intruder.

In Delphi, the site of her festival, I traced her footsteps and climbed the steep path through the archaeological site, to see and feel and sing in the theater where she staged *Prometheus Bound* decades ago. Standing there, I felt a sense of awe and of power: a double sensation of feeling humbled by my surroundings, but also of mastery of my subject—a knowledge through presence at the site that photographs or high-quality digital scans and iPhone apps alone cannot replicate. But Delphi is also the site of another figure of this study, Théodore Reianch. The marble stones with the *Hymne à Apollon* stand in a museum at the foot of the hill, and seeing them, illicitly touching them, immediately allowed me to commune with the generations of scholars of ancient Greek music who cared enough to climb the hill to see these relics. They are still as clear and easy to read today as they were a century ago or twenty centuries ago. Standing in front of the millennia-old stone tables, I sang, quietly, to myself at first, but then a bit louder as fellow tourists realized what I was doing. I went all in: I sang louder without shame. And when I reached out to touch the marble blocks, no one stopped me.[75]

In *The Symposium* Plato offers a variety of definitions of love, but one that resonates with me says love "is of engendering and begetting upon the beautiful";[76] that is to say, love is the quest, the creation, and the striving toward the beautiful, not just in physical form, as individuals make love to seek beauty and (sometimes) to create new human life. On another level, love is the quest for the engendering and the begetting upon the beautiful in wisdom. Love is the search for immortality, for when some people make love there is the potential of new life, a continuation of the tradition. So with the love of wisdom, its creation thus leads to new wisdom.

To write about someone or something, you must develop an intimacy, a love. Even with problematic subjects; antagonistic and flawed individuals; and legacies of oppressive, discriminatory, and paranoid methodologies, loving one's subject requires taking the good with the bad (and the ugly). As a scholar trying to piece together the scraps from the archive, I must reconcile my desire to take part in the past with the desire to be objective with the archive. When working on the dead we never experience the joys or disappointments of meeting the objects of our study in the past, as Henry Snibblesworth does in *The Classical Style*. Ludwig Beethoven doesn't get a chance to question your research. Performance as musicological scholarship can create spaces where those uncomfortable encounters may take place, albeit only in dreams, fantasies, and imagined spaces. Performing antiquity (or any past) is one way of making peace with the unrequited love of scholarship. Yes, love is hard work. But like all great pursuits it is worth it, not just for the pleasure of the conquest, but for the engendering and begetting of beauty, despite its risks.

NOTES

Chapter 1

1. Google Arts & Culture, Opéra national de Paris, Paris, France, accessed April 29, 2018, https://www.google.com/culturalinstitute/beta/partner/opéra-national-de-paris.

2. Google Arts & Culture, Acropolis Museum, Athina, Greece, accessed April 29, 2018, https://www.google.com/culturalinstitute/beta/partner/acropolis-museum.

3. See Elisabeth Le Guin, *Boccherini's Body: An Essay in Carnal Musicology* (Berkeley, Los Angeles, and London: University of California Press, 2006), 14.

4. Ibid., 25–26.

5. See Suzanne Cusick, "Musicology, Torture, Repair," *Radical Musicology* 3 (2008), http://www.radical-musicology.org.uk/2008/Cusick.htm; and William Cheng, *Just Vibrations: The Purpose of Sounding Good* (Ann Arbor: University of Michigan Press, 2016).

6. Eve Kosofsky Sedgwick began exploring the ideas central to her essay "Paranoid Reading and Reparative Reading; or, You're So Paranoid, You Probably Think This Essay Is About You," in *Touching Feeling: Affect, Pedagogy, Performativity* (Durham and London: Duke University Press, 2003), 123–151, in a number of earlier works: Eve Kosofsky Sedgwick and Adam Frank, "Shame in the Cybernetic Fold: Reading Silvan Tomkins," *Critical Inquiry* 21, no. 1 (1995): 496–522; Eve Kosofsky Sedgwick, "Introduction: Queerer Than Fiction," *Studies in the Novel* 28, no. 3 (1996): 277–280; and Eve Kosofsky Sedgwick, "Paranoid Reading and Reparative Reading; or, You're So Paranoid, You Probably Think This Introduction Is About You," in *Novel Gazing: Queer Readings in Fiction*, ed. Eve Kosofsky Sedgwick (Durham, NC: Duke University Press, 1997), 1–37. See Robyn Wiegman for a publication history of Sedgwick's evolving take on the reparative/paranoid. Robyn Wiegman, "The Times We're In: Queer Feminist Criticism and the Reparative 'Turn,'" *Feminist Theory* 15, no. 1 (2014): 4–25.

7. Sedgwick, "Paranoid Reading and Reparative Reading" (2003), 140–141.

8. Sedgwick, "Paranoid Reading and Reparative Reading" (1997), 35.

9. Wiegman, "Times We're In," 7.

10. [ζὰ . . . ἐλεξάμαν ὄναρ Κυπρογενηα.]. Sappho, *If Not, Winter: Fragments of Sappho*, trans. Anne Carson (New York: Alfred A. Knopf, 2002), 272–273.

11. Diana Taylor has tried to differentiate between the "performative" discursive and nondiscursive realms of performance by coining the term *performatic* to "denote the adjectival form of the nondiscrusive realm of performance." Diana Taylor, *The Archive and the Repertoire: Performing Cultural Memory in the Americas* (Durham and London: Duke University Press, 2003), 6.

12. Among some of the more important early contributions to feminist and queer musicology are Susan McClary, *Feminine Endings: Music, Gender, and Sexuality* (Minneapolis: University of Minnesota Press, 1991); Susan McClary, *George Bizet: "Carmen,"* Cambridge Opera Handbooks (Cambridge, UK: Cambridge University Press, 1992); and Philip Brett, Gary C. Thomas, and Elizabeth Wood, eds., *Queering the Pitch: The New Gay and Lesbian Musicology* (New York and London: Routledge, 1994).

13. See Peter Kivy, *Authenticities: Philosophical Reflections on Musical Performance* (Ithaca, NY, and London: Cornell University Press, 1995); Nicholas Kenyon, ed., *Authenticity and Early Music* (Oxford: Oxford University Press, 1988); John Butt, *Playing with History: The Historical Approach to Musical Performance* (Cambridge, UK, and New York: Cambridge University Press, 2002); and Nick Wilson, *The Art of Re-Enchantment: Making Early Music in the Modern Age* (Oxford and New York: Oxford University Press, 2014).

14. Richard Taruskin, "The Pastness of the Present and the Presence of the Past [1988]," in *Text and Acts: Essays on Music and Performance* (New York and Oxford: Oxford University Press, 1995), 99.

15. Ibid., 148.

16. See Carolyn Dinshaw, *Getting Medieval, Sexualities and Communities, Pre- and Postmodern* (Durham, NC: Duke University Press, 1999); and David Matthews, *Medievalism: A Critical History* (Cambridge, UK: Boydell & Brewer, 2015).

17. Katherine Bergeron, *Decadent Enchantments: The Revival of Gregorian Chant at Solesmes* (Berkeley, Los Angeles, and London: University of California Press, 1998), 93.

18. Ibid., 95.

19. Peggy Phelan, *Unmarked: The Politics of Performance* (New York and London: Routledge 1993), 146.

20. Ibid.

21. See Philip Auslander, *Liveness: Performance in a Mediatized Culture* [1999], 2nd ed. (New York: Routledge, 2008); and Rebecca Schneider "What Happened; or, Finishing Live," *Representations* 136, no. 1 (Fall 2016): 96–111.

22. Taylor, *Archive and the Repertoire*, 19.

23. Ibid., 20.

24. Ibid., 19.

25. Tribute bands, cover albums, cover bands, and cover performances, along with some drag performances, are notable exceptions to this. See George Plasketes, ed., *Play it Again: Cover Songs in Popular Music* (Abingdon and New York: Routledge, 2016); and Rusty Barrett, *From Drag Queens to Leathermen: Language, Gender, and Gay Male Subcultures* (Oxford and New York: Oxford University Press, 2017).

26. Schneider explores the accumulation of patina on live performance in "What Happened; or, Finishing Live," 96–97.

27. Taylor, *Archive and the Repertoire*, 20.

28. Michel Foucault, *The Archeology of Knowledge and the Discourse of Language*, trans. A. M. Sheridan Smith (New York: Pantheon Books, [1969, 1971], 1972), 7. More recent studies of the archive by Jacques Derrida, Arlette Farge, Helen Freshwater, Antoinette Burton, Carolyn Steedman, Lisa Moses Leff, Lisa Jardine, Rebekah Ahrendt, and David van der Linden have explored the ethics, uses, and abuses of preservation and access to the archive as well as enriching our relationship with the objects of history. See Jacques Derrida, *Archive Fever: A Freudian Impression*, translated by Eric Prenowitz (Chicago: University of Chicago Press, 1995); Arlette Farge, *The Allure of the Archives* [*Le Goût de l'archive*, 1989], trans. Thomas Scott-Railton (New Haven, CT, and London: Yale University Press, 2013); Helen Freshwater, "The Allure of the Archive," *Poetics Today* 24, no. 4 (2003): 729–758; Antoinette Burton, ed., *Archive Stories: Facts, Fictions, and the Writing of History* (Durham, NC, and London: Duke University Press, 2005); Carolyn Steedman, *Dust: The Archive and Cultural History* (New Brunswick, NJ: Rutgers University Press, 2002); Lisa Jardine, *Temptation in the Archives: Essays in Golden Age Dutch Culture* (London: University of College London Press, 2015); Lisa Moses Leff, *The Archive Thief: The Man Who Salvaged French Jewish History in the Wake of the Holocaust* (New York and Oxford: Oxford University Press, 2015); and Rebekah Ahrendt and David van der Linden, "The Postmasters' Piggy Bank: Experiencing the Accidental Archive," *French Historical Studies* 40, no. 2 (April 2017): 189–213.

29. Sappho, *If Not, Winter*, 272–273.

30. Rebecca Schneider, *Performing Remains: Art and War in Times of Theatrical Reenactment* (London and New York: Routledge, 2011), 10.

31. Some differentiate between historical re-enactors who engage in living history and historical interpreters who may employ some techniques used by re-enactors but primarily work to help visitors develop relationships to cultural, natural, and historical resources at sites (e.g. parks, historical sites, zoos, etc.) and develop relationships with the sites and their history. See Freeman Tilden, *Interpreting our Heritage* [1957], ed. R. Bruce Craig, foreword by Russell E. Dickenson, 4th ed. (Chapel Hill, NC: University of North Carolina Press, 2007); and Lois H. Silverman, "Personalizing the Past: A Review of Literature with Implications for Historical Interpretation," *Journal of Interpretation Research* 2, no. 1 (1997): 1–12.

32. Schneider, *Performing Remains*, 10.

33. Citing Christopher Hogwood; Taruskin, "Pastness of the Present and the Presence of the Past," 150.

34. Ibid., 145.

35. Schneider, *Performing Remains*, 13.

36. In opera, however this is different, and a topic discussed by Roger Parker in his book *Remaking the Song*. As Parker notes, operatic works with their multiple texts (archive and repertoire), and multiple bodies enacting these texts offer multiple choices for the performers. But while some operatic choices are part of the repertoire (i.e., traditional repeats of favorite arias in performance), most of the substitutions and variants are drawn from the archive. Roger Parker, "Remaking the Song," in *Remaking the Song: Operatic Visions and Revisions from Handel to Berio* (Berkeley, Los Angeles, and London: University of California Press, 2006), 1–21.

37. Anne Searcy has described the score to Tchaikovsky's *Swan Lake* as a "Frankenscore" due to the constant rearranging and reorchestration of the ballet's numbers. See Anne Searcy, "Russian Swans," *The Itinerant Balletomane* (blog), May 26, 2013, https://itinerantballetomane.blogspot.com/2013/05/russian-swans.html. See also Simon Morrison's discussion of the variants of the ballet at the Bolshoi. Simon A. Morrison, *Bolshoi Confidential: Secrets of the Russian Ballet from the Rule of the Tsars to Today* (New York: W. W. Norton, 2016), 162–178, 375–379, 384, and 420–421; and Alastair Macaulay, "One Classic Ballet, Many Interpretations," *New York Times*, July 4, 2011, https://www.nytimes.com/2011/07/05/arts/dance/swan-lake-one-classic-ballet-many-interpretations.html.

38. Classics and Archaeology have begun to embrace methods of performance studies as well. See Richard Hunter and Anna Uhlig, eds., *Imagining Reperformance in Ancient Culture: Studies in the Traditions of Drama and Lyric* (Cambridge, UK, and New York: Cambridge University Press, 2017); and Ingrid Berg, "Dumps and Ditches: Prisms of Archaeological Pracitice at Kalaureia in Greece," in *Making Cultural History: New Persepctives on Western Heritage*, ed. Anna Källén (Lund: Sweden: Nordic Academic Press, 2013), 173–183.

39. See Athena S. Leoussi, "Physical Anthropology and Ethnographic Art," in *Nationalism and Classicism: The Classical Body as National Symbol in Nineteenth-Century England and France* (New York: St. Martin's Press, 1998), 1–84.

40. See Christopher Evans, "Model Excavations: 'Performance' and the Three-Dimensional Display of Knowledge," in *Archives, Ancestors, Practices: Archaeology in the Light of Its History*, ed. Nathan Schlanger and Jarl Nordbladh (New York and Oxford: Berghahn Books, 2008), 147–161.

41. They also reveal the discipline's relationship to the history of architecture, in which models have always played a large pedagogical role. See Sara Perry, "Archaeological Visualization and the Manifestation of the Discipline: Model-Making at the Institute of Archaeology, London," in *Archaeology after Interpretation: Returning Materials to Archaeological Theory*, ed. Benjamin Alberti, Andrew Meirion Jones, and Joshua Pollard (Walnut Creek, CA: Left Coast Press, 2013), 282–283; and Jarl Nordbladh, "The Shape of History: To Give Physical Form to Archaeological Knowledge," in *Histories of Archaeological Practices: Reflections on Methods, Strategies and Social Organization in Past Fieldwork*, ed. Ola Wolfhechel Jensen (Stockholm, Sweden: The National Museum, 2012), 246.

42. See Noël Coye and Béatrice Vigié, "Three-Dimensional Archives: The Augier Models of the Museum of Archaeology (Marseilles, France)," *Complutum* 24, no. 2 (2013): 205–206.

43. See ibid., 211; and Nordbladh, "Shape of History," 242.

44. "Pompéi a passé vingt siècles dans les entrailles de la terre [. . .] Rome n'est qu'on vaste musée; Pompéi est une antiquité vivante." François-René Chateaubriand, *Œuvre romanesques et voyages* (Paris: Guillimard, 1969), II:1505, cited in John Haines, "Généalogies musicologiques: Aux origins d'une science de la musique vers 1900," *Acta Musicologica* 73, no. 1 (2001): 25; see also Nordbladh, "Shape of History," 254. On the use of artifacts and ruins as symbolic resources of the modern Greek state see Yannis Hamilakis, *The Nation and Its Ruins: Antiquity, Archaeology, and National Imagination in Greece* (Oxford and New York: Oxford University Press, 2007), 291.

45. See Fernand Benoit's dismissal of Augier in Fernand Benoit, "La constitution du Musée Borély et les fraudes des fouilles de Marseille," *Provence historique* 6 (1956): 5–22.

46. See Perry, "Archaeological Visualization and the Manifestation of the Discipline," 283.

47. "[L]'ensemble des diverses manifestations de la science musicale [. . .] relatives à l'histoire et à la philologie musicale." Pierre Aubry, "La musicologie médiévale: histoire et methods, cours professé à l'Institut Catholique de Paris, 1889–1899," *Mélanges de musicologie critique* (Paris: Welter, 1900), I:1, cited in Haines, "Généalogies musicologiques," 21.

48. See Bergeron, *Decadent Enchantments*, 93.

49. See Michel Duchesneau, "French Music Criticism and Musicology at the Turn of the Twentieth-Century: New Journals, New Networks," *Nineteenth-Century Music Review* 14 (2017): 9–32.

50. Jann Pasler, "Theorizing Race in Nineteenth-Century France: Music as Emblem of Identity," *Musical Quarterly* 89, no. 4 (Winter 2006): 460–461.

51. See François-Joseph Fétis, "Sur un nouveau mode de classification des races humanies d'après leurs systèms musicaux," *Bulletin de la Société d'Anthropologie* 2, no. 2 (1867): 137–141, cited in Pasler, "Theorizing Race in Nineteenth-Century France," 465–466.

52. See Natalie Zemon Davis, foreword to *The Allure of the Archives* [*Le Goût de l'archive*, 1989], by Arlette Farge, trans. Thomas Scott-Railton (New Haven, CT, and London: Yale University Press, 2013), xvi.

53. Ibid., xv.

54. Dom André Mocquereau, letter to Dom Lhoumeau, quoted in Dom Pierre Combe, *Historire de la restauration du chant grégorien d'après des documents inédits* (Solesmes: Abbaye de Solesmes, 1969), 127, trans. and cited in Bergeron, *Decadent Enchantments*, 66.

55. Christopher Pinney, "Introduction: 'How the Other Half . . . ,'" in *Photography's Other Histories*, ed. Christopher Pinney and Nicholas Peterson (Durham, NC, and London: Duke University Press, 2003), 3.

56. John Tagg explores the discursive violence of photography in *The Disciplinary Frame: Photographic Truths and the Capture of Meaning* (Minneapolis and London: University of Minnesota Press, 2009), xxvi.

57. Michael Aird's study of recognition of family in photos from the anthropological or historical archive invites viewers to experience the photo from myriad temporal and spatial perspectives. See Michael Aird, "Growing Up with Aborigines," in *Photography's Other Histories*, ed. Christopher Pinney and Nicholas Peterson (Durham, NC, and London: Duke University Press, 2003), 23–39.

58. Carolyn Abbate, "Sound Object Lessons," *Journal of the American Musicological Society* 69, no. 3 (Fall 2016): 798.

59. Ibid., 799.

60. Susan Sontag, *On Photography* (New York: Farrar, Straus and Giroux, 1977), 9.

61. Ibid., 10.

62. Schneider, "What Happened; or, Finishing Live," 108–09.

63. It is perhaps not at all coincidental that the period discussed also saw the rise of collectible pornographic postcards and the proliferation of other pornographic photographs. See Alain Corbin, *Women for Hire: Prostitution and Sexuality in France after 1850* [*Les filles de noce: Misère sexuelle et prostitution aux 19e et 20e siècles*, 1978], trans. Alan Sheridan (Cambridge, MA: Harvard University Press, 1990), 124–125; Carolyn J. Dean, *The Frail Social Body: Pornography, Homosexuality, and Other Fantasies in Interwar France* (Berkeley and Los Angeles: University of California Press, 2000), 39–41; and Lisa Z. Sigel, "Filth in the Wrong People's Hands: Postcards and the Expansion of Pornography in Britain and the Atlantic World, 1880–1914," *Journal of Social History* 33, no. 4 (Summer 2000): 859–885.

64. Sontag, *On Photography*, 12.

65. "L'accompagnement instrumental manque sur la pierre: Il a fallu le suppléer." Théodore Reinach, "Notice," *Hymn à Apollon*, 2nd rev. and corrected ed. (Paris: O. Bornemann, 1914), [i].

66. Elizabeth Wood, "Sapphonics," in *Queering the Pitch: The New Gay and Lesbian Musicology*, ed. Philip Brett, Elizabeth Wood, and Gary C. Thomas (New York and London: Routledge, 1994), 27–66.

Chapter 2

1. "[I]l avait fait construire une 'villa grecque' qui est un modèle de reconstitution archéologique." Paul Jamot, *Théodore Reinach (1860–1928)* (Paris: Gazette des Beaux Arts, 1928), 7.

2. For more on the building and design of the house, see Emmanuel Pontremoli, *KERYLOS* (Paris: Éditions des Bibliothèques Nationales de France, 1934); Astrid Arnold, *Villa Kérylos: Das Wohnhaus als Antikenkonstruktion* (München: Bierling & Brinkmann, 2003); and Régis Vian des Rives, *La Villa Kérylos* (Paris: Les Éditions de l'Amateur, 1997).

3. Carolyn Abbate, "Outside the Tomb," chap. 5 in *In Search of Opera* (Princeton and Oxford: Princeton University Press, 2001).

4. See Tamara Levitz, "Voice from the Crypt," chap. 7 in *Modernist Mysteries: "Perséphone"* (Oxford and New York: Oxford University Press, 2012), 474–560.

5. Pieter C. van den Toorn dissects the analytic conundrums theorists face in the neoclassical music of Stravinsky: the "nonorganic" nature of these works (their mixture of old and new, tonal and nontonal) resisst classification and any one analytical method. Pieter C. van den Toorn, "Neoclassicism and Its Definitions," in *Music Theory in Concept and Practice*, ed. James M. Baker, David W. Beach, and Jonathan W. Bernard (Rochester, NY: University of Rochester Press, 1997), 131–137.

6. See Scott Messing, "Polemic as History: The Case of Neoclassicism," *Journal of Musicology* 9, no. 4 (Autumn 1991): 481–497; Richard Taruskin, "Back to Whom? Neoclassicism and Ideology," *19th-Century Music* 16, no. 3 (Spring 1993): 286–302; Martha M. Hyde, "Neoclassic and Anachronistic Impulses in Twentieth-Century Music," *Music Theory Spectrum* 18, no. 2 (Autumn 1996): 200–235; Abbate, "Outside the Tomb," 193; and Levitz, "Voice from the Crypt."

7. See Samuel N. Dorf, "Eroticizing Antiquity: Madame Mariquita, Régina Badet and the Dance of the Exotic Greeks from Stage to Popular Press," in *Opera, Exoticism and*

Visual Culture, ed. Hyunseon Lee and Naomi Segal (Bern, Oxford, and New York: Peter Lang, 2015); and Samuel N. Dorf, "Seeing Sappho in Paris: Operatic and Choreographic Adaptations of Sapphic Lives and Myths," *Music and Art: International Journal for Music Iconography* 38 (2009): 289–308.

8. He penned a seven-volume history of the affair: Joseph Reinach, *Histoire de l'affaire Dreyfus* (Paris: Fasquelle, 1902–1930); see also Leslie Derfler, *The Dreyfus Affair* (Westport, CT: Greenwood Press, 2002), 31–50.

9. See Aron Rodrigue, "Totems, Taboos, and Jews: Salomon Reinach and the Politics of Scholarship in Fin-de-Siècle France," *Jewish Social Studies* 10, no. 2 (Winter 2004): 1–19.

10. The Reinach family ended tragically. Joseph's son Adolphe died in World War I, Salomon did not have children, and Théodore's son Léon along with his wife Béatrice Reinach (née de Camondo) and two children Fanny and Bertrand were murdered at Auschwitz. Filippo Tuena's Italian novel, *Le varizioni Reinach*, brings the story of Léon and Béatrice to life. See Filippo Tuena, *Le varizioni Reinach* (Milan: Rizzoli, 2005).

11. *Pavane* was premiered publicly in 1888 and privately in 1891 by the Comtesse de Greffulhe.

12. "L'accompagnement instrumental manque sur la pierre: il a fallu le suppléer." Théodore Reinach, "Notice," in *Hymn à Apollon*, 2nd rev. and corrected ed. (Paris: O. Bornemann, 1914), [i]; see also Jean-Michel Nectoux, *Gabriel Fauré: A Musical Life*, trans. Roger Nichols (Cambridge, UK: Cambridge University Press, 1991), 544–545.

13. See Annie Bélis, "Les deux hymnes delphiques à Apollon," in *Corpus des inscriptions de Delphes* III (Paris: Boccard, 1992); and Egert Pöhlmann, *Denkmäler altgreichischer Musik* (Nuremberg: H. Carl, 1970), 58–76; and Egert Pöhlmann and Martin L. West, eds., *Documents of Ancient Greek Music: The Extant Melodies and Fragments Edited and Transcribed with Commentary* (New York and Oxford: Oxford University Press, 2001), 70.

14. See Bélis, "Les deux hymnes delphiques à Apollon," 48 and 53; and Pöhlmann and West, *Documents of Ancient Greek Music*, 71.

15. See Martin L. West, *Ancient Greek Music* (Oxford and New York: Oxford University Press, 1992), 140–141 and 289.

16. Pöhlmann and West identify these as frags. 3 and 4. See Pöhlmann and West, *Documents of Ancient Greek Music*, 72–73.

17. For the sake of simplicity, I have retained Pöhlmann and West's pitch designations, since both Bélis and Reinach employ them as well. Martin West's 1992 edition and the Fauré/Reinach versions of 1894 and 1914 transpose all pitches up a major 6th.

18. Note that B♭ is absent, thus creating the pentatonic feel. See Pöhlmann and West, *Documents of Ancient Greek Music*, 73.

19. Ibid., 73.

20. Pöhlmann and West concur with Reinach's restoration of this text. Pöhlmann and West, *Documents of Ancient Greek Music*, 71. See also Théodore Reinach, "Hymnes avec notes musicales [1911]," *Fouilles de Delphes* 3, fasc. 2 (1909–1913): 148.

21. West argues that the sequence at the end of line 24 on the word "συριγμαθ' [hissing]" represents another example of text paining, but the common usage of that gesture (D E♭ C D E♭), does not seem to support this claim. See West, *Ancient Greek Music*, 292.

22. Henri Weil, "Hymne à Apollon: Inscriptions de Delphes, nouveaux fragments d'hymnes accompagnés de notes de musique," *Bulletin de Correspondance Hellénique* 17 (1893): 569–583; and Théodore Reinach, "La musique des hymnes de Delphes," *Bulletin de Correspondance Hellénique* 17 (1893): 584–610. These essays were reproduced in Henri Weil and Théodore Reinach, *Hymne à Apollon: Inscriptions de Delphes, nouveaux fragments d'hymnes accompagnés de notes de musique, par Henri Weil; La musique des hymnes de Delphes, par Théodore Reinach* (Paris: Thorin et fils, 1894). Henri Weil (1818–1909) was a German-born philologist who worked in France. Like the Reinachs he was also Jewish. He earned the cross of the Legion of Honor in 1887. See Frederick T. Haneman, "Weil, Henri," in *The Jewish Encyclopedia*, ed. Isidore Singer (New York and London: Funk and Wagnalls Co., 1901–1906), 12:491–492.

23. Théodore Reinach, Gabriel Fauré, and Henri Weil, *Hymne à Apollon, Chant Grec du IIIe Siècle avant J.C, découvert à Delphes par l'Ecole Française d'Athènes* (Paris: O. Bornemann, 1894).

24. Reinach, "Hymnes avec notes musicales," 147–169.

25. Théodore Reinach, Gabriel Fauré, and Henri Weil, *Hymne à Apollon, Chant Grec du IIe Siècle avant J.C, découvert à Delphes par l'Ecole Française d'Athènes*, 2nd rev. and corrected ed. (Paris: O. Bornemann, 1914).

26. Nectoux dedicates one sentence and a footnote to the work in a chapter on *Prométhée*. See Nectoux, *Gabriel Fauré*, 193 and 574n1.

27. Graham Johnson, *Gabriel Fauré: The Songs and Their Poets*, with translations of the song texts by Richard Stokes (Farnham, UK, and Burlington, VT: Ashgate; London: Guildhall School of Music & Drama, 2009), 252–253.

28. See Carolyn Abbate, "Music—Drastic or Gnostic?," *Critical Inquiry* 30 (Spring 2004): 505–536; and Michael Gallope et al., "Vladimir Jankélévitch's Philosophy of Music," *Journal of the American Musicological Society* 65, no. 1 (Spring 2012): 215–256.

29. Karol Berger, "Musicology According to Don Giovanni, or: Should We Get Drastic?," *Journal of Musicology* 22 (Summer 2005): 497.

30. See Théodore Reinach, *La Musique Grecque et L'Hymne à Apollon: Conférence faite à l'Association pour l'encouragement des etudes grecques* (Paris: Ernest Leroux, 1894), 16; and Jon Solomon, "The Reception of Ancient Greek Music in the Late Nineteenth Century," *International Journal of the Classical Tradition* 17, no. 4 (December 2010): 510–511.

31. See Nick Wilson, *The Art of Re-enchantment: Making Early Music in the Modern Age* (Oxford and New York: Oxford University Press, 2014), 212–228.

32. Rebecca Schneider, *Performing Remains: Art and War in Times of Theatrical Reenactment* (London and New York: Routledge, 2011), 2.

33. Ibid., 10.

34. Philip Gossett, *Divas and Scholars: Performing Italian Opera* (Chicago and London: University of Chicago Press, 2006), ix.

35. See "fan, n.2," in *Oxford English Dictionary Online*, Oxford University Press, March 2017, www.oed.com. We can contrast the "fan" from the "fetishist," who "irrationally" worships an object, or someone who finds sexual desire stimulated through a non-sexual object or body part. See "fetish, n." and "fetishist, n.," in *Oxford English Dictionary Online*, Oxford University Press, March 2017, www.oed.com. See also

William Pietz, "The Problem of the Fetish, I," *RES: Anthropology and Aesthetics* 9 (Spring 1985): 5–17.

36. "Toutefois, dans le cas présent, j'incline à me prononcer en faveur du *chroma* tonique, non seulement parce qu'il est le seul qui puisse s'exécuter sur un de nos instruments à tempérament, mais encore parce qu'il est le moins difficile à chanter et que dans un morceau de ce genre le compositeur n'a pas dû accumuler les difficultés." Reinach, "La musique des hymnes de Delphes," 593.

37. This process is not unlike Dom Pothier's readings of chant sources. See Katherine Bergeron, *Decadent Enchantments: The Revival of Gregorian Chant at Solesmes* (Berkeley, Los Angeles, and London: University of California Press, 1998), 104–112.

38. "Malheureusement nous n'avons pas la fin de notre morceau; à défaut de ce critérium décisif, nous ne pouvons donc fonder notre détermination du mode que sur trois éléments: 1° l'impression tonale produite sur une oreille moderne; 2° la terminaison des membres de phrase et surtout des grandes reprises; 3° la note qui revient le plus fréquemment." Reinach, "La musique des hymnes de Delphes," 597.

39. "L'impression tonale est nettement celle de notre ton d'Ut mineur; si l'on voulait harmoniser la mélodie, les trois accords qui reviendraient constamment seraient les accords parfaits mineurs de Ut et de Fa et l'accord parfait majeur de Sol, c'est à dire précisément les trois accords fondamentaux du ton d'Ut mineur." Reinach, "La musique des hymnes de Delphes," 597.

40. "[L]'octave-type de notre morceau n'est pas seulement semblable, mais identique, à notre gamme d'Ut mineur. Il y a là une coïncidence bien remarquable, qui prouve l'ancienneté et la persistance du sentiment musical actuel." Reinach, "La musique des hymnes de Delphes," 600.

41. "C'est certainement ce que notre air contient de plus nouveau et de plus étranger à nos habitudes musicales modernes." Reinach, "La musique des hymnes de Delphes," 601.

42. "[V]ous reconnaîtrez, je l'espère, un ancêtre direct de la musique européenne. On cherchera, on a déjà cherché des analogues à cet air dans la musique moderne et même contemporaine: j'ai indiqué moi-même, sans y insister d'ailleurs, la mélodie du pâtre, pour cor anglais *solo*, qui ouvre le IIIe acte de *Tristan et Yseult*." Reinach, *La Musique Grecque et L'Hymne à Apollon*, 16; and "Si quelque chose rappelle le *mélos* de notre hymne dans la musique moderne, ce sont certains 'airs de pâtres' des pays de montagnes, d'un accent si naïf et si mélancolique, et les compositions savantes qui s'en sont inspirées, par exemple la mélodie pour cor anglais *solo* qui ouvre le 3e acte de *Tristan et Iseult* de Richard Wagner." Reinach, "La musique des hymnes de Delphes," 602.

43. "Je me contenterai de faire observer qu'elle n'a rien de commun avec les vagues et flottantes psalmodies de la musique orientale moderne, dont une théorie superficielle voudrait rapprocher la musique des Grecs: elle se distingue au contraire par la netteté et la précision des contours." Reinach, "La musique des hymnes de Delphes," 602.

44. "Mais quelle que soit la valeur de ces rapprochements, un fait demeure certain, qui achève de donner à la trouvaille de Delphes son haut intérêt historique et esthétique: c'est que l'idéal musical des Grecs du IIIe siècle [*sic*] avant notre ère était très voisin qu'on ne pouvait le soupçonner jusqu'à présent, de notre idéal mélodique actuel: les principes sont identiques, les procédés même offrent de surprenantes analogies." Reinach, *La Musique Grecque et L'Hymne à Apollon*, 16.

45. Reinach, "La musique des hymnes de Delphes," 603–604.

46. See Ibid., 604.

47. "L'orchestre des Grecs n'était pas moins imparfait que leur harmonie. Certes, ils ne dédaignaient pas la musique purement instrumentale; ils avaient, comme nous, des salles de concert et des virtuoses applaudis, et leurs auteurs nous ont transmis les noms d'une variété infinie d'instruments. Mais sous les étiquettes regardez les choses: vous verrez que tous ces instruments—du moins ceux d'un emploi usuel—se ramenaient à deux types: la lyre ou cithare, et la flûte. Or, la lyre avait moins d'étendue que notre harpe, et la flûte moins de sonorité que notre clarinette." Théodore Reinach, *La Musique Grecque et L'Hymne à Apollon*, 2.

48. See Tony Bennett, *The Birth of the Museum: History, Theory, Politics* (London and New York, Routledge, 1995), 2–5.

49. Reinach,"La musique des hymnes de Delphes," 586–588.

50. "Ancient dances" here refers to *ancien régime* rather than ancient Greek. Nectoux, *Gabriel Fauré*, 108–109.

51. See Jann Pasler, "Countess Greffulhe as Entrepreneur: Negotiating Class, Gender and Nation," in *Writing through Music: Essays on Music, Culture, and Politics* (Oxford and New York: Oxford University Press, 2008), 285–317.

52. Fauré had been passed over by the Institut twice (the seat went to Théodore Dubois in 1894 and to Charles Lenepveu in 1896) before his election on March 13, 1909. This was the same year Théodore Reinach earned election to the Institut as well. See Carlo Caballero, *Fauré and French Musical Aesthetics* (Cambridge, UK, and New York, Cambridge University Press, 2001), 59–66.

53. Ibid., 64.

54. See Nectoux, *Gabriel Fauré*, 193 and 574n1.

55. See Elinor Olin, "Le ton et la parole: melodrama in France 1871–1913" (PhD diss., Northwestern University, 1991), 76; and Christopher Moore, "Regionalist Frictions in the Bullring: Lyric Theater in Béziers at the *Fin de Siècle*," *19th-Century Music* 37, no. 3 (Spring 2014): 211–241.

56. See Théodore Reinach, "Hymnes avec notes musicales," 154; and Pöhlmann and West, *Documents of Ancient Greek Music*, 63.

57. "[P]our m'aider à combler les lacunes de la mélodie, j'ai profité à diverses reprises de la collaboration de mon ami M. Eugène d'Eichthal." Reinach, "Hymnes avec notes musicales," 148.

58. Nectoux, *Gabriel Fauré*, 56–57 and 511–512.

59. Reinach's critical note only says that "La note Γ est certaine et non I comme on avait lu d'abord." Reinach, "Hymnes avec notes musicales," 155.

60. See Pöhlmann and West, *Documents of Ancient Greek Music*, 66; and Bélis, "Les deux hymnes delphiques à Apollon," 71–72.

61. "Le signe [Special symbol 1] (Ré bémol) est sûr; mais c'est certainement une bévue du lapicide pour ⅄ (La bémol). D'ailleurs, dans cette inscription, le signe ⅄ se fait exactement comme un Λ, avec une haste en plus." Reinach, "Hymnes avec notes musicales," 155.

62. See Reinach, "La musique des hymnes de Delphes," 597.

63. "In this way the Gaul's war-fury, that impiously crossed into this land." Translation by Martin L. West in *Ancient Greek Music*, 289–292.

64. "[F]ournit un indice matériel." Weil, "Hymne à Apollon," 570–571.

65. Richard Leppert, "Sexual Identity, Death, and the Family Piano," *19th-Century Music* 16, no. 2 (Autumn 1992): 105.

66. Ibid., 124.

67. Max Horkheimer and Theodor W. Adorno, *Dialectic of Enlightenment*, trans. John Cumming (New York, 1972), 32–37 and 43–80, cited in Leppert, "Sexual Identity, Death and the Family Piano," 123–124.

68. Homer, *The Odyssey*, trans. Emily Wilson (New York: W. W. Norton, 2018), 307.

69. Judith A. Peraino, *Listening to the Sirens: Musical Technologies of Queer Identity from Homer to Hedwig* (Berkeley: University of California Press, 2005), 14–15.

70. Igor Stravinsky, quoted in Vittorio Tranquilli, "Avvenimenti della vita teatrale cittadina: Strawinsky in prosa," *Il Piccolo di Trieste*, April 23, 1931, cited and translated in Tamara Levitz, *Modernist Mysteries: "Perséphone"* (Oxford and New York: Oxford University Press, 2012), 527–528.

Chapter 3

1. Serious scholarship on Barney's writings and her circle began in the 1990s with translations, collections, and reprints of works by Barney and other writers associated with her. More recent biographical studies have similarly focused on Barney's love life, and to a lesser extent on her writing; however, her contributions to music and dance performance have been largely ignored. Tamara Levitz made passing references to Barney in her discussion of Ida Rubinstein in *Modernist Mysteries*. While the dance scholar Ann Cooper Albright has explored some aspects of Barney's connection to the dances of Eva Palmer in her biography of the American dancer Loïe Fuller, musicologists have yet to seriously investigate these issues. See Tamara Levitz, *Modernist Mysteries: "Perséphone"* (Oxford and New York: Oxford University Press, 2012); Ann Cooper Albright, *Traces of Light: Absence and Presence in the Work of Loïe Fuller* (Middletown, CT: Wesleyan University Press, 2007), chap. 4; Natalie Clifford Barney, *Adventures of the Mind* [*Aventures de l'esprit*, 1929], trans. with annotations by John Spalding Gatton (New York and London: New York University Press, 1992); Natalie Clifford Barney, *A Perilous Advantage: The Best of Natalie Clifford Barney*, ed. and trans. Anna Livia (Norwich, VT: New Victoria Publishers, 1992); Djuna Barnes, *Ladies Almanack: Showing Their Signs and Their Tides, Their Moons and Their Changes, the Seasons as It Is with Them, Their Eclipses and Equinoxes, as Well as a Full Record or Diurnal and Nocturnal Distempers* [1928] (Elmwood, IL: Dalkey Archive Press, 1992); and Natalie Clifford Barney, *Women Lovers, or The Third Woman*, ed. and trans. Chelsea Ray (Madison: University of Wisconsin Press, 2016). See also Jean Chalon, *Portrait of a Seductress: The World of Natalie Barney*, trans. Carol Barko (New York: Crown, 1979); Karla Jay, *The Amazon and the Page: Natalie Clifford Barney and Renée Vivien* (Bloomington: Indiana University Press, 1988); Suzanne Rodriguez, *Wild Heart, a Life: Natalie Clifford Barney's Journey from Victorian America to Belle Époque Paris* (New York: Ecco, 2002); and Diana Souhami, *Wild Girls: Paris, Sappho and Art— The Lives and Loves of Natalie Barney and Romaine Brooks* (London: Weidenfeld & Nicolson, 2004).

2. She did not preserve any of her own musical compositions (if she ever formally wrote any). This doesn't necessarily mean that Barney did not write music; it only means

that nothing she created has been preserved in music notation or on recording in an archive.

3. See Sandra Boehringer, "Female Homoeroticism," in *A Companion to Greek and Roman Sexualities*, ed. Thomas K. Hubbard (Chichester, UK: Wiley Blackwell, 2014), 154–156; André Lardinois, "Lesbian Sappho and Sappho of Lesbos," in *From Sappho to de Sade: Moments in the History of Sexuality*, ed. Jan Bremmer (London: Routledge, 1989), 15–35; Dimitrios Yatromanolakis, *Sappho in the Making: The Early Reception*, Hellenic Studies Series 28 (Washington, DC: Center for Hellenic Studies, 2008), 23; and Kate Gilhuly, "Lesbians Are Not from Lesbos," in *Ancient Sex: New Essays*, ed. Ruby Bondell and Kirk Ormand (Columbus: The Ohio State University, 2015), 173.

4. Diana Taylor, *The Archive and the Repertoire: Performing Cultural Memory in the Americas* (Durham, NC, and London: Duke University Press, 2003), 19–20.

5. Jill Lepore, "Historians Who Love Too Much: Reflections on Microhistory and Biography," *Journal of American History* 88, no. 1 (June 2001): 129.

6. Barney is notable for being the first Ohioan honored with an Ohio Historical Marker almost entirely for her LGBTQ identity. It is also the first of the State's historical markers to mention an honoree's sexuality. Standing next to the main branch of the Dayton Public Library, the marker is five blocks away from where the Barney family home once stood at 33 North Perry Street. The marker's text reads in part, "Natalie, who knew that she was a lesbian by age twelve, lived an outspoken and independent life unusual for a woman of this time period. Her openness and pride about her sexuality, without shame, was at least one hundred years ahead of its time" (Ohio Historical Marker 16-57).

7. Mitchell Morris, "Calling Names, Taking Names," in "Colloquy: Music and Sexuality," *Journal of the American Musicological Society* 66, no. 3 (Fall 2013): 835.

8. See Suzanne Cusick, "On a Lesbian Relationship with Music: A Serious Effort Not to Think Straight," in *Queering the Pitch: The New Gay and Lesbian Musicology*, ed. Philip Brett, Elizabeth Wood, and Gary C. Thomas (New York: Routledge, 1994), 67–84.

9. Jane McIntosch Snyder, *Lesbian Desire in the Lyrics of Sappho* (New York: Columbia University Press, 1997), 1.

10. Elizabeth Wood, "Sapphonics," in *Queering the Pitch: The New Gay and Lesbian Musicology*, ed. Philip Brett, Elizabeth Wood, and Gary C. Thomas (New York and London: Routledge, 1994), 27.

11. Ibid., 27–28.

12. See Bruce W. Holsinger, *Music, Body, and Desire in Medieval Culture: Hildegard of Bingen to Chaucer* (Stanford, CA: Stanford University Press, 2001), 129; Judith A. Peraino, *Listening to the Sirens: Musical Technologies of Queer Identity from Homer to Hedwig* (Berkeley, Los Angeles, and London: University of California Press, 2006); Stacy Wolf, *A Problem Like Maria: Gender and Sexuality in the American Musical* (Ann Arbor: University of Michigan Press, 2002); Debi Withers, "Kate Bush: Performing and Creating Queer Subjectivities on *Lionheart*," *Nebula* 3, nos. 2–3 (September 2006): 125–141; Gillian Rodger, "Drag, Camp, and Gender Subversion in the Music and Videos of Annie Lennox," *Popular Music* 23 (2004): 17–29; Mike Daley, "Patti Smith's *Gloria*: Intertextual Play in a Rock Vocal Performance," *Popular Music* 16, no. 3 (October 1997): 238; and Alice A. Kuzniar, "Zarah Leander and Transgender Specularity," *Film Criticism* 23, nos. 2–3 (Winter/Spring 1999): 74–93.

13. See Wood, "Sapphonics"; Sophie Fuller, "'Devoted Attention': Looking for Lesbian Musicians in *Fin-de-siècle* Britain," in *Queer Episodes in Music and Modern Identity*, ed. Sophie Fuller and Lloyd Whitsell (Urbana and Chicago: University of Illinois Press, 2002), 94; Corinne E. Blackmer and Patricia Juliana Smith, introduction to *En Travesti: Women, Gender Subversion, Opera*, ed. Corinne E. Blackmer and Patricia Juliana Smith (New York: Columbia University Press, 1995), 3; and Karen Henson, "Victor Capoul, Marguerite Olagnier's *Le Saïs*, and the Arousing of Female Desire," *Journal of the American Musicological Society* 52, no. 3 (Autumn 1999): 431.

14. See Wayne Koestenbaum, *The Queen's Throat: Opera Homosexuality and the Mystery of Desire* [1993] (New York: Vintage Books, 1994); Sam Abel, *Opera in the Flesh: Sexuality in Operatic Performance* (Boulder, CO: Westview Press, 1996); Terry Castle, "In Praise of Brigitte Fassbaender: Reflections on Diva-Worship," in *En Travesti: Women, Gender Subversion, Opera*, ed. Corinne E. Blackmer and Patricia Juliana Smith (New York: Columbia University Press, 1995), 20–58; and Wolf, *A Problem Like Maria*.

15. Wood, "Sapphonics," 29.

16. Peraino, *Listening to the Sirens*, 26–28. Also see Snyder, *Lesbian Desire in the Lyrics of Sappho*. For more on parsing sexual and political identities in ancient Greece, see David M. Halperin, "Sex Before Sexuality: Pederasty, Politics, and Power in Classical Athens," in *Hidden from History: Reclaiming the Gay and Lesbian Past*, ed. Martin Duberman, Martha Vicinus, and George Chauncey Jr. (New York and London: Meridian, 1990), 37–53.

17. Wood, "Sapphonics," 28.

18. Natalie Clifford Barney, *Éparpillements* (Paris: E. Sansot, 1910), 60.

19. A typescript copy of Barney's unpublished childhood memoires exists as part of the Renée Lang Collection in the Department of Special Collections, Memorial Library, University of Wisconsin-Madison. Another copy resides at the Bibliothèque littéraire Jacques Doucet. The typescript in Paris is dated 1949; the version I consulted in Madison was dated 1950 and includes a number of minor corrections by the author in pencil. Natalie Clifford Barney, "Nos secrètes amours ou L'Amant féminin ou Mémoires secrets" (unpublished typescript with author's autograph corrections, October 31, 1950), Renée Lang Collection, box 15, folder 17, Department of Special Collections, Memorial Library, University of Wisconsin-Madison, 23.

20. I refer to her as "Eva Palmer" when discussing her prior to her marriage and "Eva Palmer Sikelianos" after her marriage.

21. Barney, "Nos secrètes amours," 23.

22. "Bar Harbour," *New York Times*, August 26, 1900, 14.

23. "Il s'en suivit une liaison où le poésie, le Banquet de Platon, et le nudisme eurent leur part, dans une vie devenue arcadienne." Barney, "Nos secrètes amours," 39.

24. Ibid., 40.

25. Rodriguez, *Wild Heart*, 89–90.

26. Ibid., 100.

27. "Mon amour pour Elle [Natalie Barney] est déjà chuchoté à Londres, cela empêchera ma sœur de se marier, cela achèvera d'affoler ma mère, très nerveuse, cela m'interdira presque toute société humaine—on me dit que cela me mènera à la folie—, et je l'aime, voyez-vous, d'une passion si tenace et si terrible que RIEN ne peut me séparer

d'elle—que je brave toutes les conséquences—, que je choisirais la folie et la mort et la désolation des êtres qui sont liés à mon existence plutôt que d'arracher cet amour douloureux. Je puis tout supporter pour Elle seule, la perte d'Elle me jetterait à l'abîme (24 mars 1901)." Jean-Paul Goujon, *Tes blessures sont plus douces que leurs caresses: Vie de Renée Vivien* (Paris: Régine Deforges, 1986), 164–165.

28. Ibid., 158.

29. "Aux yeux de Vivien, Charles-Brun possédait un rayonnement intellectuel qui faisait de lui bien autre chose que le simple professeur de lycée qu'il était dans le civil. Cette sorte d'aura explique que Vivien ait été très attirée par son esprit et ait choisi de se l'attacher pour ses travaux littéraires. Mais leurs relations ne se limitèrent pas à la littérature, et Charles-Brun devint bientôt un sorte de confident, comme le montrent les lettres que Vivien lui adressa." Goujon, *Tes blessures*, 159–160. Charles-Brun served as a confidant to Renée Vivien, and unlike others, he refused to write a tell-all biography of his infamous protégée despite Salomon Reinach's urgings. See Goujon, *Tes blessures*, 160.

30. Rodriguez, *Wild Heart*, 117.

31. For more on their relationship after Eva Palmer's move to Greece and her marriage to Angehlos Sikelianos, see chapter 5.

32. Rodriguez, *Wild Heart*, 117.

33. Jay, *Amazon and the Page*, 62.

34. See Jean L. Kling, *Alice Pike Barney: Her Life and Art*, introduced by Wanda M. Corn (Washington, DC: National Museum of American Art and Smithsonian Institution Press, 1994).

35. See Smithsonian Institution Archives, Barney, Alice Pike, 1857–1931, Alice Pike Barney Papers, c. 1890–1994, accession number 96-154, box 1.

36. For example, Alice Pike Barney hosted a lecture recital on *Parsifal* presented by Walter Damrosch for the benefit of the firemen of Baltimore, MD, and Washington, DC. The event was held in 1904 at the Lafayette Opera House.

37. See Mary Simonson, "Dancing the Future, Performing the Past: Isadora Duncan and Wagnerism in the American Imagination," *Journal of the American Musicological Society* 65, no. 2 (Summer 2012): 511–556; and Louis K. Epstein, "Toward a Theory of Patronage: Funding for Music Composition in France, 1918–1939" (PhD diss., Harvard University, 2013).

38. See Kling, *Alice Pike Barney*, 251–257.

39. See ibid., 108–110.

40. "Et parmi les derniers arpèges de la harpe noyés sous les applaudissements, Anne [Anne was the pseudonym for Eva Palmer in Barney's memoire] quitta la scène pour me rejoindre à l'écart; et fière de son succès qu'elle vint m'offrir je reçus son corps vibrant dans mes bras." Barney, "Nos secrètes amours," 39.

41. Marian Wilson Kimber, "In a Woman's Voice: Musical Recitation and the Feminization of American Melodrama," in *Melodramatic Voices: Understanding Music Drama*, ed. Sarah Hibberd (Surrey, UK, and Burlington, VT: Ashgate, 2011), 61. See also Marian Wilson Kimber, *The Elocutionists: Women, Music, and the Spoken Word* (Urbana, Chicago, and Springfield: University of Illinois Press, 2017).

42. See Mary Simonson, "Dance Pictures: The Cinematic Experiments of Anna Pavlova and Rita Sacchetto," *Screening the Past* 40 (September 15, 2015), http://www.screeningthepast.com/2015/08/dance-pictures-the-cinematic-experiments-of-anna-

pavlova-and-rita-sacchetto/; and Nancy Lee Chalfa Ruyter, introduction to "Essays on François Delsarte," ed. Nancy Lee Chalfa Ruyter, special issue, *Mime Journal* 23 (2004/2005): 4–5.

43. See Carrie J. Preston, *Modernism's Mythic Pose: Gender, Genre, Solo Performance* (Oxford and New York: Oxford University Press, 2011), 58–67.

44. See Carrie J. Preston, "Posing Modernism: Delsartism in Modern Dance and Silent Film," chapter 2 in *Modernism's Mythic Pose: Gender, Genre, Solo Performance* (Oxford and New York: Oxford University Press, 2011), 58–99; Suzanne Bordelon, "Embodied *Ethos* and Rhetorical Accretion: Genevieve Stebbins and the *Delsarte System of Expression*," *Rhetoric Society Quarterly* 46, no. 2 (2016): 105–130; Nancy Lee Chalfa Ruyter, "The Genteel Transition: American Delsartism," in *Reformers and Visionaries: The Americanization of the Art of Dance* (Brooklyn, NY: Dance Horizons, 1979), 17–32; Joseph Fahey, "Quiet Victory: The Professional Identity American Women Forged Through Delsartism," in "Essays on François Delsarte," ed. Nancy Lee Chalfa Ruyter, special issue, *Mime Journal* 23 (2004/2005): 43–84; Taylor Susan Lake, "The Delsarte Attitude on the Legitimate Stage: Mary Anderson's Galatea and the Trope of the Classical Body," in "Essays on François Delsarte," ed. Nancy Lee Chalfa Ruyter, special issue, *Mime Journal* 23 (2004/2005): 113–135; and Taylor Susan Lake, "American Delsartism and the Bodily Discourse of Respectable Womanliness" (PhD diss., University of Iowa, 2002), 99. See also Karen J. Blair, *The Torchbearers: Women and Their Amateur Arts Associations in America, 1890–1930* (Bloomington: Indiana University Press, 1994), 27–75; and Ted Shawn's influential book, *Every Little Movement: A Book about François Delsarte, the Man and His Philosophy, His Science of Applied Aesthetics, the Application of This Science to the Art of the Dance, the Influence of Delsarte on American Dance* (New York: Dance Horizons, 1954).

45. Caroline B. Le Row, "Recitations with Music," *Werner's Voice Magazine* 13 (November 1891): 300, cited in Marian Wilson Kimber, "The Peerless Reciter: Reconstructing the Lost Art of Elocution with Music," in *Performance Practice: Issues and Approaches*, ed. Timothy D. Watkins (Ann Arbor, MI: Steglein Publishing, 2009), 205.

46. See Ibid., 205.

47. See Jay, *Amazon and the Page*, 66. See Ovid, *Heroides. Amores*, translated by Grant Showerman, revised by G. P. Goold, Loeb Classical Library 41 (Cambridge MA, and London: Harvard University Press, 1914), 180–196. Here, Ovid's portrays Sappho resolved to throw herself off a cliff when abandoned by her male loved Phaon. See Alphonse Daudet, *Sapho: Mœurs Parisiennes* (Paris: G. Charpentier, 1884). In the novel, Daudet positions the happy, simple, rural, clean, and moral Jean Gaussin against the dissolute, wild, urban, dirty, immoral prostitute Fanny. The courtesan terrorizes him from the very beginning of the novel.

48. See Sappho, *Sappho: Memoir, Text, Selected Renderings, and a Literal Translation by Henry Thorton Wharton*, 3rd ed. (London: John Lane, 1895), 45–46; Wharton numbers the fragment as 122. Modern editions identify it as frag. 156, see Sappho frag. 156: "πόλυ πάκτιδος ἀδυμελεστέρα/χρύσω χρυσοτέρα" ["far more sweetsounding than a lyre / golder than gold"], translated by Anne Carson. See Sappho, *If Not, Winter: Fragments of Sappho*, trans. Anne Carson (New York: Alfred A. Knopf, 2002), 314–315.

49. Rodriguez, *Wild Heart*, 155; Colette, *Mes apprentissages, Trois Six Neuf, Discours de Réception à l'Académie Royale Belge*, Œuvres Complètes (Genève: Éditions de Crémille, 1970), 158.

50. Renée Fleury, an actress who appeared in a few films of the 1930s, may be the "Fleury" listed as the other friend of Sappho.

51. Identified in the script as "Ramberg."

52. Barney lists Phaon as played by M. Vania. Natalie Clifford Barney, *Actes et Entrt'actes* (Paris: Sansot, 1910), 49.

53. See Artemis Leontis, "Eva Palmer Sikelianos Before Delphi," in *Americans and the Experience of Delphi*, ed. Paul Lorenz and David Roessels (Boston: Somerset Hall Press, 2013), 21–23. For more on Eva Palmer Sikelianos see chapter 5.

54. Marie Rambert, *Quicksilver* (London: MacMillan, 1972), 33–34.

55. Ibid., 34–35.

56. As Joan DeJean writes, "[Daudet's Fanny] is the exemplary male fantasy of woman in Daudet's day, a prostitute." *Fictions of Sappho, 1546–1937* (Chicago: University of Chicago Press, 1989), 259. Jules Massenet composed an opera by the same name in 1897.

57. "Why Miss Barney's Sapho Had to Move," *Dayton Journal*, 2nd ed., November 14, 1909, 13.

58. Ibid., 13. Penelope Duncan was born in Lefkada, Greece in the Ionian Sea where Sappho supposedly leapt to her death.

59. See Kimber, *Elocutionists*, 29–33.

60. See Nancy Lee Chalfa Ruyter, *The Cultivation of Body and Mind in Nineteenth-Century American Delsartism* (Westport, CT, and London: Greenwood Press, 1999), 91–92.

61. Joan DeJean posits that the changing orthography of "Sappho" in French scholarship from "Sapho" to "Sapphô" coincided with a "tolerance of sexual diversity" as twentieth-century scholars began to accept the possibility of the poet's non-heteronormative sexual life. See DeJean, *Fictions of Sappho*, 56.

62. Jay, *Amazon and the Page*, 68.

63. See Leontis, "Eva Palmer Sikelianos Before Delphi," 21–23.

64. "ERANNA: Leurs regards nuptiaux sauront t'humilier/Si tu restes . . . SAPPHO: Je reste . . . GORGO: Et tu crois oublier! / Songeant au proche hymen, ton front penché se trouble. / SAPPHO: Je ne sais que choisir car ma pensée est double." Barney, *Actes et Entr'actes*, 57.

65. Οὐκ οἶδ' ὅττι θέω, δύο μοι τὰ νοήματα. Translation from Sappho, *Sappho: A New Translation*, trans. Diane J. Raynor and André Lardinois (Cambridge, UK, and New York: Cambridge University Press, 2014), 51.

66. "GORGO: Ta vie est ton poème/Le plus beau; ton chef-d'œuvre éternel, c'est toi-même. ERANNA: Et tes chants, messagers de ta gloire, diront / Aux siècles à venir ta grandeur." Barney, *Actes et Entr'actes*, 60.

67. J. Jack Halberstam's discussions of queer time can shed light on the ways Barney carved out a uniquely queer space, walled off from the rest of the world, through the reperformance of antiquity. Halberstam writes of queerness in the shadow of the AIDS epidemic as "strange temporalities, imaginative life schedules, and eccentric economic practices," in many ways divorced from sexual identities. Judith [Jack] Halberstam, *In a Queer Time and Place: Transgender Bodies, Subcultural Lives* (New York: New York University Press, 2005), 1.

68. Barney did benefit from the conventions of family (connections to artists), inheritance (from her father) and childrearing (a mother who supported her). While Halberstam

identifies a decidedly contemporary formulation of queer time and space radically shaped by the HIV/AIDS epidemic, Halberstam nonetheless connects this process to the work of Carolyn Dinshaw in *Getting Medieval*. Halberstam, *In a Queer Time and Place*, 2–3.

69. Barney's characters' suicides could also be read in light of Lee Edelman's *No Future: Queer Theory and the Death Drive* (Durham, NC: Duke University Press, 2004).

70. For more on the idea of the ludic in music especially as it relates to keyboard music, see Roger Moseley, *Keys to Play: Music as a Ludic Medium from Apollo to Nintendo* (Oakland, CA: University of California Press, 2018).

71. Tes Slominski, "Doin' Time with Meg and Cris, Thirty Years Later: The Queer Temporality of Pseudonostalgia," *Women and Music* 19 (2015): 86–94.

72. Ibid., 88.

73. Wood, "Sapphonics," 27.

74. On the utopian potential of queerness in performance, see José Esteban Muñoz, *Cruising Utopia: The Then and There of Queer Futurity* (New York and London: New York University Press, 2009).

75. See Halberstam, *In a Queer Time and Place*, 185.

76. Rebecca Schneider, *Performing Remains: Art and War in Times of Theatrical Reenactment* (London and New York: Routledge, 2011), 2.

77. Both Elizabeth Freeman and David Román have addressed queerness in the type of temporal re-enactment described by Schneider. Freeman uses "temporal drag," while Román writes of "archival drag." Freeman's work reclaims a generational model of queer politics that allows an iteration, repetition, and citation of previous generations of queer mothers/sisters that is not ironic: "They do not necessarily aim to reveal the original as always already a copy, but instead engage with prior time as genuinely elsewhere." Román demonstrates how "archival drag" has been used to inspire creativity in the past. "They drag back into the public sphere artists who have either died or retired, refusing to acknowledge the finality of death—the death of the artist, of the avant-garde, of queer culture. Their archival drag reinvokes past genius, and not simply as an insider joke. The arts once mattered, they remind us, and they can matter again." See Elizabeth Freeman, "Packing History, Count(er)ing Generations," *New Literary History* 31, no. 4 (Autumn 2000): 734–735; and later in Elizabeth Freeman, "Deep Lez: Temporal Drag and the Specters of Feminism," in *Time Binds: Queer Temporalities, Queer Histories* (Durham, NC and London: Duke University Press, 2010), 59–94; and David Román, "Archival Drag: Or, The Afterlife of Performance," in *Performance in America: Contemporary US Culture and the Performing Arts* (Durham, NC: Duke University Press, 2005), 174.

78. William Cheng, "Pleasure's Discontents," in "Colloquy: Music and Sexuality," *Journal of the American Musicological Society* 66, no. 3 (Fall 2013): 841–842.

79. Ibid., 844.

80. See Carolyn Dinshaw, *Getting Medieval, Sexualities and Communities, Pre- and Postmodern* (Durham, NC: Duke University Press, 1999), 1.

81. For more on the idea of "touch" see chapter 6.

82. [*Sic*], "L'amour est un oiseau rebelle" from Bizet's *Carmen*.

83. Sappho frag. 49 reads: "I loved you, Atthis, once long ago/a little child you seemed to me and graceless." Translated by Anne Carson, in Sappho, *If Not, Winter*, 103.

84. Chalon, *Portrait of a Seductress*, 76–77.

85. Ibid., 61.

86. ἄγι δὴ χέλυ δῖα μοι λέγε / φωνάεσσα δὲ γίνεο. Sappho, *If Not, Winter*, 240–241.

87. Schneider, *Performing Remains*, 14.

88. City of Light: Paris, 1900–1950 (website), accessed August 31, 2015, http://www.philharmonia.co.uk/paris.

89. Louis Epstein, "Musical Geography: Mapping the Sounds of Paris, 1924," accessed August 24, 2015, http://pages.stolaf.edu/musicalgeography/. Danielle and Eric Fosler-Lussier have created another noteworthy digital musical cartography project of Cold-War-Era cultural presentations sponsored by the United States Department of State. Danielle Fosler-Lussier and Eric Fosler-Lussier, "Database of Cultural Presentations: Accompaniment to *Music in America's Cold War Diplomacy*," version 1.1, last modified 1 April 1, 2015, http://musicdiplomacy.org/database.html.

90. Amy Wells-Lynn, "The Intertextual, Sexually-Coded Rue Jacob: A Geocritical Approach to Djuna Barnes, Natalie Barney, and Radclyffe Hall," *South Central Review* 22, no. 3 (Fall 2005): 79.

91. Taylor, *Archive and the Repertoire*, 24.

92. Ibid., 143.

93. See Richard Dyer, "Judy Garland and Gay Men," in *Heavenly Bodies: Films Stars and Society*, 2nd ed. (London and New York: Routledge, 2004), 137–191; David M. Halperin, "The Queen Is Not Dead," in *How to Be Gay* (Cambridge, MA, and London: Belknap Press of Harvard University Press, 2012), 109–125.; and Peraino, *Listening to the Sirens*, 119–120.

94. Barney, *Éparpillements*, 60.

95. Margaret Reynolds, *The Sappho History* (New York: Palgrave, 2003), 10.

96. For more on Salomon Reinach and Natalie Clifford Barney's relationship, see chapter 6.

97. Sappho, *If Not, Winter*, 240–241.

98. See Nina Wakeford, "Anna Livia," *Guardian*, September 26, 2007, https://www.theguardian.com/news/2007/sep/26/guardianobituaries.booksobituaries; and University of California Berkeley, Faculty Senate, memorial page to Livia, accessed May 29, 2018, https://senate.universityofcalifornia.edu/_files/inmemoriam/html/annaliviajulianbrawn.html.

99. Anna Livia, *Minimax* (Portland, OR: The Eighth Mountain Press, 1991), 2.

100. Natalie Clifford Barney, *Quelques Potraits-Sonnets de Femmes* (Paris: Ollendorf, 1900).

101. Livia, *Minimax*, 3. "Che farò senza Euridice" is from Gluck's *Orfeo ed Euridice* (1762) and "Ardon gl'incensi" is from Donizetti's *Lucia di Lammermoor* (1835).

102. Ibid., 34.

103. Ibid., 56.

104. Ibid., 83.

105. Ibid., 122.

106. Ibid., 145.

107. Ibid., 158–159.

108. Ibid., 195.

109. Ibid., 210.

Chapter 4

1. "The 'Dance Your Ph.D.' Contest," accessed June 25, 2015, www.gonzolabs.org/dance/.

2. Cedric Kai Wei Tan, "Sperm Competition between Brothers and Female Choice," accessed June 25, 2015, https://vimeo.com/77304026.

3. Jenna Kloosterman, "Terahertz Arrays for Heterodyne Receivers," accessed June 25, 2015, https://vimeo.com/107441342.

4. Repeated attempts to talk with Bohannon via email and telephone about why the arts and humanities have been snubbed were unsuccessful.

5. See also chapter 6.

6. French institutionalized musical historiography came into being in the 1890s as the Sorbonne accepted the first dissertations in musicology from Jules Combarieu (1893), Romain Rolland (1895), Maurice Emmanuel (1895), and Louis Laloy (1904). See also chapter 1.

7. Composed between 1921 and 1923, orchestrated in 1924, revised in 1927, and premiered at the Opéra on June 19, 1929. His first opera, *Prométhée enchaîné*, composed between 1916 and 1918, did not premiere until 1959.

8. Other opera composers/librettists/musicologists contemporary to Emmanuel include Boris Asafyev, Wilhelm Grosz, and most recently Kendra Preston Leonard, George Lewis and Mitchell Morris. Thanks to Anne Searcy, Alexandra Monchick, Marcos Balter, and Erica Scheinberg for pointing them out to me.

9. Exceptions include Ronald Stevenson. See Ronald Stevenson, "Maurice Emmanuel: A Belated Apologia," *Music and Letters* 40, no. 2 (April 1959): 154–165; and the work of Christophe Corbier. The French Radio and Television National Orchestra (Orchestre national de la RTF) led by Tony Austin recorded the opera in 1958.

10. Léandre Vaillat, *Ballets de l'Opéra de Paris (ballets dans les opéras; nouveaux ballets)* (Paris: Compagnie française des arts graphiques, 1947), 104.

11. "Mais n'est-ce pas étrange de refuser aux artistes la faculté de la pensée et de la réflexion? [. . .] Je fais de la philosophie parce qu'il m'importe, à moi qui suis artiste, de savoir qui je suis, d'où je viens; parce que mes convictions se reflèteront des mes œuvres, parce que je croirai ou non à l'idéal. Je fais de la littérature parce que j'apprends à y connaître l'âme dans ces manifestations de chaque jour et qu'il m'importe, à moi qui suis artiste, de connaître ce cœur à qui je veux parler. Je fais des sciences, parce que la Nature m'éblouit par ses splendeurs et que je trouve en l'étudiant quelque chose de cette beauté idéale que je dois refléter dans mes œuvres et qu'il m'importe à moi qui suis artiste d'aller chercher à toutes ses sources. Je crois donc [. . .] qu'on peut être un artiste, un philosophe, un savant, et qu'il est d'autant plus nécessaire d'être tout cela à la fois dans de certaines limites, que la nature humaine étant bornée, l'artiste doit souvent s'aider du savant, et le savant du philosophe." Letter to his father, July 3, 1882, coll. Anne Eichner, cited in Christophe Corbier, *Maurice Emmanuel* (Paris: bleu nuit, 2007), 28–29.

12. See ibid., 48–50.

13. Anecdotes cited in ibid., 54–56.

14. The English translation by Harriet Jean Beauley corrupts the text in many key sections, distorting and at times completely misunderstanding Emmanuel's ideas. See Maurice Emmanuel, *The Antique Greek Dance after Sculptured and Painted Figures*, trans. Harriet Jean Beauley (New York and London: John Lane Company, 1916).

15. Maurice Emmanuel, *La Danse grecque antique d'après les monuments figures; Traité de la musique grecque antique; Le Rythme d'Euripide à Debussy* (Genève: Slatkine Reprints, 1984), 119.

16. "Imaginons l'exaltation d'Emmanuel, voyant des images figées depuis l'Antiquité s'animer sous ses yeux." Corbier, *Maurice Emmanuel*, 56.

17. Marta Braun, *Picturing Time: The Work of Étienne-Jules Marey (1830–1904)* (Chicago and London: University of Chicago Press, 1992), xiii and xvii.

18. Chronophotography affected other fields of knowledge as well as politics. The French nation looked to Marey's technology to train both athletes and soldiers, and soon painters and sculptors looked to his images (as well as Edward Muybridge's) for inspiration and an authoritative source on the moving body, free of aesthetic judgments. Ibid., xix.

19. Étienne-Jules Marey, *Le Mouvement* [1894], preface by André Miquel (Nîmes: Éditions Jacqueline Chambon, 1994), 185; and Étienne-Jules Marey, *Movement* [*Le Mouvement*, 1894], trans. Eric Pritchard (New York: D. Appleton and Company, 1895), 170.

20. Marey, *Le Mouvement*, 186; and Marey, *Movement*, 170.

21. See Corbier, *Maurice Emmanuel*, 25–26.

22. Marey, *Le Mouvement*, 195.

23. Marey's work inspired Léon Heuzey, an archaeologist who helped discover sites at Delphi and also a scholar of ancient Greek costume. See Léon Alexandre Heuzey, *Histoire du costume antique d'après des études sur le modèle vivant* (Paris: Édouard Champion, 1922).

24. Marey, *Movement*, 184. [M. Maurice Emmanuel, qui prépare un important travail sur la danse dans l'antiquité, nous a prié de fixer par la photographie instantanée certains attitudes qu'il a relevées, soit sur des bas-reliefs, soit sur des vases grecs. Sur ces images photographiques on saisit, dans son ensemble, l'harmonie des plis du costume avec l'expression particulière que leur donne le mouvement de la danse. La succession même d'une phrase de chorégraphie se peut suivre dans une série d'images chronophotographiques.] Marey, *Le Mouvement*, 195.

25. See Corbier, *Maurice Emmanuel*, 57.

26. [Leur œil exercé savait voir; avec un peu d'argile, ils exprimaient la chose vue. La comparaison des images orchestiques que nous leur devons, avec celles que la photographie nous permet d'obtenir sera la garantie de leur exactitude.] Maurice Emmanuel, *La Danse grecque antique d'après les monuments figures* (Paris: Hachette, 1896), 26.

27. For more on Emmanuel's inspirations for his use of modern technology to study ancient dance, see Frederick Naerebout, "'In Search of a Dead Rat': The Reception of Ancient Greek Dance in Late Nineteenth-Century Europe and America," in *The Ancient Dancer in the Modern World: Responses to Greek and Roman Dance*, ed. Fiona Macintosh (Oxford and New York: Oxford University Press, 2010), 43–49.

28. Susan Sontag, *On Photography* (New York: Farrar, Straus and Giroux, 1977), 6.

29. Roland Barthes, *Camera Lucida: Reflections on Photography* [1980], trans. Richard Howard (New York: Hill and Wang, 1982), 76.

30. Sontag, *On Photography*, 14.

31. Siegfried Kracauer, "Photography" [1927], trans. Thomas Y. Levin, *Critical Inquiry* 19, no. 3 (Spring 1993): 422; see also Mary Ann Doane, "Temporality, Storage, Legibility: Freud, Marey, and the Cinema," *Critical Inquiry* 22, no. 2 (Winter 1996): 313–343.

32. Corbier, *Maurice Emmanuel*, 57–58.

33. Emmanuel, *La Danse grecque antique*, 27.

34. Isadora Duncan, "The Dance of the Future [1902 or 1903, 1909]," in *The Art of the Dance*, ed. and introduced Sheldon Cheney (New York: Theatre Arts, Inc., 1928), 54.

35. Ibid., 57.

36. Ibid., 62.

37. In 1855 an article described Madame Mariquita as a costume designer and "antiquarian" as well as choreographer and dancer. See "Paris," *The Musical World* 33, no. 32 (August 11, 1855): 520. See also Sarah Gutsche-Miller, "Madame Mariquita, the French Fokine," in *Proceedings of the Society of Dance History Scholars, Thirty-Third Annual Conference, Stanford University, Palo Alto and San Francisco, CA* ([Riverside, CA]: Society of Dance History Scholars, 2009), 106–111; Gutsche-Miller, "Pantomime-Ballet on the Music-Hall Stage: The Popularisation of Classical Ballet in Fin-de-Siècle Paris" (PhD diss., McGill University, 2010); and Gutsche-Miller, *Parisian Music-Hall Ballet, 1871–1913* (Rochester, NY: University of Rochester Press, 2015).

38. "Maraquita, Noted Ballet Mistress, Is Dead in Paris," *New York Herald*, October 14, 1922. The New York Public Library for the Performing Arts, Jerome Robbins Dance Collection, Mariquita, 1830–1922. [Clippings].

39. "Je me suis aussitôt empressée de visiter des musées, j'ai regardé des vases antiques, des fresques, des statues . . . et dans des documents longuement examinés, étudiés avec soin, j'ai trouvé des poses, des attitudes, des gestes, sur quoi reposera tout mon divertissement. . . . Que voulez-vous, je ne suis qu'une interprète! . . . Je n'ai ni inventé, ni créé l'art grec. . . . Je m'efforce seulement d'en exprimer toute la beauté par la danse en m'inspirant des chefs-d'œuvre qu'il nous a laissés, figés dans la splendeur des pierres ou des marbres, dans la magnificence éteinte des fresques!" Georges Talmont [and Madame Mariquita], "Comment Madame Mariquita monte un ballet," *Comœdia Illustré* 1e Année 1, no. 1 (December 15, 1908): 22–23.

40. See Annegret Fauser, "Visual Pleasures—Musical Signs: Dance at the Paris Opéra," *South Atlantic Quarterly* 104, no. 1 (Winter 2005): 99–121; Mary Ann Smart, *Mimomania: Music and Gesture in Nineteenth-Century Opera* (Berkeley, Los Angeles, and London: University of California Press, 2004); and Gutsche-Miller, "Madame Mariquita, the French Fokine."

41. They are organized in terms of their level of importance: first the "*Figures*" (the painted vases, bas-reliefs, etc.), followed by "The *Rhythms* of the poets" (lyrics, tragedies, comedies, ballads, etc.), and finally the few "*Writings*" from antiquity relating to dance. Emmanuel decided to organize his material thematically by gesture rather than chronologically, placing preclassical next to late Hellenist images. "We are looking less to follow the transformations of the types of dance, than to recover, through their variations, gymnastics, which apply to all dances." Emmanuel, *La Danse grecque antique*, 26.

42. "Si l'on peut établir—et cette étude n'a pas d'autre but,—qu'abstraction faite de la fantaisie ou de l'inexpérience des artistes, les mouvements de danse qu'ils ont fixés sur les vases et les reliefs sont souvent bien vus et fidèlement traduits, on admettra volontiers

que des représentations exactes des scènes orchestiques soient les documents les plus précieux que nous puissions consulter." Emmanuel, *La Danse grecque antique*, 3.

43. "Mon excuse est que, à coté de disciples fervents et fidèles, vous avez à Paris de gauches imitateurs, et quelques 'démarqueurs' impudents, qui détournent l'attention ou entravent la sympathie." Maurice Emmanuel, "Le 'Rythme et la Musique' (lettre ouverte)," *Le Rythme, Nouvelles de l'Institut Jacques-Dalcroze* 12 (February 1924): 21.

44. See Gutsche-Miller, "Pantomime-Ballet on the Music-Hall Stage"; and Ann Cooper Albright, *Traces of Light: Absence and Presence in the Work of Loïe Fuller* (Middletown, CT: Wesleyan University Press, 2007), 123.

45. "La danseuse (fig. 193) dont la cambrure est si forte et qui se contoune étrangement, est une de ces Bacchantes dont le délire orgiastique faisait des folles ou des malades. Le Dr. Meige n'hésite pas à reconnaître dans cette représentation, et dans d'autres, analogues, un état de crise pathologique, et une déformation due à un état nerveux spécial. [. . .] le *Corps camber*, sans être réservé exclusivement aux danseurs bachiques, joue un rôle considérable dans l'orchestique dionysiaque (388 à 399, 404, 405)." Emmanuel, *La Danse grecque antique*, 101–102.

46. Henry Meige, a student of Dr. Jean-Martin Charcot, teamed up with Marey to analyze and document hysterical subjects in order to pathologize and constrain these types of performances. See Jonathan Marshall, "The Priestesses of Apollo and the Heirs of Aesculapius: Medical Art-Historical Approaches to Ancient Choreography after Charcot," *Forum for Modern Language Studies* 43, no. 4 (October 2007): 410–426.

47. Ibid., 422.

48. "Mais à défaut d'un traité méthodique—qui semble n'avoir jamais été composé,—ils permettent de connaître les idées des Grecs sur l'orchestique et de délimiter le domaine de cet art. Ils nous le montrent singulièrement vaste et beau, et s'ils nous renseignent mal sur les procédés gymnastiques de la danse, ils nous apprennent qu'elle est un art divin, et qu'elle joue dans l'éducation de l'homme un rôle considérable." Emmanuel, *La Danse grecque antique*, 5.

49. Ibid., 5–6.

50. Ibid., 20–21.

51. See Tony Bennett, introduction to *The Birth of the Museum: History, Theory, Politics* (London and New York: Routledge, 1995).

52. See Stevenson, "Maurice Emmanuel," 159.

53. Emmanuel, *La Danse grecque antique*, 20–21.

54. Émile Vuillermoz even characterized the choruses of the final act as reminiscent of the death of Adonis in Debussy's *Le Martyre de Saint-Sébastien* (1911), another antiquity-themed work with modern music. "Et il est curieux de constater combien les chœurs de Maurice Emmanuel évoquent par instant la couleur si particulière de ceux du *Martyre de Saint-Sébastien* au moment de la plainte funèbre évoquant la *Mort d'Adonis*. La science et l'instinct nous donnent ici le spectacle d'une de leurs plus émouvantes rencontres." Émile Vuillermoz, "Salamine," *Candide*, no. 276 (June 27, 1929): 15.

55. Maurice Emmanuel, *Salamine, tragédie lyrique en trois actes d'après les "Perses" d'Eschyle* (Paris: Choudens, 1929), 1.

56. Corbier, *Maurice Emmanuel*, 142–144.

57. "Mais le rôle, *parlé en mesure*, du Coryphée, subsiste: aussi bien n'est-il pas sans exemple sur la scène de l'Opéra; et l'accompagnement instrumental, qui le soutient, assure la continuité musicale de l'ensemble." Emmanuel, *Salamine*, 1.

58. David A. Grayson, "The Opera: Genesis and Sources," in *Claude Debussy: Pelléas et Mélisande*, ed. Roger Nichols and Richard Langham Smith, Cambridge Opera Handbooks (Cambridge, UK: Cambridge University Press, 1989), 47.

59. See Julie McQuinn, "Exploring the Erotic in Debussy's Music," *The Cambridge Companion to Debussy*, ed. Simon Trezise (Cambridge, UK: Cambridge University Press, 2003), 131–133; and Katherine Bergeron, "Mélisande's Hair, or the Trouble in Allemonde: A Postmodern Allegory at the Opéra-Comique," in *Siren Songs: Representations of Gender and Sexuality in Opera*, ed. Mary Ann Smart (Princeton, NJ, and Oxford: Princeton University Press, 2000), 160–185.

60. McQuinn "Exploring the Erotic in Debussy's Music."

61. "Euripide avait tourné le dos à Eschyle. En faisant passer à travers le quadrillage des barres de mesure, qui ne sont pas pour lui les signaux de temps percutés, des rythmes sans cesse ondoyants, Debussy tourne le dos à Wagner, qui, novateur dans l'agencement et la longueur de ses périodes, *non carrées*, demeure, par la persistance, l'insistance de ses formules rythmiques, un disciple des grands classiques allemands." Maurice Emmanuel, *Le Rythme d'Euripide à Debussy* (Geneva: Congrès du rythme, 1926); and reprint in *La Danse grecque antique d'après les monuments figures; Traité de la musique grecque antique; Le Rythme d'Euripide à Debussy*, Genève, Slatkine Reprints, 1984), 554.

62. This is also similar to Duncan's own interest in "evolution" in her writings, but as discussed previously, Emmanuel and Duncan reach very different interpretations. See Christophe Corbier, "Continuité, tradition, nouveauté: Essai sur l'esthétique de Maurice Emmanuel," in *Tradition et innovation en histoire de l'art*, ed. Jean-René Gaborit (Grenoble: Collection Actes des Congrès des Sociétés historiques et scientifiques [CD-ROM], 2006), 201–212.

63. "Et dans l'éternel tournoiement des siècles elles reviennent, discrètes, sans imposer à notre vanité le joug des vieilles choses. Elles nous laissent créer du vieux neuf." Maurice Emmanuel, *Histoire de la langue musicale* (Paris: Henri Laurens, 1911), 572.

64. "Histoire ancienne et qui se renouvellera, tant que des artistes originaux surgiront, et que l'art connaîtra, grâce à eux, le renouvellement nécessaire." Maurice Emmanuel, *Pelléas et Mélisande de Claude Debussy: Étude et analyse* (Paris: Mellottée, 1926), 211.

65. Ibid., 135.

66. This is coincidently not that different from the approach of sixteenth-century French musicians who experimented with measured music also designed to recreate music-speech: *vers mesuré à l'antique*.

67. "Les rythmes reflètent ceux d'Eschyle, mais ne prétendent à rien de plus." Emmanuel, *Salamine*, 1.

68. Emmanuel, *La Danse grecque antique*, 3–4.

69. "[L]a poésie véritablement orchestique, celle dont l'allure plus libre ne s'astreint pas à des types métriques, la poésie des chœurs d'Eschyle, d'Aristophane ou de Pindare, n'a pu être soumise à une analyse exacte. Déjà d'admirables travaux en ont fait des ensembles métriques qui paraissaient n'être que confusion. [. . .] En dépit des lacunes qui subsistent et qu'il sera peut-être difficile de combler, la Rythmique grecque, dans ce

que la poésie nous en révèle, est une source d'information directe et féconde à laquelle doit puiser l'historien de la danse." Ibid., 4–5.

70. The Archive Guerra cited in Francesca Falcone's article is currently housed in a private collection in Rome. See Maurice Emmanuel, letter to Nicola Guerra (4 June 1929), Archive Guerra, cited in Francesca Falcone, "Nicola Guerra maître de ballet all'Opéra di Parigi: Gli anni 1927–1929," *Chorégraphie* 12, no. 6 (1998): 55.

71. "[A]ttitudes lentes, sur le thème des doigts allongés (index et médius) [. . .] les petites [. . .] seulement exécuter des mouvements du torse et des bras" Emmanuel, letter to Nicola Guerra.

72. "A côté de ce type, il s'en forme un autre dès le VIᵉ siècle (10): le personnage qui prend part à la lamentation funèbre porte une main à sa chevelure, dans un mouvement plein de calme et dont la noblesse révèle le sens purement mimique; et il étend l'autre bras dans la direction du mort." Emmanuel, *La Danse grecque antique*, 272–274.

73. André Levinson, "Grecs et barbares," *Candide*, no. 276 (June 27, 1929): 15.

74. "[L]es pleureuses asiatiques n'y accomplissent qu'une brève et sommaire mimique funèbre. Mais les gestes consacrés de leurs rites font que nous nous souvenons de ce que doivent à M. Emmanuel tous ceux que passionne l'art de la danse. [. . .] Bref, son traité est comme la réfutation anticipée de cette conception d'une danse grecque anarchique et impressionniste, chère aux gymnasiarques anglo-saxons, et que devait personnifier Isadora Duncan dansant, pieds nus." Levinson, "Grecs et barbares," 15.

75. André Levinson, "Some Commonplaces on the Dance," *Broom* 4, no. 1 (December 1922): 17; See also André Levinson, *Ballet Old and New*, trans. Susan Cook (Summer, NY: Dance Horizons, 1982), 77–78 and 93; and André Levinson. "Précisions sur la danse: Le Concours de l'Opéra," *Comoedia* (December 21, 1928): 15.

76. Lívia Fuchs, "Hungry: On Hungarian Dance," in *Europe Dancing: Perspectives on Theatre Dance and Cultural Identity*, ed. Andrée Grau and Stephanie Jordan (London and New York: Routledge, 2000), 80.

77. Giannandrea Poesio, "Italy: The Cinderella of the Arts," in *Europe Dancing: Perspectives on Theatre Dance and Cultural Identity*, ed. Andrée Grau and Stephanie Jordan (London and New York: Routledge, 2000), 102.

78. On the other hand, Guerra did choreograph Ida Rubinstein (en pointe throughout) in a mixed cast version of Florent Schmitt's *La Tragédie de Salome* (1919) that included both "rhythmic" and "classical" dance. See Lynn Garafola, "Forgotten Interlude: Eurhythmic Dancers at the Paris Opéra," in *Legacies of Twentieth-Century Dance* (Middletown, CT: Wesleyan University Press, 2005), 93; Michel de Cossart, *Ida Rubinstein (1885–1960): A Theatrical Life* (Liverpool, UK: Liverpool University Press, 1987), 75; and Poesio, "Italy: The Cinderella of the Arts," 102.

79. Ágnes Körtvélyes, "Guerra Miklós ballettmester operaházi müködése," in *A magjar balett történetébö*, ed. Vályi Rózsi (Budapest: Zenemükiádó, 1956), 188.

80. "La danse classique a ses racines dans l'Olympe, et nous a été enseignée par les dieux. La danse moderne n'est pas même bacchique, elle est tout au plus sélénique." G. Manacorda, "Danse classique ou Danse moderne? Interview de M. Guerra, directeur de l'Académie de danse à l'Opéra de Paris," in *Illustration théâtrale internationale* [s.d.]: 135, Archives Guerra cited in Francesca Falcone, "Nicola Guerra (1865–1942): Un maestro italiano dimenticato," November 30, 2010, http://www.augustevestris.fr/article198.html.

81. André Levinson deplored this mixing of styles. He wrote how he hoped Yvonne Daunt would come to her senses, forget the "outmoded childishness of Duncanism," and accept that she was "a remarkable classical dancer." Quoted in Garafola, "Forgotten Interlude," 98.

82. Earlier choreographies in the 1920s were danced by Régina Badet and choreographed by Madame Mariquita.

83. See Garafola, "Forgotten Interlude," 98–99.

84. André Levinson, "La Danse: Épitaphe," *Comoedia*, September 21, 1925, 3.

85. Corbier, *Maurice Emmanuel*, 146.

86. André Levinson, *La Danse d'aujourd'hui: Études, notes, portraits* (Paris: Duchartere et Van Buggenhoudt, 1929), 201, cited in Garafola "Forgotten Interlude," 99.

87. Ibid., 99.

88. Ibid., 100.

89. Richard Schechner, *Performance Studies: An Introduction*, 3rd ed. (London and New York: Routledge, 2013), ix.

Chapter 5

1. See David Roessels, introduction to *Americans and the Experience of Delphi*, ed. Paul Lorenz and David Roessels (Boston: Somerset Hall Press, 2013), ix.

2. See Maria Tsouvala et al., "Opening Plenary Panel: The State of Dance Studies in Greece" (opening plenary session at "Cut & Paste: Dance Advocacy in the Age of Austerity," the 2015 Joint Conference of the Society of Dance History Scholars and the Congress on Research in Dance, Athens, Greece, June 4, 2015).

3. Natalie Clifford Barney, "Nos secrètes amours ou L'Amant féminin ou Mémoires secrets" (unpublished typescript with author's autograph corrections, October 31, 1950), 193 found in the Renée Lang Collection, box 15, folder 17, Department of Special Collections, Memorial Library, University of Wisconsin-Madison.

4. "Viens poupoule, viens poupoule, viens! / Quand j'entends des chansons ça me rend tout polisson / Ah! viens poupoule, viens poupoule, viens! / Souviens-toi que c'est comme ça que j'suis devenu papa."

5. "Et lorsque nous foulâmes cette poussière consacrée par les sandales de Sapho et de ses poétesses, nous reprîmes conscience de notre pèlerinage malgré les irruptions modernes." Barney, "Nos secrètes amours," 193.

6. Ibid., 193–194.

7. Kate Gilhuly, "Lesbians Are Not from Lesbos," in *Ancient Sex: New Essays*, ed. Ruby Bondell and Kirk Ormand (Columbus: The Ohio State University, 2015), 173.

8. See Berthold Seewald, "Griechenland zerstörte schon einmal Europas Ordnung," *Die Welt*, June 11, 2015, http://www.welt.de/geschichte/article142305296/Griechenland-zerstoerte-schon-einmal-Europas-Ordnung.html.

9. Eva Palmer-Sikelianos, *Upward Panic: The Autobiography of Eva Palmer-Sikelianos*, ed. with an introduction by John P. Anton (Chur, Switzerland, and Philadelphia: Harwood Academic Publishers, 1993), 51.

10. Barney to Palmer Sikelianos, October 21, 1930; ΑΡΧΕΙΟ ΕΥΑΣ PALMER ΣΙΚΕΛΙΑΝΟΥ [Eva Palmer Sikelianos Archive] 189/5 no. 494–650. Museum Benaki, Delta House, Kifisia.

11. Artemis Leontis, "Eva Palmer Sikelianos Before Delphi," in *Americans and the Experience of Delphi*, ed. Paul Lorenz and David Roessels (Boston: Somerset Hall Press, 2013), 3.

12. For more on Mrs. Patrick Campbell, see Penny Farfan, *Performing Queer Modernism* (New York: Oxford University Press, 2017), 11–26.

13. Courtland Palmer Jr., a student of Ignacy Paderewski, was a well-respected pianist. His compositions were less warmly received. Apparently he also suffered from crippling stage fright. See Guido M. Gatti, "The Academy of St. Cecilia and the Augusteo in Rome," *Musical Quarterly* 8, no. 3 (1922): 329.

14. Eva Palmer [Sikelianos] to Natalie Clifford Barney, March 7, 1902, BLJD, Fonds Natalie Clifford Barney, NCB C 2920, 30–35.

15. Palmer Sikelianos, *Upward Panic*, 32.

16. See Leontis, "Eva Palmer Sikelianos Before Delphi," 13–14.

17. Ibid., 24.

18. Vanessa Agnew, "Introduction: What Is Reenactment?," *Criticism* 46, no. 3 (Summer 2004): 330.

19. Palmer Sikelianos, *Upward Panic*, 75.

20. Ibid., 76.

21. Sappho, *Sappho: A New Translation*, trans. Diane J. Raynor and André Lardinois (Cambridge, UK, and New York: Cambridge University Press, 2014), 70. Anne Carson's translation differs in gender: "[S]weet mother I cannot work the loom / I am broken with longing for a boy by slender Aphrodite. [γλύκηα μᾶτερ, οὔτοι δύναμαι κρέκην τὸν ἴστον / πόθῳ δάμεισα παῖδος βραδίναν δι᾽ Ἀφροδίταν]" See Sappho, *If Not, Winter: Fragments of Sappho*, trans. Anne Carson (New York: Alfred A. Knopf, 2002), 202–203.

22. In her memoir, written in the 1930s and 1940s, she argued that America and the Soviet Union shared equal blame for the rise of such machines. Palmer Sikelianos, Upward Panic, 79.

23. Ibid., 79.

24. Ibid., 80.

25. The composer, Erik Satie's fear of modern technology (as well as his perverse embrace of it during his flirtation with Dadaism) is one notable example. See Robert Orledge, *Satie the Composer* (Cambridge, UK, and New York: Cambridge University Press, 1990), 263.

26. John P. Anton, introduction to *Upward Panic: The Autobiography of Eva Palmer-Sikelianos*, ed. with an introduction by John P. Anton (Chur, Switzerland, and Philadelphia: Harwood Academic Publishers, 1993), xii–xiii.

27. Ibid., xii–xiii.

28. Lynn Garafola, *Diaghilev's Ballets Russes* (New York: Da Capo, 1989), 98.

29. Palmer Sikelianos, *Upward Panic*, 193.

30. See Diana Taylor, *The Archive and the Repertoire: Performing Cultural Memory in the Americas* (Durham, NC, and London: Duke University Press, 2003).

31. Jacqueline Decter, *Nicholas Roerich: The Life and Art of a Russian Master* (Rochester, VT: Park Street Press, 1989), 19.

32. Lynn Garafola, "The Enigma of Nicholas Roerich," *Dance Chronicle* 13, no. 3 (1990–1991): 402.

33. Nicholas Roerich, *N. K. Rerikh: Iz literaturnogo naslediya* (Moscow: Izobrazitel'noe iskusstvo, 1974), 84, cited in Decter, *Nicholas Roerich*, 19.

34. Millicent Hodson, "Nijinsky's Choreographic Method: Visual Sources from Roerich for *Le Sacre du printemps*," *Dance Research Journal* 18, no. 2 (Winter 1986–1987): 7.

35. Interview with Kenneth Archer (London, April 3, 1981), cited in Hodson, "Nijinsky's Choreographic Method," 7.

36. Bronislava Nijinska, *Bronislava Nijinska: Early Memoirs*, ed. Irina Nijinska and Jean Rawlison (New York: Holt, Rinehart and Wilson, 1981), 461.

37. Roger Fry, "M. Larionow and the Russian Ballet," *Burlington Magazine* (March 1919), 112.

38. Palmer Sikelianos, *Upward Panic*, 109.

39. Ibid., 110.

40. Garafola, *Diaghilev's Ballets Russes*, 17.

41. Quoted in Natalia Roslavleva, *Era of the Russian Ballet 1770–1965* (London: Gollancz, 1966), 175.

42. Garafola, *Diaghilev's Ballets Russes*, 12.

43. See Simon Morrison, "The Origins of *Daphnis et Chloé* (1912)," *19th-Century Music* 28, no. 1 (2004): 52.

44. See Maurice Ravel, "Une esquisse autobiographique de Ravel [1928]," *La Revue musicale* 19 (1938): 17–23; English translation in Arbie Orenstein, ed., *A Ravel Reader: Correspondence, Articles, Interviews* (New York: Columbia University Press, 1990). 29–37, cited in Deborah Mawer, "Ballet and the Apotheosis of the Dance," in *Cambridge Companion to Ravel*, ed. Deborah Mawer (Cambridge, UK: Cambridge University Press, 2000), 143.

45. Nijinska notes that her brother, "from the very beginning, without any preparation, [was] in complete mastery of the new technique." Lynn Garafola sees this statement reinforcing Arnold Haskells's assertion that Bakst developed these innovative movements and poses, which he then handed to Nijinsky to implement. See Garafola, *Diaghilev's Ballets Russes*, 53.

46. "Elles sont le résultat d'une savante compilation archéologique: ce pli du jarret vient d'un musée allemand, ce fléchissement de l'épaule a été noté au Louvre et c'est à la National Gallery qu'a été relevé ce geste de l'avant-bras." [Willy] Henry Gauthier-Villars, "Deux Ballets Russes de Musiciens Français," *Comœdia Illustré* 4e année, no. 18 (June 15, 1912): [2].

47. Koula Pratsika, "Anamnesis apo tis protes Delfikes Eortes tou 1927," [Recollections from the first Delphic Festivals of 1927], in *Angelos Sikelianos, Eua Palmer-Sikelianu, Delphikes Eortes. Eidikon Aphieroma Tes Epitheoreseos Eos* (Athens: Papaedema, 1998), 127, cited and translated in Leontis, "Eva Palmer Sikelianos Before Delphi," 2.

48. The festival was supposed to be a first step in founding a university and a school of music, but ultimately it became a grand spectacle founded on similar conflicting ideologies as the modern Olympic movement: strident individualism and international harmony. See Palmer-Sikelianos, *Upward Panic*, 103–119; Ann Cooper Albright, *Traces of Light: Absence and Presence in the Work of Loïe Fuller* (Middletown, CT: Wesleyan University Press, 2007) 165–173; Artemis Leontis, "Eva Palmer's Distinctive Greek

Journey," in *Women Writing Greece: Essays on Hellenism, Orientalism and Travel*, ed. Vassiliki Kolocotroni and Efterpi Mitsi (Amsterdam and New York: Rodopi, 2008); and Allen Guttmann, *The Olympics: A History of the Modern Games* (Urbana: University of Illinois Press, 1992).

49. Agnew, "Introduction: What Is Reenactment?" 330.

50. Palmer Sikelianos, *Upward Panic*, 113.

51. Bruce G. Trigger, "Alternative Archaeologies: Nationalist, Colonialist, Imperialist," *Man, New Series* 19, no. 3 (September 1984): 355–370; Artemis Leontis, "The Alternative Archaeologies of Eva Palmer Sikelianos" (lecture presented at the American School of Classical Studies at Athens, Athens, Greece, May 6, 2014). See also Leontis's forthcoming biography Artemis Leontis: *Eva Palmer Sikelianos: A Life in Ruins* (Princeton, NJ: Princeton University Press, 2019 [forthcoming]).

52. Artemis Leontis, "Alternative Archaeologies of Eva Palmer Sikelianos," 2014.

53. See Taylor, *Archive and Repertoire*, 2003.

54. Richard Schechner, *Between Theatre and Anthropology* (Chicago: University of Chicago Press, 1985), 36.

55. Rebecca Schneider, *Performing Remains: Art and War in Times of Theatrical Reenactment* (London and New York: Routledge, 2011), 10.

56. Palmer Sikelianos, *Upward Panic*, 47.

57. Léon Heuzey, *Histoire du costume antique d'après des études sur le modèle vivant* (Paris: Édouard Champion, 1922).

58. Palmer Sikelianos, *Upward Panic*, 48.

59. Ibid., 48–49.

60. Leontis, "Eva Palmer Sikelianos Before Delphi," 1.

61. Palmer Sikelianos, *Upward Panic*, 219.

62. Ibid., 219.

63. NB: from John Keats, "On First Looking into Chapman's Homer" (1816).

64. Palmer Sikelianos, *Upward Panic*, 49–50.

65. Isadora Duncan, *My Life* (New York: Boni and Liveright, 1927), 129–130.

66. Palmer Sikelianos, *Upward Panic*, 185.

67. Ibid., 186.

68. Ibid., 50.

69. Ibid., 115.

70. Ibid., 115.

71. See Aeschylus, *Hoi tragōdies tou Aischylou*, [trans.] Ionnes Gryparō (Athens: Delphikes Heortes, 1930).

72. Palmer Sikelianos, *Upward Panic*, 108.

73. Ibid., 109. The reference to "gymnastic-exercises" alludes to the work of François Delsarte, whose movement styles were still in vogue for "Hellenic" dances. See Albright, *Traces of Light*, 151.

74. Angelos dreamed of establishing a Delphic University. His plans never came to fruition. See Lia Papadaki, *To efivikó prótypo kai i Delfikí prospátheia tou Ággelou Sikelianoú* (Athens: Genikí grammateía néas geniás, 1995), 122–124.

75. Palmer Sikelianos, *Upward Panic*, 125.

76. Ibid., 125.

77. Ibid., 134.

78. Ibid., 135.

79. The film is silent. *Prometheus Bound* [videorecording], directed and produced by Eva Sikelianos and Angelos Sikelianos, [based on the play] by Aeschylus (Delphi, Greece, 1930), The New York Public Library of the Performing Arts, Dance Collection (*MGZIDVD 5-1758).

80. For more on the stage setting, particualry the focus on circular and centripetal movement, see Gonda Van Steen, "'The World's a Circular Stage': Aeschylean Tragedy through the Eyes of Eva Palmer-Sikelianou," *International Journal of the Classical Tradition* 8, no. 3 (Winter 2002): 375–393.

81. Even musically, one could imagine Stravinsky resetting Palmer Sikelianos's awkward monophonic melodies composed later for an American production of *Prometheus Bound* with the textures, rhythms, and formal play of *Les Noces*.

82. *Pythian Games* [videorecording], produced by Eva and Angelos Sikelianos (Delphi, Greece, 1930), The New York Public Library of the Performing Arts, Dance Collection (*MGZIDVD 5-1758).

83. See Dimitris Damaskos, "The Uses of Antiquity in Photographs by Nelly: Imported Modernism and Home-Grown Ancestor Worship in Inter-War Greece," in *A Singular Antiquity: Archaeology and Hellenic Identity in Twentieth-Century Greece*, ed. Dimitris Damaskos and Dimitris Plantzos (Athens: Mouseio Benaki, 2008), 321–336.

84. See Pantelis Michelakis, *Greek Tragedy on Screen* (Oxford and New York: Oxford University Press, 2013), 112–117; and Pantelis Michelakis, "Dancing with Prometheus: Performance and Spectacle in the 1920s," in *The Ancient Dancer in the Modern World: Responses to Greek and Roman Dance*, ed. Fiona Macintosh (Oxford and New York: Oxford University Press, 2010), 224–235.

85. Michelakis, *Greek Tragedy on Screen*, 115.

86. Ibid., 117; see also Albright, *Traces of Light*; and Frederick Naerebout, "'In Search of a Dead Rat': The Reception of Ancient Greek Dance in Late Nineteenth-Century Europe and America," in *The Ancient Dancer in the Modern World: Responses to Greek and Roman Dance*, ed. Fiona Macintosh (Oxford and New York: Oxford University Press, 2010), 39–56.

87. Christopher Pinney, "Introduction: 'How the Other Half . . . ,'" in *Photography's Other Histories*, ed. Christopher Pinney and Nicholas Peterson (Durham, NC, and London: Duke University Press, 2003), 6–7.

88. Robert Payne, *The Splendor of Greece* (New York: Harper, 1960), 102.

89. Ann Cooper Albright, "The Tanagra Effect: Wrapping the Modern Body in the Folds of Ancient Greece," in *The Ancient Dancer in the Modern World: Responses to Greek and Roman Dance*, ed. Fiona Macintosh (Oxford and New York: Oxford University Press, 2010), 71.

90. See Palmer Sikelianos, *Upward Panic*, 143–144.

91. Both Maria Tsouvala and Natlie Zervou highlighted the Delphic Festivals in their discussions of modern dance studies in Greece during the opening plenary panel for the 2015 Society of Dance History Scholars Conference in Athens, Greece, "The State of Dance Studies in Greece," on June 4, 2015.

92. See Marta E. Savigliano, *Tango and the Political Economy of Passion* (Boulder, CO, and Oxford: Westview Press, 1995).

93. Ann Cooper Albright, "On the Ground in Greece," *Choros International Dance Journal* 2 (Spring 2013): 128.

94. Ibid., 131.

95. Michael Scott, *Delphi and Olympia: The Spatial Politics of Panhellenism in the Archaic and Classical Periods* (Cambridge, UK, and New York: Cambridge University Press, 2010), 135; Guillaume Thibault and Jean-Luc Martinez, "La reconstitution de la colonne des danseuses a Delphes," in *Actes du colloque Virtual Retrospect 2007* (Bordeaux: Edition Ausonius, 2008), 231–238.

96. See Ioanna Tzartzani, "Embodying the Crisis: The Body as a Site of Resistance in Post-Bailout Greece," *Choros International Dance Journal* 2 (Spring 2014): 40–49.

Chapter 6

1. Susan Sontag, "Unguided Tour," *New Yorker*, October 31, 1977, 40.

2. Salomon Reinach was one of Théodore Reinach's older brothers (see chapters 2 and 4).

3. Now available in an expanded edition: Charles Rosen, *The Classical Style: Haydn, Mozart, Beethoven*, expanded ed. (New York and London: W.W. Norton, 1998).

4. Jeremy Denk, "Jeremy Denk Responds," *Musicology Now*, June 24, 2014, http://musicologynow.ams-net.org/2014/06/jeremy-denk-responds.html.

5. For Charles Rosen's unflinchingly critical review of Taruskin's *Oxford History of Western Music*, see Charles Rosen, "Western Music: The View from California," in *Freedom and the Arts: Essays on Music and Literature* (Cambridge, MA: Harvard University Press, 2012), 210–239. The review was originally published in the *New York Review of Books*. See Charles Rosen, "From the Troubadours to Frank Sinatra," Part II, *New York Review of Books* 53, no. 4 (March 9, 2006). Taruskin naturally responded with a similarly unflinchingly critical review of Rosen. See Richard Taruskin, "Afterword: *Nicht blubefleckt?*," *Journal of Musicology* 26, no. 2 (2009): 274–284.

6. Kristi Brown-Montesano, "*The Classical Style*, of Sorts," *Musicology Now*, June 20, 2014, http://musicologynow.ams-net.org/2014/06/the-classical-style-of-sorts.html.

7. Steven Stucky, *The Classical Style: An Opera (of Sorts)*, libretto by Jeremy Denk, inspired by the book by Charles Rosen ([King of Prussia, PA]: Theodore Presser Company, [2015]), 189–191; quoting Rosen, *The Classical Style*, 460.

8. Anthony Tommasini, "We're Nothing but Busts, Mozart. Busts! 'The Classical Style,' an Opera Buffa at Zankel Hall," *New York Times*, December 5, 2014, http://www.nytimes.com/2014/12/06/arts/music/the-classical-style-an-opera-buffa-at-zankel-hall.html.

9. See Sara Ahmed, *Living a Feminist Life* (Durham, NC: Duke University Press, 2017); and William Cheng, *Just Vibrations: The Purpose of Sounding Good* (Ann Arbor: University of Michigan Press, 2016). Media depictions of the sexy scholar (e.g., George Lucas's Indiana Jones or Dan Brown's Robert Langdon, from *The Da Vinci Code*) are sexy because they are doers, adventurers, despite the fact (not because) they can both read ancient Aramaic.

10. Stucky, *Classical Style: An Opera (of Sorts)*, 94–95.

11. Suzanne Cusick, "On a Lesbian Relationship with Music: A Serious Effort Not to Think Straight," in *Queering the Pitch*, ed. Philip Brett, Gary Thomas, and Elizabeth Wood (New York and London: Routledge, 1994), 78.

12. Suzanne Cusick, "Let's Face the Music and Dance (or, Challenges to Contemporary Musicology)," in *AMS at 75*, ed. Jane Bernstein (Brunswick, ME: American Musicological Society, 2011), 27.

13. Ibid., 32.

14. Suzanne Cusick, "Musicology, Torture, Repair," *Radical Musicology* 3 (2008), par. 14, http://www.radical-musicology.org.uk/2008/Cusick.htm.

15. Cheng, *Just Vibrations*, 46.

16. There are only a few practical guides. James Grier's *The Critical Editing of Music*, for example, covers the ins and outs of transcribing and editing musical sources for the scholar of music. James Grier, *The Critical Editing of Music: History, Method, and Practice* (Cambridge, UK, and New York: Cambridge University Press, 1996). Graduate programs in musicology are starting to remedy this trend. In spring 2018 Glenda Goodman offered a seminar at the University of Pennsylvania titled "Sounding Archives."

17. Deidre Shauna Lynch, *Loving Literature: A Cultural History* (Chicago and London: University of Chicago Press, 2015).

18. See Rosen, "Western Music," 210–239.

19. Richard Taruskin, *Oxford History of Western Music*, 6 vols. (Oxford: Oxford University Press, 2005), 1:xvii.

20. Taruskin, "Afterword: *Nicht blubefleckt?*," 278–279.

21. For example, see Philip V. Bohlman, "Musicology as a Political Act," *Journal of Musicology* 11, no. 4 (Autumn 1993): 411–436; Susan McClary, *Feminine Endings: Music, Gender, and Sexuality* (Minneapolis: University of Minnesota Press, 1991); Ruth A. Solie, "What Do Feminists Want? A Reply to Pieter van den Toorn," *Journal of Musicology* 9 (1991): 399–410; and Pieter Van den Toorn, "Politics, Feminism, and Contemporary Music Theory," *Journal of Musicology* 9 (1991): 275–299. See also James Currie, *Music and the Politics of Negation* (Bloomington: Indiana University Press, 2012); Cusick, "Musicology, Torture, Repair"; and Cheng, *Just Vibrations*.

22. Rosen, "Western Music,", 238.

23. Elizabeth Le Guin, *Boccherini's Body: An Essay in Carnal Musicology* (Berkeley, Los Angeles, and London: University of California Press, 2006), 14.

24. Ibid., 234–253.

25. Elizabeth Freeman, *Time Binds: Queer Temporalities, Queer Histories* (Durham, NC, and London: Duke University Press, 2010), 95.

26. Ibid., 95–96.

27. See Carolyn Dinshaw, *Getting Medieval, Sexualities and Communities, Pre- and Postmodern* (Durham, NC: Duke University Press, 1999); and Ari Friedlander, "Desiring History and Historicizing Desire," *Journal for Early Modern Cultural Studies* 16, no. 2 (Spring 2016): 1–20.

28. Freeman, *Time Binds*, 100.

29. Arlette Farge, *The Allure of the Archives* [*Le Goût de l'archive*, 1989], trans. Thomas Scott-Railton (New Haven, CT, and London: Yale University Press, 2013), 11.

30. Sappho, *Sappho: A New Translation*, trans. Diane J. Raynor and André Lardinois (Cambridge, UK, and New York: Cambridge University Press, 2014), 72.

31. Eva Palmer Sikelianos, *Upward Panic: The Autobiography of Eva Palmer-Sikelianos*, ed. John P. Anton (Chur, Switzerland, and Philadelphia: Harwood, 1993), 37–38.

32. He took a particular interest in Liane de Pougy, the celebrated dancer, courtesan, and lover of Barney around 1900, whose notoriety is illustrated by a confession she made to a priest: "Father, I have lived very freely. Except for murder and robbery I've done everything." [Mon père j'ai vécu très librement. Sauf tuer et voler, j'ai tout fait.] Liane de Pougy, *Mes Cahiers bleus* (Paris: Plon, 1977), 27.

33. [Vous ne voulez pas écrire sur elle [Pauline Tarn/Renée Vivien] ce que je serais affligé de lire. D'abord, mon culte pour elle n'est pas une idolâtrie; je la juge sévèrement quand je songe à sa santé ruinée, à sa vie gâchée. Quittée par Flossie [Natalie Clifford Barney], elle devait rester *veuve* ou se marier; ses années *à passantes* sont lamentables. En second lieu, rien de ce qui concerne un si grand génie n'est indifférent, pas même ses humiliations consenties. Mais ne conçois que vous ne désiriez pas vider la corne de vos souvenirs entre mes mains. Ecrivez donc, sur elle aussi, quelques pages que je ne lirai pas. Racontez votre brouille et ses causes; fouillez votre mémoire; dites tous. Mais ne dites que ce que vous savez vous-même; les bons juges ne retiennent pas le *hearsay*.] Salomon Reinach to Liane de Pougy, January 19, 1920, in Max Jacob and Salomon Reinach, *Lettres à Liane de Pougy* (Paris: Plon, 1980), 164.

34. See Salomon Reinach, *Bibliographie de Salomon Reinach* (Paris: Société d'Édition Les Belles-Lettres, 1936).

35. One early communication was a picture postcard of the Cincinnati Art Museum in Eden Park, the city where Barney spent much of her childhood. On the back he wrote in English: "A queer art museum?" Undated letter from Salomon Reinach to Natalie Clifford Barney, Bibliothèque littéraire Jacques Doucet (hereafter BLJD), Fonds Natalie Clifford Barney, NCB C 1615. "Queer" had been in use to describe homosexuals since at least the 1890s. See "queer, n.2," in *Oxford English Dictionary Online*, Oxford University Press, March 2017, http://www.oed.com/view/Entry/156235.

36. He then shares a personal story from when he was twenty and a university student. He tells her that he only has a little experience with what he calls "the treasure," a euphemism for same-sex desire, and tells her how two comrades he was interested in were "more interested in each other." When the couple broke up he comforted one of the heartbroken boys with lines from Racine. BLJD, NCB C 1624.

37. BLJD, NCB C 1640.

38. Sappho frag. 134: μνάσασθαί τινά φαιμι καὶ ἔτερον ἀμμέων/ζὰ . . . ἐλεξάμαν ὄναρ Κυπρογενηα. Sappho, *If Not, Winter: Fragments of Sappho*, trans. Anne Carson (New York: Alfred A. Knopf, 2002), 103.

39. BLJD, NCB C 1641. Barney was actually born in Dayton, Ohio. Her family moved to Cincinnati when she was in her teens.

40. Sappho frag. 49 reads: "I loved you, Atthis, once long ago/a little child you seemed to me and graceless." Sappho, *If Not, Winter*, 103.

41. BLJD, NCB C 1641.

42. [Le cœur d'un savant est un puits ténébreux où sont engloutis bien des sentiments avortés qui remontent à la surface en guise d'arguments. Ces concepts qu'il croit atteindre par raissonement témoignent d'instincts, éveillés à travers ce même esprit qui voulut les condamner au néant. Et certes, je n'ai pas résisté à toute

croyance pour croire à l'infaillibilité de l'esprit humain quelque savant qu'il soit.] Natalie Clifford Barney, *L'Aventures de l'esprit* (Paris: Éditions Émile-Paul Frères, 1929), 251–252; and Natalie Clifford Barney, *Adventures of the Mind* [*L'Aventures d'esprit*, 1929], trans. John Spalding Gatton (New York and London: New York University Press, 1992), 184.

43. [Avidité qu'il cache aussi mal qu'il la satisfait en baisant le menu péché de leurs mains. Et n'est-ce pas par une jalousie d'amoureux qu'il tâche d'amasser des reliques et de les défendre avec tant d'âpreté, jusqu'au moment où il est sûr de ne plus souffrir de leur exploitation, jusqu'à l'an "deux mille."] Barney, *L'Aventures de l'esprit*, 252; and Barney, *Adventures of the Mind*, 184–185.

44. [Et c'est également à l'an 2000 qu'il destine les lettres d'amour que ses contemporaines voudront confier à son musée secret. Si je me sentais capable de faire moi-même à présent ce livre qui me concerne sur Renée Vivien, me prêterait-il seulement les notes et documents qu'il a collectionnés sur elle? Certaines lettres que Renée Vivien m'écrivit et que j'avais permis à Salomon Reinach de relever me sont revenues, mais sur leur fronton gravé d'une guirlande de violettes, il avait inscrit, en lettres minuscules il est vrai, mais perceptibles, au coin de chaque page: *copié*. Rien ne sort indemne des mains de la science!] Barney, *L'Aventures de l'esprit*, 252; and Barney, *Adventures of the Mind*, 185.

45. In a series of letters written many years after Salomon Reinach's death, Barney used her own manipulative methods to shape the never-completed biographical project begun by comparative literature scholar Renée Lang (1902–2003). Throughout the 1950s Barney tried to manipulate Lang with flattery and flirtation in attempts to control her legacy. Ultimately, Lang broke Barney's confidence, and without her support the biographical project fell apart. Their correspondence is housed at the University of Wisconsin–Madison. See Faith B. Miracle, "Lang, Renée (A Farewell)," *Milwaukee Journal Sentinel*, June 23, 2003; and the Barney/Lang correspondence in the Renée B. Lang Collection, Department of Special Collections, Memorial Library, University of Wisconsin–Madison.

46. Barney preferred to craft her own narrative, her own life story, through a number of memoirs: *Je me souviens* (1910), *Pensées d'une Amazone* (1920), *Aventures de l'Esprit* (1929), *Nouvelles Pensées de l'Amazone* (1939), *Souvenirs Indiscrets* (1960), and the unpublished "Nos secrètes amours ou L'Amant féminin ou Mémoires secrets" (ca. 1950)

47. Cusick, "Let's Face the Music and Dance," 32.

48. See William H. Stiebing Jr., *Uncovering the Past: A History of Archaeology* (New York and Oxford: Oxford University Press, 1993), 131.

49. Schliemann did the same thing in his discoveries at Troy. See Heinrich Schliemann, *Myth, Scandal, and History: The Heinrich Schliemann Controversy and a First Edition of the Mycenaean Diary*, ed. William Calder and David Traill (Detroit: Wayne State University Press, 1986); see also the special issue of *Archaeology* dedicated to Schliemann's forgeries: Spencer P. M. Harrington, "Behind the Mask of Agamemnon," *Archaeology* 52, no. 4 (July/August 1999): 51–59.

50. See Stiebing, *Uncovering the Past*, 138–139, 78–82, 99, and 106–107.

51. [Rechercher ces inscriptions et les photographier avec soin serait une tâche bien séduisante pour un voyageur de bonne volonté; il n'aurait pas besoin, comme l'épigraphiste, d'une connaissance même sommaire des langues classiques et d'une

préparation assez fastidieuse; l'habitude seule de la photographie sur papier sensible le mettrait en mesure de rendre les plus grands services et de combler une véritable lacune dans notre connaissance, si incomplète encore, des monuments figures de l'antiquité.] Salomon Reinach, *Conseils aux Voyageurs archéologues en Grèce et dans l'Orient hellénique* (Paris: Ernest Leroux, 1886), 74–75.

52. See Carlo Maurilio Lerici, "How to Steal Antiquities," in *Hand on the Past: Pioneer Archaeologists Tell Their Own Story*, ed. C. W. Ceram (New York: Knopf, 1966).

53. Stiebing, *Uncovering the Past*, 51–54.

54. [L'exportation des œuvres d'art antiques étant interdite par les lois grecques et turques, nous ne conseillons pas au voyageur d'acheter les antiquités qu'on lui offrirait. S'il a la chance de trouver une *Venus de Milo*, le courage et l'habileté de la transporter en lieu sûr, nous lui adresserons tous nos compliments; mais les présents conseils n'ont pas la prétention d'enseigner ou d'encourager la contrebande.] Reinach, *Conseils aux Voyageurs archéologues*, 85.

55. His instructions in all their illicit detail are reminiscent of the infamous prostitution guidebooks like the 1883 *The Pretty Girls of Paris*. See *The Pretty Women of Paris: Their Names and Addresses, Qualities and Faults, Being a Complete Directory or Guide to Pleasure for Visitors to the Gay City* [1883] (Ware: Wordsworth Editions, 1996); see also Willy's guide to homosexual life in Paris: Willy [Henry Gauthier-Villars], *The Third Sex* [1927], trans. and with an introduction and notes by Lawrence R. Schehr (Urbana and Chicago: University of Illinois Press, 2007).

56. See chapter 4. [Que voulez-vous, je ne suis qu'une interprète!... Je n'ai ni inventé, ni créé l'art grec.] Georges Talmont [and Madame Mariquita], "Comment Madame Mariquita monte un ballet," *Comœdia Illustré* 1, no. 1 (December 15, 1908): 23.

57. However, some critics did not appreciate the mixture of Gluck's music with "ancient" dances, seeing it as completely inauthentic. Reviewing Mariquita's dances for Gluck's ballets from his eighteenth-century "Greek" operas, Georges Servières criticized her work as "highly objectionable: however ingenious. [. . .] Gluck could never have meant his ballets to be serious restorations of Greek dances." [Cette tentative est fort critiquable: si ingénieuse que puisse être la chorégraphie inventée par Mme Mariquita, elle constitue une transposition d'époque qui viole, selon moi, les intentions du compositeur. Jamais dans ses ballets, Gluck n'a pu avoir en vue une reconstitution sérieuse des danses grecques.] Georges Servières, "Les Ballets de Gluck," *Musica* 8, no. 77 (February 1909): 56–57.

58. [On s'enfonce dans les textes ardus, on "potasse" les gravures qui les commentent; on "pioche" la mythologie. On questionne les amis bacheliers.] Régina Badet, "Danses grecques & danses modernes," *Musica* 7, no. 75 (Christmas Supplement, December 1908): 242.

59. [Et, la première répétition passée, tandis que la danseuse qui s'en moque s'écrie: "Comment qu'on dit *la barbe*, en grec?" la danseuse qui ne s'en moque pas, la consciencieuse, l'ambitieuse, court acheter les livres révélateurs. C'est ainsi qu'on peut voir—tableau bien parisien—telle jolie silhouette de petite femme passer, pressée, sur le boulevard, en tenant précieusement M. Salomon Reinach—imprimé bien entendu.] Badet, "Danses grecques & danses modernes," 242.

60. Ibid., 242.

61. See Marc Slobin, "Ethical Issues," in *Ethnomusicology: An Introduction*, ed. Helen Myers (New York and London: W. W. Norton and Company, 1992), 329–336.

62. Susan Sontag, *On Photography* (New York: Farrar, Straus and Giroux, 1977), 14.

63. John Caldwell, "Toccata," in *Oxford Music Online: Grove Music Online*, Oxford University Press, accessed June 6, 2017 http://www.oxfordmusiconline.com/subscriber/article/grove/music/28035.

64. See Carolyn Dinshaw's concept of "touch," a "queer historical impulse" that makes connections across time. Dinshaw, *Getting Medieval*, 1.

65. Carolyn Abbate, "Sound Object Lessons," *Journal of the American Musicological Society* 69, no. 3 (Fall 2016): 803, citing Vladimir Jankélévitch, *Music and the Ineffable* [*La Musique et l'Ineffable*], translated by Carolyn Abbate (Princeton: Princeton University Press, [1961] 2003), 27.

66. Ibid., 803.

67. Eve Kosofsky Sedgwick, *Touching Feeling: Affect, Pedagogy, Performativity* (Durham, NC, and London: Duke University Press, 2003), 146.

68. Ibid., 140–141.

69. Robyn Wiegman, "The Times We're In: Queer Feminist Criticism and the Reparative 'Turn,'" *Feminist Theory* 15, no. 1 (2014): 7.

70. Eve Kosofsky Sedgwick, "Paranoid Reading and Reparative Reading; or, You're So Paranoid, You Probably Think This Introduction Is About You," in *Novel Gazing: Queer Readings in Fiction*, ed. Eve Kosofsky Sedgwick (Durham, NC: Duke University Press, 1997), 35.

71. Wiegman, "The Times We're In," 7.

72. Citing Melanie Klein (1946), Sedgwick writes, "Among Klein's names for the reparative process is love." Sedgwick, *Touching Feeling*, 128.

73. Cusick, "Musicology, Torture, Repair," par. 20.

74. Cheng, *Just Vibrations*, 98.

75. Perhaps my criticism of Emmanuel's *Salamine* is tainted by my lack of a physical connection to him. I never had an opportunity to walk through his house, see his grave, or touch his photographs.

76. Plato, *Plato in Twelve Volumes*, trans. Harold N. Fowler (Cambridge, MA: Harvard University Press; London: William Heinemann Ltd., 1925), 9:206e.

BIBLIOGRAPHY

Archival Collections

Alice Pike Barney Papers, Smithsonian Institution Archives, Accession 96-153 and 96-154, Washington, DC.

Bibliothèque littéraire Jacques Doucet, Paris, France. (BLJD)

Eva Palmer Sikelianos Archive, Museum Benaki, Delta House, Kifisia, Greece

The New York Public Library for the Performing Arts, Jerome Robbins Dance Collection, New York City, NY.

Renée B. Lang Collection, Department of Special Collections, Memorial Library, University of Wisconsin–Madison, Madison, WI.

Books, Articles, and Scores

Abbate, Carolyn. "Music—Drastic or Gnostic?" *Critical Inquiry* 30 (Spring 2004): 505–536.

———. "Outside the Tomb." Chap. 5 in *In Search of Opera*. Princeton, NJ, and Oxford: Princeton University Press, 2001.

———. "Sound Object Lessons." *Journal of the American Musicological Society* 69, no. 3 (Fall 2016): 793–829.

Abel, Sam. *Opera in the Flesh: Sexuality in Operatic Performance*. Boulder, CO: Westview Press, 1996.

Aeschylus. *Hoi tragōdies tou Aischylou*. [Translated by] Ionnes Gryparō. Athens: Delphikes Heortes, 1930.

Agnew, Vanessa. "Introduction: What Is Reenactment?" *Criticism* 46, no. 3 (Summer 2004): 327–339.

Ahmed, Sara. *Living a Feminist Life*. Durham, NC: Duke University Press, 2017.

Ahrendt, Rebekah, and David van der Linden. "The Postmasters' Piggy Bank: Experiencing the Accidental Archive." *French Historical Studies* 40, no. 2 (April 2017): 189–213.

Aird, Michael. "Growing Up with Aborigines." In *Photography's Other Histories*, edited by Christopher Pinney and Nicholas Peterson, 23–39. Durham, NC, and London: Duke University Press, 2003.

Albright, Ann Cooper. "On the Ground in Greece." *Choros: International Dance Journal* 2 (Spring 2013): 128–132.

———. "The Tanagra Effect: Wrapping the Modern Body in the Folds of Ancient Greece." In *The Ancient Dancer in the Modern World: Responses to Greek and Roman Dance*, edited by Fiona Macintosh, 57–76. Oxford and New York: Oxford University Press, 2010.

———. *Traces of Light: Absence and Presence in the Work of Loïe Fuller*. Middletown, CT: Wesleyan University Press, 2007.

Anton, John P. Introduction to *Upward Panic: The Autobiography of Eva Palmer-Sikelianos*. Edited with an introduction by John P. Anton. Chur, Switzerland, and Philadelphia: Harwood Academic Publishers, 1993.

Arnold, Astrid. *Villa Kérylos: Das Wohnhaus als Antikenkonstruktion*. München: Bierling & Brinkmann, 2003.

Auslander, Philip. *Liveness: Performance in a Mediatized Culture* [1999]. 2nd ed. New York: Routledge, 2008.

Badet, Régina. "Danses Grecques & Danses Modernes." *Musica* 7, no. 75 (Christmas issue, December 1908): 242.

Barnes, Djuna. *Ladies Almanack: Showing Their Signs and Their Tides, Their Moons and Their Changes, the Seasons as It Is with Them, Their Eclipses and Equinoxes, as Well as a Full Record or Diurnal and Nocturnal Distempers* [1928]. Elmwood, IL: Dalkey Archive Press, 1992.

Barney, Natalie Clifford. *Actes et Entrt'actes*. Paris: Sansot, 1910.

———. *Adventures of the Mind* [*Aventures de l'esprit*, 1929]. Translated with annotations by John Spalding Gatton. New York and London: New York University Press, 1992.

———. *L'Aventures de l'esprit*. Paris: Éditions Émile-Paul Frères, 1929.

———. *Éparpillements*. Paris: E. Sansot, 1910.

———. "Nos Secretes Amours ou L'Amant Feminin ou Memires Secrets." Unpublished typescript with author's autograph corrections, October 31, 1950.

———. *Un panier de framboises*. Edited by Jean Chalon. Paris: Mercure, 1979.

———. *A Perilous Advantage: The Best of Natalie Clifford Barney*. Edited and translated by Anna Livia, with an introduction by Karla Jay. Norwich, VT: New Victoria Publishers, 1992.

———. *Quelques Potraits-Sonnets de Femmes*. Paris: Ollendorf, 1900.

———. *Women Lovers, or The Third Woman*. Edited and translated by Chelsea Ray. Madison: University of Wisconsin Press, 2016.

Barrett, Rusty. *From Drag Queens to Leathermen: Language, Gender, and Gay Male Subcultures*. Oxford and New York: Oxford University Press, 2017.

Barthes, Roland. *Camera Lucida: Reflections on Photography* [1980]. Translated by Richard Howard. New York: Hill and Wang, 1982.

Bélis, Annie. "Les deux hymnes delphiques à Apollon." In *Corpus des inscriptions de Delphes* III. Paris: Boccard, 1992.

Bennett, Tony. *The Birth of the Museum: History, Theory, Politics*. London and New York: Routledge, 1995.

Benoit, Fernand. "La constitution du Musée Borély et les fraudes des fouilles de Marseille." *Provence historique* 6 (1956): 5–22.

Berg, Ingrid. "Dumps and Ditches: Prisms of Archaeological Practice at Kalaureia in Greece." In *Making Cultural History: New Perspectives on Western Heritage*, edited by Y. Anna Källén, 173–183. Lund: Sweden: Nordic Academic Press, 2013.

Berger, Karol. "Musicology According to Don Giovanni, or: Should We Get Drastic?" *Journal of Musicology* 22 (Summer 2005): 490–501.

Bergeron, Katherine. *Decadent Enchantments: The Revival of Gregorian Chant at Solesmes*. Berkeley, Los Angeles, and London: University of California Press, 1998.

———. "Mélisande's Hair, or the Trouble in Allemonde: A Postmodern Allegory at the Opéra-Comique." In *Siren Songs: Representations of Gender and Sexuality in Opera*, edited by Mary Ann Smart, 160–185. Princeton, NJ, and Oxford: Princeton University Press, 2000.

Blackmer, Corinne E., and Patricia Juliana Smith, eds. *En Travesti: Women, Gender Subversion, Opera*. New York: Columbia University Press, 1995.

Blair, Karen J. *The Torchbearers: Women and Their Amateur Arts Associations in America, 1890–1930*. Bloomington: Indiana University Press, 1994.

Boehringer, Sandra. "Female Homoeroticism." In *A Companion to Greek and Roman Sexualities*, edited by Thomas K. Hubbard, 154–167. Chichester, UK: Wiley Blackwell, 2014.

Bohlman, Philip V. "Musicology as a Political Act." *Journal of Musicology* 11, no. 4 (Autumn 1993): 411–436.

Bordelon, Suzanne. "Embodied *Ethos* and Rhetorical Accretion: Genevieve Stebbins and the *Delsarte System of Expression*." *Rhetoric Society Quarterly* 46, no. 2 (2016): 105–130.

Braun, Marta. *Picturing Time: The Work of Étienne-Jules Marey (1830–1904)*. Chicago and London: University of Chicago Press, 1992.

Brett, Philip, Gary C. Thomas, and Elizabeth Wood, eds. *Queering the Pitch: The New Gay and Lesbian Musicology*. New York and London: Routledge, 1994.

Brown-Montesano, Kristi. "*The Classical Style*, of Sorts." *Musicology Now*, June 20, 2014. http://musicologynow.ams-net.org/2014/06/the-classical-style-of-sorts.html.

Burton, Antoinette, ed. *Archive Stories: Facts, Fictions, and the Writing of History*. Durham, NC, and London: Duke University Press, 2005.

Butt, John. *Playing with History: The Historical Approach to Musical Performance*. Cambridge, UK, and New York: Cambridge University Press, 2002.

Caballero, Carlo. *Fauré and French Musical Aesthetics*. Cambridge, UK, and New York: Cambridge University Press, 2001.

Castle, Terry. "In Praise of Brigitte Fassbaender: Reflections on Diva-Worship." In *En Travesti: Women, Gender Subversion, Opera*, edited by Corinne E. Blackmer and Patricia Juliana Smith, 20–58. New York: Columbia University Press, 1995.

Chalon, Jean. *Portrait of a Seductress: The World of Natalie Barney*. Translated by Carol Barko. New York: Crown, 1979.

Cheng, William. *Just Vibrations: The Purpose of Sounding Good*. Ann Arbor: University of Michigan Press, 2016.

———. "Pleasure's Discontents." In "Colloquy: Music and Sexuality." *Journal of the American Musicological Society* 66, no. 3 (Fall 2013): 841–844.

Colette. *Mes apprentissages, Trois Six Neuf, Discours de Réception à l'Académie Royale Belge*. Œuvres Complètes. Genève: Éditions de Crémille, 1970.

Combe, Dom Pierre. *Historire de la restauration du chant grégorien d'après des documents inédits.* Solesmes: Abbaye de Solesmes, 1969.

Corbier, Christophe. "Continuité, tradition, nouveauté: Essai sur l'esthétique de Maurice Emmanuel." In *Tradition et innovation en histoire de l'art,* edited by Jean-René Gaborit, 201–212. Grenoble: Collection Actes des Congrès des Sociétés historiques et scientifiques [CD-ROM], 2006.

———. *Maurice Emmanuel.* Paris: bleu nuit, 2007.

Corbin, Alain. *Women for Hire: Prostitution and Sexuality in France after 1850* [*Les filles de noce: Misère sexuelle et prostitution aux 19e et 20e siècles,* 1978]. Translated by Alan Sheridan. Cambridge, MA: Harvard University Press, 1990.

Cossart, Michel de. *Ida Rubinstein (1885–1960): A Theatrical Life.* Liverpool, UK: Liverpool University Press, 1987.

Coye, Noël, and Béatrice Vigié. "Three-Dimensional Archives: The Augier Models of the Museum of Archaeology (Marseilles, France)." *Complutum* 24, no. 2 (2013): 203–212.

Currie, James. *Music and the Politics of Negation.* Bloomington: Indiana University Press, 2012.

Cusick, Suzanne. "Let's Face the Music and Dance (or, Challenges to Contemporary Musicology)." In *AMS at 75,* edited by Jane Bernstein, 25–32. Brunswick, ME: American Musicological Society, 2011.

———. "Musicology, Torture, Repair." *Radical Musicology* 3 (2008), http://www. radical- musicology.org.uk/2008/Cusick.htm.

———. "On a Lesbian Relationship with Music: A Serious Effort Not to Think Straight." In *Queering the Pitch: The New Gay and Lesbian Musicology,* edited by Philip Brett, Elizabeth Wood, and Gary C. Thomas, 67–84. New York: Routledge, 1994.

Daley, Mike. "Patti Smith's *Gloria*: Intertextual Play in a Rock Vocal Performance." *Popular Music* 16, no. 3 (October 1997): 235–253.

Damaskos, Dimitris. "The Uses of Antiquity in Photographs by Nelly: Imported Modernism and Home-Grown Ancestor Worship in Inter-War Greece." In *A Singular Antiquity: Archaeology and Hellenic Identity in Twentieth-Century Greece,* edited by Dimitris Damaskos and Dimitris Plantzos, 321–336. Athens: Mouseio Benaki, 2008.

Daudet, Alphonse. *Sapho: Mœurs Parisiennes.* Paris: G. Charpentier, 1884.

Davis, Natalie Zemon. "Foreword." In Arlette Farge. *The Allure of the Archives* [*Le Goût de l'archive,* 1989]. Translated by Thomas Scott-Railton. Foreword by Natalie Zemon Davis. New Haven, CT, and London: Yale University Press, 2013.

Dean, Carolyn J. *The Frail Social Body: Pornography, Homosexuality, and Other Fantasies in Interwar France.* Berkeley and Los Angeles: University of California Press, 2000.

Decter, Jacqueline. *Nicholas Roerich: The Life and Art of a Russian Master.* Rochester, VT: Park Street Press, 1989.

DeJean, Joan. *Fictions of Sappho, 1546–1937.* Chicago: University of Chicago Press, 1989.

Denk, Jeremy. "Jeremy Denk Responds." *Musicology Now,* June 24, 2014. http:// musicologynow.ams-net.org/2014/06/jeremy-denk-responds.html.

Derfler, Leslie. *The Dreyfus Affair.* Westport, CT: Greenwood Press, 2002.

Derrida, Jacques. *Archive Fever: A Freudian Impression*. Translated by Eric Prenowitz. Chicago: University of Chicago Press, 1995.

Dinshaw, Carolyn. *Getting Medieval, Sexualities and Communities, Pre- and Postmodern*. Durham, NC: Duke University Press, 1999.

Doane, Mary Ann. "Temporality, Storage, Legibility: Freud, Marey, and the Cinema." *Critical Inquiry* 22, no. 2 (Winter 1996): 313–343.

Dorf, Samuel N. "Eroticizing Antiquity: Madame Mariquita, Régina Badet and the Dance of the Exotic Greeks from Stage to Popular Press." In *Opera, Exoticism and Visual Culture*, edited by Hyunseon Lee and Naomi Segal, 73–92. Bern, Oxford, and New York: Peter Lang, 2015.

———. "Eva Palmer-Sikelianos Dances Aeschylus: The Politics of Historical Reenactment When Staging the Rites of the Past." *Choros: International Dance Journal* 5 (Spring 2016): 1–11.

———. "Seeing Sappho in Paris: Operatic and Choreographic Adaptations of Sapphic Lives and Myths." *Music and Art: International Journal for Music Iconography* 38 (2009): 289–308.

Duchesneau, Michel. "French Music Criticism and Musicology at the Turn of the Twentieth- Century: New Journals, New Networks." *Nineteenth-Century Music Review* 14 (2017): 9–32.

Duncan, Isadora. "The Dance of the Future [1902 or 1903, 1909]." In *The Art of the Dance*, edited and introduced by Sheldon Cheney, 54–63. New York: Theatre Arts, Inc., 1928.

———. *My Life*. New York: Boni and Liveright, 1927.

Dyer, Richard. "Judy Garland and Gay Men." In *Heavenly Bodies: Films Stars and Society*. 2nd ed. London and New York: Routledge, 2004.

Edelman, Lee. *No Future: Queer Theory and the Death Drive*. Durham, NC: Duke University Press, 2004.

Emmanuel, Maurice. *The Antique Greek Dance after Sculptured and Painted Figures*. Translated by Harriet Jean Beauley. New York and London: John Lane Company, 1916.

———. *La Danse grecque antique d'après les monuments figures*. Paris: Hachette, 1896.

———. *La Danse grecque antique d'après les monuments figures; Traité de la musique grecque antique; Le Rythme d'Euripide à Debussy*. Genève: Slatkine Reprints, 1984.

———. *Histoire de la langue musicale*. Paris: Henri Laurens, 1911.

———. *Pelléas et Mélisande de Claude Debussy: Étude et analyse*. Paris: Mellottée, 1926.

———. "Le 'Rythme et la Musique' (lettre ouverte)." *Le Rythme, Nouvelles de l'Institut Jacques Dalcroze* 12 (February 1924): 21–23.

———. *Le Rythme d'Euripide à Debussy*. Geneva: Congrès du rythme, 1926.

———. *Salamine, tragédie lyrique en trois actes d'après les "Perses" d'Eschyle*. Paris: Choudens, 1929.

Epstein, Louis K. "Toward a Theory of Patronage: Funding for Music Composition in France, 1918–1939." PhD diss., Harvard University, 2013.

Evans, Christopher. "Model Excavations: 'Performance' and the Three-Dimensional Display of Knowledge." In *Archives, Ancestors, Practices: Archaeology in the Light of Its History*, edited by Nathan Schlanger and Jarl Nordbladh, 147–161. New York and Oxford: Berghahn Books, 2008.

Fahey, Joseph. "Quiet Victory: The Professional Identity American Women Forged Through Delsartism." In "Essays on François Delsarte," edited by Nancy Lee Chalfa Ruyter. Special issue, *Mime Journal* 23 (2004/2005): 43–84.

Falcone, Francesca. "Nicola Guerra maître de ballet all'Opéra di Parigi: Gli anni 1927– 1929." *Chorégraphie* 12, no. 6 (1998): 39–78.

———. "Nicola Guerra (1865–1942): Un maestro italiano dimenticato." November 30, 2010. http://www.augustevestris.fr/spip.php?article198.

Farfan, Penny. *Performing Queer Modernism*. New York: Oxford University Press, 2017.

Farge, Arlette. *The Allure of the Archives* [*Le Goût de l'archive*, 1989]. Translated by Thomas Scott-Railton. Foreword by Natalie Zemon Davis. New Haven, CT, and London: Yale University Press, 2013.

Fauser, Annegret. "Visual Pleasures—Musical Signs: Dance at the Paris Opéra." *South Atlantic Quarterly* 104, no. 1 (Winter 2005): 99–121.

Fosler-Lussier, Danielle, and Eric Fosler-Lussier. "Database of Cultural Presentations: Accompaniment to *Music and America's Cold War Diplomacy*." Version 1.1. Last modified April 1, 2015. http://musicdiplomacy.org/database. html.

Foucault, Michel. *The Archeology of Knowledge and the Discourse of Language*. Translated by A. M. Sheridan Smith. New York: Pantheon Books, 1972 [1969, 1971].

Freeman, Elizabeth. "Deep Lez: Temporal Drag and the Specters of Feminism." In *Time Binds: Queer Temporalities, Queer Histories*, 62–65. Durham, NC, and London: Duke University Press, 2010.

———. "Packing History, Count(er)ing Generations." *New Literary History* 31, no. 4 (Autumn 2000): 727–744.

———. *Time Binds: Queer Temporalities, Queer Histories*. Durham, NC, and London: Duke University Press, 2010.

Freshwater, Helen. "The Allure of the Archive." *Poetics Today* 24, no. 4 (2003): 729–758.

Friedlander, Ari. "Desiring History and Historicizing Desire." *Journal for Early Modern Cultural Studies* 16, no. 2 (Spring 2016): 1–20.

Fry, Roger. "M. Larionow and the Russian Ballet." *Burlington Magazine* (March 1919): 112–118.

Fuchs, Lívia. "Hungry: On Hungarian Dance." In *Europe Dancing: Perspectives on Theatre Dance and Cultural Identity*, edited by Andrée Grau and Stephanie Jordan, 79–99. London and New York: Routledge, 2000.

Fuller, Sophie. "'Devoted Attention:' Looking for Lesbian Musicians in *Fin-de-siècle* Britain." In *Queer Episodes in Music and Modern Identity*, edited by Sophie Fuller and Lloyd Whitsell, 79–101. Urbana and Chicago: University of Illinois Press, 2002.

Gallope, Michael, Brian Kane, Steven Rings, James Hepokoski, Judy Lochhead, Michael J. Puri, and James R. Currie. "Vladimir Jankélévitch's Philosophy of Music." *Journal of the American Musicological Society* 65, no. 1 (Spring 2012): 215–256.

Garafola, Lynn. *Diaghilev's Ballets Russes*. New York: Da Capo, 1989.

———. "The Enigma of Nicholas Roerich." *Dance Chronicle* 13, no. 3 (1990–1991): 401–412.

———. "Forgotten Interlude: Eurhythmic Dancers at the Paris Opéra." In *Legacies of Twentieth- Century Dance*, 85–106. Middletown, CT: Wesleyan University Press, 2005.

Gatti, Guido M. "The Academy of St. Cecilia and the Augusteo in Rome." *Musical Quarterly* 8 no. 3 (1922): 323–345.

Gibbons, William. *Building the Operatic Museum: Eighteenth-Century Opera in Fin-de-Siècle Paris*. Rochester, NY: University of Rochester Press, 2013.

Gilhuly, Kate. "Lesbians Are Not from Lesbos." In *Ancient Sex: New Essays*, edited by Ruby Bondell and Kirk Ormand, 143–176. Columbus: The Ohio State University, 2015.

Gossett, Philip. *Divas and Scholars: Performing Italian Opera*. Chicago and London: University of Chicago Press, 2006.

Goujon, Jean-Paul. *Tes blessures sont plus douces que leurs caresses: Vie de Renée Vivien*. Paris: Régine Deforges, 1986.

Grayson, David A. "The Opera: Genesis and Sources." In *Claude Debussy: Pelléas et Mélisande*, edited by Roger Nichols and Richard Langham Smith, 30–61. Cambridge Opera Handbooks. Cambridge, UK: Cambridge University Press, 1989.

Grier, James. *The Critical Editing of Music: History, Method, and Practice*. Cambridge, UK, and New York: Cambridge University Press, 1996.

Gutsche-Miller, Sarah. "Madame Mariquita, the French Fokine." In *Proceedings of the Society of Dance History Scholars, Thirty-Third Annual Conference, Stanford University, Palo Alto and San Francisco, CA*, 106–111. Riverside, CA: Society of Dance History Scholars, 2009.

———. "Pantomime-Ballet on the Music-Hall Stage: The Popularisation of Classical Ballet in Fin-de-Siècle Paris." PhD diss., McGill University, 2010.

———. *Parisian Music-Hall Ballet, 1871–1913*. Rochester, NY: University of Rochester Press, 2015.

Guttmann, Allen. *The Olympics: A History of the Modern Games*. Urbana: University of Illinois Press, 1992.

Haines, John. "Antiquarian Nostalgia and the Institutionalization of Early Music." In *The Oxford Handbook of Music Revival*, edited by Caroline Bithell and Juniper Hill, 73–93. New York and Oxford: Oxford University Press, 2014.

———. "Généalogies musicologiques: Aux origins d'une science de la musique vers 1900." *Acta Musicologica* 73, no. 1 (2001): 21–44.

Halberstam, Judith [Jack]. *In a Queer Time and Place: Transgender Bodies, Subcultural Lives*. New York: New York University Press, 2005.

Halperin, David M. *How to Be Gay*. Cambridge, MA, and London: Belknap Press of Harvard University Press, 2012.

———. "The Queen Is Not Dead." In *How to Be Gay*, 109–128. Cambridge, MA, and London: Belknap Press of Harvard University Press, 2012.

———. "Sex Before Sexuality: Pederasty, Politics, and Power in Classical Athens." In *Hidden from History: Reclaiming the Gay and Lesbian Past*, edited by Martin Duberman, Martha Vicinus, and George ChaunceyJr., 37–53. New York and London: Meridian, 1990.

Hamilakis, Yannis. *The Nation and Its Ruins: Antiquity, Archaeology, and National Imagination in Greece.* Oxford and New York: Oxford University Press, 2007, 291.

Haneman, Frederick T. "Weil, Henri." In *The Jewish Encyclopedia*, edited by Isidore Singer, 12:491–492. New York and London: Funk and Wagnalls Co., 1901–1906.

Harrington, Spencer P. M. "Behind the Mask of Agamemnon." *Archaeology* 52, no. 4 (July/August 1999): 51–59.

Henson, Karen. "Victor Capoul, Marguerite Olagnier's *Le Saïs*, and the Arousing of Female Desire." *Journal of the American Musicological Society* 52, no. 3 (Autumn 1999): 419–463.

Heuzey, Léon Alexandre. *Histoire du costume antique d'après des études sur le modèle vivant.* Paris: Édouard Champion, 1922.

Hibberd, Sarah, ed. *Melodramatic Voices: Understanding Music Drama.* Surrey, UK, and Burlington, VT: Ashgate, 2011.

Hodson, Millicent. "Nijinsky's Choreographic Method: Visual Sources from Roerich for *Le Sacre du printemps*." *Dance Research Journal* 18, no. 2 (Winter 1986–1987): 7–15.

Holsinger, Bruce W. *Music, Body, and Desire in Medieval Culture: Hildegard of Bingen to Chaucer.* Stanford, CA: Stanford University Press, 2001.

Homer. *The Odyssey.* Translated by Emily Wilson. New York: W. W. Norton, 2018.

Hunter, Richard, and Anna Uhlig. Editors. *Imagining Reperformance in Ancient Culture: Studies in the Traditions of Drama and Lyric.* Cambridge, UK, and New York: Cambridge University Press, 2017.

Hyde, Martha M. "Neoclassic and Anachronistic Impulses in Twentieth-Century Music." *Music Theory Spectrum* 18, no. 2 (Autumn 1996): 200–235.

Jacob, Max, and Salomon Reinach. *Lettres à Liane de Pougy.* Preface by Jean Chalon. Introduction by Paul Bernard. Paris: Plon, 1980.

Jamot, Paul. *Théodore Reinach (1860–1928).* Paris: Gazette des Beaux Arts, 1928.

Jardine, Lisa. *Temptation in the Archives: Essays in Golden Age Dutch Culture.* London: University of College London Press, 2015.

Jay, Karla. *The Amazon and the Page: Natalie Clifford Barney and Renée Vivien.* Bloomington: Indiana University Press, 1988.

Johnson, Graham. *Gabriel Fauré: The Songs and Their Poets.* With translations of the song texts by Richard Stokes. Farnham, UK, and Burlington, VT: Ashgate; London: Guildhall School of Music & Drama, 2009.

Kenyon, Nicholas, ed. *Authenticity and Early Music.* Oxford: Oxford University Press, 1988.

Kimber, Marian Wilson. *The Elocutionists: Women, Music, and the Spoken Word.* Urbana, Chicago, and Springfield: University of Illinois Press, 2017.

———. "In a Woman's Voice: Musical Recitation and the Feminization of American Melodrama." In *Melodramatic Voices: Understanding Music Drama*, edited by Sarah Hibberd, 61–82. Surrey, UK, and Burlington, VT: Ashgate, 2011.

———. "The Peerless Reciter: Reconstructing the Lost Art of Elocution with Music." In *Performance Practice: Issues and Approaches*, edited by Timothy D. Watkins, 202–223. Ann Arbor, MI: Steglein Publishing, 2009.

Kivy, Peter. *Authenticities: Philosophical Reflections on Musical Performance.* Ithaca, NY, and London: Cornell University Press, 1995.

Kling, Jean L. *Alice Pike Barney: Her Life and Art*. Introduced by Wanda M. Corn. Washington, DC: National Museum of American Art and Smithsonian Institution Press, 1994.

Koestenbaum, Wayne. *The Queen's Throat: Opera Homosexuality and the Mystery of Desire* [1993]. Reprint. New York: Vintage Books, 1994.

Körtvélyes, Ágnes. "Guerra Miklós ballettmester operaházi müködése." In *A magjar balett történetébö*, edited by Vályi Rózsi, 175–190. Budapest: Zenemükiádó, 1956.

Kracauer, Siegfried. "Photography" [1927]. Translated by Thomas Y. Levin. *Critical Inquiry* 19, no. 3 (Spring 1993): 421–436.

Kuzniar, Alice A. "Zarah Leander and Transgender Specularity." *Film Criticism* 23, nos. 2–3 (Winter/Spring 1999): 74–93.

Lake, Taylor Susan. "American Delsartism and the Bodily Discourse of Respectable Womanliness." PhD diss., University of Iowa, 2002.

———. "The Delsarte Attitude on the Legitimate Stage: Mary Anderson's Galatea and the Trope of the Classical Body." In "Essays on François Delsarte," edited by Nancy Lee Chalfa Ruyter. Special issue, *Mime Journal* 23 (2004/2005): 113–135.

Lardinois, André. "Lesbian Sappho and Sappho of Lesbos." In *From Sappho to de Sade: Moments in the History of Sexuality*, edited by Jan Bremmer, 15–35. London: Routledge, 1989.

Le Guin, Elisabeth. *Boccherini's Body: An Essay in Carnal Musicology*. Berkeley, Los Angeles, and London: University of California Press, 2006.

Leff, Lisa Moses. *The Archive Thief: The Man Who Salvaged French Jewish History in the Wake of the Holocaust*. New York and Oxford: Oxford University Press, 2015.

Leontis, Artemis. "The Alternative Archaeologies of Eva Palmer Sikelianos." Lecture presented at the American School of Classical Studies at Athens, Athens, Greece, May 6, 2014.

———."Eva Palmer's Distinctive Greek Journey." In *Women Writing Greece: Essays on Hellenism, Orientalism and Travel*, edited by Vassiliki Kolocotroni and Efterpi Mitsi, 159–184. Amsterdam and New York: Rodopi, 2008.

———. "Eva Palmer Sikelianos Before Delphi." In *Americans and the Experience of Delphi*, edited by Paul Lorenz and David Roessels, 1–49. Boston: Somerset Hall Press, 2013.

———. *Eva Palmer Sikelianos: A Life in Ruins*. Princeton, NJ: Princeton University Press, 2019 [In Press].

Leoussi, Athena S. *Nationalism and Classicism: The Classical Body as National Symbol in Nineteenth-Century England and France*. New York: St. Martin's Press, 1998.

———. "Physical Anthropology and Ethnographic Art." In *Nationalism and Classicism: The Classical Body as National Symbol in Nineteenth-Century England and France*. New York: St. Martin's Press, 1998.

Lepore, Jill. "Historians Who Love Too Much: Reflections on Microhistory and Biography." *Journal of American History* 88, no. 1 (June 2001): 129–144.

Leppert, Richard. "Sexual Identity, Death, and the Family Piano." *19th-Century Music* 16, no. 2 (Autumn 1992): 105–128.

Lerici, Carlo Maurilio. "How to Steal Antiquities." In *Hand on the Past: Pioneer Archaeologists Tell Their Own Story*, edited by C. W. Ceram. 18–26. New York: Knopf, 1966.

Levinson, André. *Ballet Old and New*. Translated by Susan Cook. Summer, NY: Dance Horizons, 1982.

———. *La Danse d'aujourd'hui: Études, notes, portraits*. Paris: Duchartere et Van Buggenhoudt, 1929.

———. "La Danse: Épitaphe." *Comoedia*, September 21, 1925, 3.

———. "Grecs et barbares." *Candide*, no. 276 (June 27, 1929): 15.

———. "Précisions sur la danse: Le Concours de l'Opéra." *Comoedia*. December 21, 1928, 15.

———. "Some Commonplaces on the Dance." *Broom* 4, no. 1 (December 1922): 17.

Levitz, Tamara. *Modernist Mysteries: "Perséphone."* Oxford and New York: Oxford University Press, 2012.

———. "Voice from the Crypt." Chap. 7 in *Modernist Mysteries: "Perséphone."* Oxford and New York: Oxford University Press, 2012.

Livia, Anna. *Minimax*. Portland, OR: The Eighth Mountain Press, 1991.

Lorenz, Paul, and David Roessels, eds. *Americans and the Experience of Delphi*. Boston: Somerset Hall Press, 2013.

Lynch, Deidre Shauna. *Loving Literature: A Cultural History*. Chicago and London: University of Chicago Press, 2015.

Macaulay, Alastair. "One Classic Ballet, Many Interpretations." *New York Times*, July 4, 2011. https://www.nytimes.com/2011/07/05/arts/dance/swan-lake-one-classic-ballet-many-interpretations.html.

Macintosh, Fiona, ed. *The Ancient Dancer in the Modern World: Responses to Greek and Roman Dance*. Oxford and New York: Oxford University Press, 2010.

Marey, Étienne-Jules. *Movement [Le Mouvement, 1894]*. Translated by Eric Pritchard. New York: D. Appleton and Company, 1895.

———. *Le Mouvement* [1894]. Preface by André Miquel. Nîmes: Éditions Jacqueline Chambon, 1994.

Marshall, Jonathan. "The Priestesses of Apollo and the Heirs of Aesculapius: Medical Art-Historical Approaches to Ancient Choreography after Charcot." *Forum for Modern Language Studies* 43, no. 4 (October 2007): 410–426.

Matthews, David. *Medievalism: A Critical History*. Cambridge, UK: Boydell & Brewer, 2015.

Mawer, Deborah. "Ballet and the Apotheosis of the Dance." In *Cambridge Companion to Ravel*, edited by Deborah Mawer, 140–161. Cambridge, UK: Cambridge University Press, 2000.

McClary, Susan. *Feminine Endings: Music, Gender, and Sexuality*. Minneapolis: University of Minnesota Press, 1991.

———. *George Bizet: "Carmen."* Cambridge Opera Handbooks. Cambridge, UK: Cambridge University Press, 1992.

McQuinn, Julie. "Exploring the Erotic in Debussy's Music." In *The Cambridge Companion to Debussy*, edited by Simon Trezise, 117–136. Cambridge, UK: Cambridge University Press, 2003.

Messing, Scott. "Polemic as History: The Case of Neoclassicism." *Journal of Musicology* 9, no. 4 (Autumn 1991): 481–497.

Michelakis, Pantelis. "Dancing with Prometheus: Performance and Spectacle in the 1920s." In *The Ancient Dancer in the Modern World: Responses to Greek and*

Roman Dance, edited by Fiona Macintosh, 224–235. Oxford and New York: Oxford University Press, 2010.

———. *Greek Tragedy on Screen*. Oxford and New York: Oxford University Press, 2013.

Moore, Christopher. "Regionalist Frictions in the Bullring: Lyric Theater in Béziers at the *Fin de Siècle*." *19th-Century Music* 37, no. 3 (Spring 2014): 211–241.

Morris, Mitchell. "Calling Names, Taking Names." In "Colloquy: Music and Sexuality." *Journal of the American Musicological Society* 66, no. 3 (Fall 2013): 831–835.

Morrison, Simon A. *Bolshoi Confidential: Secrets of the Russian Ballet from the Rule of the Tsars to Today*. New York: W. W. Norton, 2016.

———. "The Origins of *Daphnis et Chloé* (1912)." *19th-Century Music* 28, no. 1 (2004): 50–76.

Moseley, Roger. *Keys to Play: Music as a Ludic Medium from Apollo to Nintendo*. Oakland, CA: University of California Press, 2018.

Muñoz, José Esteban. *Cruising Utopia: The Then and There of Queer Futurity*. New York and London: New York University Press, 2009.

Naerebout, Frederick. "'In Search of a Dead Rat': The Reception of Ancient Greek Dance in Late Nineteenth-Century Europe and America." In *The Ancient Dancer in the Modern World: Responses to Greek and Roman Dance*, edited by Fiona Macintosh, 39–56. Oxford and New York: Oxford University Press, 2010.

Nectoux, Jean-Michel. *Gabriel Fauré: A Musical Life*. Translated by Roger Nichols. Cambridge, UK: Cambridge University Press, 1991.

Nijinska, Bronislava. *Bronislava Nijinska: Early Memoirs*. Edited by Irina Nijinska and Jean Rawlison. Introduction by Anna Kisselgoff. New York: Holt, Rinehart and Wilson, 1981.

Nordbladh, Jarl. "The Shape of History: To Give Physical Form to Archaeological Knowledge." In *Histories of Archaeological Practices: Reflections on Methods, Strategies and Social Organization in Past Fieldwork*, edited by Ola Wolfhechel Jensen, 241–258. Stockholm: The National Museum, 2012.

Olin, Elinor. "Le ton et la parole: Melodrama in France 1871–1913." PhD diss., Northwestern University, 1991.

———. "Reconstructing Greek Drama: Saint-Saëns and the Melodramatic Ideal." In *Melodramatic Voices: Understanding Music Drama*, edited by Sarah Hibberd, 45–60. Surrey, UK, and Burlington, VT: Ashgate, 2011.

Orledge, Robert. *Satie the Composer*. Cambridge, UK, and New York: Cambridge University Press, 1990.

Ovid. *Heroides. Amores*. Translated by Grant Showerman. Revised by G. P. Goold. Loeb Classical Library 41. Cambridge, MA, and London: Harvard University Press, 1914.

Palmer-Sikelianos, Eva. *Upward Panic: The Autobiography of Eva Palmer-Sikelianos*. Edited with an introduction by John P. Anton. Chur, Switzerland, and Philadelphia: Harwood Academic Publishers, 1993.

Palmer Sikelianos, Eva, and Natalie Clifford Barney. *Grámmata tīs Eúas Palmer Sikelianoú stī Natalie Clifford Barney*. Translated and edited by Lia Papadaki. Athens: Th. Kastaniōtīs, 1995.

Papadaki, Lia. *To efivikó prótypo kai ī Delfikī prospátheia tou Ággelou Sikelianoú*. Athens: Genikī grammateía néas geniás, 1995.

Parker, Roger. "Remaking the Song." In *Remaking the Song: Operatic Visions and Revisions from Handel to Berio*, 1–21. Berkeley, Los Angeles, and London: University of California Press, 2006.

Pasler, Jann. "Countess Greffulhe as Entrepreneur: Negotiating Class, Gender and Nation." In *Writing through Music: Essays on Music, Culture, and Politics*, 285–317. Oxford and New York: Oxford University Press, 2008.

———. "Theorizing Race in Nineteenth-Century France: Music as Emblem of Identity." *Musical Quarterly* 89, no. 4 (Winter 2006): 459–504.

Payne, Robert. *The Splendor of Greece*. New York: Harper, 1960.

Peraino, Judith A. *Listening to the Sirens: Musical Technologies of Queer Identity from Homer to Hedwig*. Berkeley: University of California Press, 2005.

Perry, Sara. "Archaeological Visualization and the Manifestation of the Discipline: Model-Making at the Institute of Archaeology, London." In *Archaeology After Interpretation: Returning Materials to Archaeological Theory*, edited by Benjamin Alberti, Andrew Meirion Jones, and Joshua Pollard, 281–304. Walnut Creek, CA: Left Coast Press, 2013.

Phelan, Peggy. *Unmarked: The Politics of Performance*. London and New York: Routledge, 1993.

Pietz, William. "The Problem of the Fetish, I." *RES: Anthropology and Aesthetics* 9 (Spring 1985): 5–17.

Pinney, Christopher. "Introduction: 'How the Other Half . . . .'" In *Photography's Other Histories*, edited by Christopher Pinney and Nicholas Peterson, 1–14. Durham, NC, and London: Duke University Press, 2003.

Pinney, Christopher, and Nicholas Peterson, eds. *Photography's Other Histories*. Durham, NC, and London: Duke University Press, 2003.

Plasketes, George, ed. *Play it Again: Cover Songs in Popular Music*. Abingdon and New York: Routledge, 2016.

Plato, *Plato in Twelve Volumes*. Translated by Harold N. Fowler. Cambridge, MA: Harvard University Press; London: William Heinemann, 1925.

Poesio, Giannandrea. "Italy: The Cinderella of the Arts." In *Europe Dancing: Perspectives on Theatre Dance and Cultural Identity*, edited by Andrée Grau and Stephanie Jordan, 100–118. London and New York: Routledge, 2000.

Pöhlmann, Egert. *Denkmäler altgreichischer Musik*. Nuremberg: H. Carl, 1970.

Pöhlmann, Egert, and Martin L. West, eds. *Documents of Ancient Greek Music: The Extant Melodies and Fragments Edited and Transcribed with Commentary*. New York and Oxford: Oxford University Press, 2001.

Pontremoli, Emmanuel. *KERYLOS*. Paris: Éditions des Bibliothèques Nationales de France, 1934.

Pougy, Liane de. *Mes Cahiers bleus*. Paris: Plon, 1977.

Preston, Carrie J. *Modernism's Mythic Pose: Gender, Genre, Solo Performance*. Oxford and New York: Oxford University Press, 2011.

———. "Posing Modernism: Delsartism in Modern Dance and Silent Film." Chap. 2 in *Modernism's Mythic Pose: Gender, Genre, Solo Performance*. Oxford and New York: Oxford University Press, 2011.

The Pretty Women of Paris: Their Names and Addresses, Qualities and Faults, Being a Complete Directory or Guide to Pleasure for Visitors to the Gay City [1883]. Introduction by Robin De Beaumont. Ware: Wordsworth Editions, 1996.

Rambert, Marie. *Quicksilver.* London: Macmillan, 1972.

Reinach, Joseph. *Histoire de l'affaire Dreyfus.* Paris: Fasquelle, 1902–1930.

Reinach, Salomon. *Bibliographie de Salomon Reinach.* Paris: Société d'Édition Les Belles-Lettres, 1936.

———. *Conseils aux Voyageurs archéologues en Grèce et dans l'Orient hellénique.* Paris: Ernest Leroux, 1886.

———. *Esquisses Archéologiques.* Paris: Ernest Leroux, 1888.

Reinach, Théodore. *Hymn à Apollon.* 2nd rev. and corrected ed. Restituted by Henri Weil. Transcribed by Théodore Reinach. Accompanied by Gabriel Fauré. Paris: O. Bornemann, 1914.

———. "Hymnes avec notes musicales [1911]." *Fouilles de Delphes* 3, fasc. 2 (1909–1913): 147–169.

———. "La musique des hymnes de Delphes." *Bulletin de Correspondance Hellénique* 17 (1893): 584–610.

———. *La Musique Grecque et L'Hymne à Apollon: Conférence faite à l'Association pour l'encouragement des etudes grecques.* Paris: Ernest Leroux, 1894.

Reinach, Théodore, Gabriel Fauré, and Henri Weil. *Hymne à Apollon, Chant Grec du IIIe Siècle avant J.C, découvert à Delphes par l'Ecole Française d'Athènes.* Paris: O. Bornemann, 1894.

———. *Hymne à Apollon, Chant Grec du IIe Siècle avant J.C, découvert à Delphes par l'Ecole Française d'Athènes.* 2nd rev. and corrected ed. Paris: O. Bornemann, 1914.

———. "Notice." In *Hymne à Apollon, Chant Grec du IIe Siècle avant J.C, découvert à Delphes par l'Ecole Française d'Athènes.* 2nd rev. and corrected ed. Paris: O. Bornemann, 1914.

Reynolds, Margaret. *The Sappho History.* New York: Palgrave, 2003.

Rodger, Gillian. "Drag, Camp, and Gender Subversion in the Music and Videos of Annie Lenox." *Popular Music* 23 (2004): 17–29.

Rodrigue, Aron. "Totems, Taboos, and Jews: Salomon Reinach and the Politics of Scholarship in Fin-de-Siècle France." *Jewish Social Studies* 10, no. 2 (Winter 2004): 1–19.

Rodriguez, Suzanne. *Wild Heart, a Life: Natalie Clifford Barney's Journey from Victorian America to Belle Époque Paris.* New York: Ecco, 2002.

Roessels, David. Introduction to *Americans and the Experience of Delphi.* Edited by Paul Lorenz and David Roessels. Boston: Somerset Hall Press, 2013.

Román, David. "Archival Drag: Or, The Afterlife of Performance." In *Performance in America: Contemporary US Culture and the Performing Arts.* Durham, NC: Duke University Press, 2005.

———. *Performance in America: Contemporary US Culture and the Performing Arts.* Durham, NC: Duke University Press, 2005.

Rosen, Charles. *The Classical Style: Haydn, Mozart, Beethoven* [1971]. Expanded ed. New York and London: W.W. Norton, 1998.

———. "From the Troubadours to Frank Sinatra." Part II. *New York Review of Books* 53, no. 4 (March 9, 2006). http://www.nybooks.com/articles/2006/03/09/from-the-troubadours-to-sinatra-part-ii/

———. "Western Music: The View from California." In *Freedom and the Arts: Essays on Music and Literature*, 210–239. Cambridge, MA: Harvard University Press, 2012.

Roslavleva, Natalia. *Era of the Russian Ballet 1770–1965*. Foreword by Ninette de Valois. London: Gollancz, 1966.

Ruyter, Nancy Lee Chalfa. *The Cultivation of Body and Mind in Nineteenth-Century American Delsartism*. Westport, CT, and London: Greenwood Press, 1999.

———, ed. "Essays on François Delsarte." Special issue, *Mime Journal* 23 (2004/2005).

———. "The Genteel Transition: American Delsartism." In *Reformers and Visionaries: The Americanization of the Art of Dance*. 17–30. Brooklyn, NY: Dance Horizons, 1979.

———. *Reformers and Visionaries: The Americanization of the Art of Dance*. Brooklyn, NY: Dance Horizons, 1979.

Sappho. *If Not, Winter: Fragments of Sappho*. Translated by Anne Carson. New York: Alfred A. Knopf, 2002.

———. *Sappho: A New Translation*. Translated by Diane J. Raynor and André Lardinois. Cambridge, UK, and New York: Cambridge University Press, 2014.

———. *Sappho: Memoir, Text, Selected Renderings, and a Literal Translation by Henry Thorton Wharton*. 3rd ed. London: John Lane, 1895.

Sappho and Alcaeus. *Greek Lyric I: Sappho and Alcaeus*. Edited and translated by David A. Campbell. Loeb Classical Library 42. Cambridge, MA, and London: Harvard University Press, 1990.

Savigliano, Marta E. *Tango and the Political Economy of Passion*. Boulder, CO, and Oxford: Westview Press, 1995.

Schechner, Richard. *Between Theatre and Anthropology*. Chicago: University of Chicago Press, 1985.

———. *Performance Studies: An Introduction*. 3rd ed. Sara Brady, media ed. London and New York: Routledge, 2013.

Schliemann, Heinrich. *Myth, Scandal, and History: The Heinrich Schliemann Controversy and a First Edition of the Mycenaean Diary*. Edited by William Calder and David Traill. Detroit: Wayne State University Press, 1986.

Schneider, Rebecca. *Performing Remains: Art and War in Times of Theatrical Reenactment*. London and New York: Routledge, 2011.

———. "What Happened; or, Finishing Live." *Representations* 136, no. 1 (Fall 2016): 96–111.

Scott, Michael. *Delphi and Olympia: The Spatial Politics of Panhellenism in the Archaic and Classical Periods*. Cambridge, UK, and New York: Cambridge University Press, 2010.

Searcy, Anne. "Russian Swans." *The Itinerant Balletomane* (blog), May 26, 2013. https://itinerantballetomane.blogspot.com/2013/05/russian-swans.html.

Sedgwick, Eve Kosofsky. "Introduction: Queerer Than Fiction." *Studies in the Novel* 28, no. 3 (1996): 277–280.

———. "Paranoid Reading and Reparative Reading; or, You're So Paranoid, You Probably Think This Introduction Is about You." In *Novel Gazing: Queer Readings in Fiction*, edited by Eve Kosofsky Sedgwick, 1–37. Durham, NC: Duke University Press, 1997.

———. "Paranoid Reading and Reparative Reading; or, You're So Paranoid, You Probably Think This Essay Is about You." In *Touching Feeling: Affect, Pedagogy, Performativity*, 123–151. Durham, NC, and London: Duke University Press, 2003.

———. *Touching Feeling: Affect, Pedagogy, Performativity*. Durham, NC, and London: Duke University Press, 2003.

Sedgwick, Eve Kosofsky, and Adam Frank. "Shame in the Cybernetic Fold: Reading Silvan Tomkins." *Critical Inquiry* 21, no. 1 (1995): 496–522.

Seewald, Berthold. "Griechenland zerstörte schon einmal Europas Ordnung." *Die Welt*, June 11, 2015. http://www.welt.de/geschichte/article142305296/Griechenland-zerstoerte-schon-einmal-Europas-Ordnung.html.

Servières, Georges. "Les Ballets de Gluck." *Musica* 8, no. 77 (February 1909): 56–57.

Shawn, Ted. *Every Little Movement: A Book about François Delsarte, the Man and His Philosophy, His Science of Applied Aesthetics, the Application of This Science to the Art of the Dance, the Influence of Delsarte on American Dance*. New York: Dance Horizons, 1954.

Sigel, Lisa Z. "Filth in the Wrong People's Hands: Postcards and the Expansion of Pornography in Britain and the Atlantic World, 1880–1914." *Journal of Social History* 33, no. 4 (Summer, 2000): 859–885.

Silverman, Lois H. "Personalizing the Past: A Review of Literature with Implications for Historical Interpretation." *Journal of Interpretation Research* 2, no. 1 (1997): 1–12.

Simonson, Mary. "Dance Pictures: The Cinematic Experiments of Anna Pavlova and Rita Sacchetto." *Screening the Past* 40. September 15, 2015. http://www.screeningthepast.com/2015/08/dance-pictures-the-cinematic-experiments-of-anna-pavlova-and-rita-sacchetto/.

———. "Dancing the Future, Performing the Past: Isadora Duncan and Wagnerism in the American Imagination." *Journal of the American Musicological Society* 65, no. 2 (Summer 2012): 511–556.

Slobin, Marc. "Ethical Issues." In *Ethnomusicology: An Introduction*, edited by Helen Myers, 329–336. New York and London: W. W. Norton and Company, 1992.

Slominski, Tes. "Doin' Time with Meg and Cris, Thirty Years Later: The Queer Temporality of Pseudonostalgia." *Women and Music* 19 (2015): 86–94.

Smart, Mary Ann. *Mimomania: Music and Gesture in Nineteenth-Century Opera*. Berkeley, Los Angeles, and London: University of California Press, 2004.

Snyder, Jane McIntosch. *Lesbian Desire in the Lyrics of Sappho*. New York: Columbia University Press, 1997.

Solie, Ruth A. "What Do Feminists Want? A Reply to Pieter van den Toorn." *Journal of Musicology* 9 (1991): 399–410.

Solomon, Jon. "The Reception of Ancient Greek Music in the Late Nineteenth Century." *International Journal of the Classical Tradition* 17, no. 4 (December 2010): 497–525.

Sontag, Susan. *On Photography*. New York: Farrar, Straus and Giroux, 1977.

———. "Unguided Tour." *New Yorker*, October 31, 1977, 40–45.

Souhami, Diana. *Wild Girls: Paris, Sappho and Art—The Lives and Loves of Natalie Barney and Romaine Brooks*. London: Weidenfeld & Nicolson, 2004.

Steedman, Carolyn. *Dust: The Archive and Cultural History*. New Brunswick, NJ: Rutgers University Press, 2002.

Stevenson, Ronald. "Maurice Emmanuel: A Belated Apologia." *Music and Letters* 40, no. 2 (April 1959): 154–165.

Stiebing, William H., Jr. *Uncovering the Past: A History of Archaeology*. New York and Oxford: Oxford University Press, 1993.

Stucky, Steven. *The Classical Style: An Opera (of Sorts)*. Libretto by Jeremy Denk. Inspired by the book by Charles Rosen. [King of Prussia, PA]: Theodore Presser Company, [2015].

Tagg, John. *The Disciplinary Frame: Photographic Truths and the Capture of Meaning*. Minneapolis and London: University of Minnesota Press, 2009.

Talmont, Georges [and Madame Mariquita]. "Comment Madame Mariquita monte un Ballet." *Comœdia Illustré* 1e année, no. 1 (December 15, 1908): 21–24.

Taruskin, Richard. "Afterword: *Nicht blubefleckt?*" *Journal of Musicology* 26, no. 2 (2009): 274–284.

———. "Back to Whom? Neoclassicism and Ideology." *19th-Century Music* 16, no. 3 (Spring 1993): 286–302.

———. *Oxford History of Western Music*. 6 vols. Oxford: Oxford University Press, 2005.

———. "The Pastness of the Present and the Presence of the Past [1988]." In *Text and Acts: Essays on Music and Performance*. 90–154. New York and Oxford: Oxford University Press, 1995.

———. *Text and Act: Essays on Music and Performance*. New York and Oxford: Oxford University Press, 1995.

Taylor, Diana. *The Archive and the Repertoire: Performing Cultural Memory in the Americas*. Durham, NC, and London: Duke University Press, 2003.

Thibault, Guillaume, and Jean-Luc Martinez. "La reconstitution de la colonne des danseuses a Delphes." In *Actes du colloque Virtual Retrospect 2007*, 231–238. Bordeaux: Edition Ausonius, 2008.

Tilden, Freeman. *Interpreting our Heritage* [1957]. Edited by R. Bruce Craig. Foreword by Russell E. Dickenson. 4th ed. Chapel Hill, NC: University of North Carolina Press, 2007.

Trigger, Bruce G. "Alternative Archaeologies: Nationalist, Colonialist, Imperialist." *Man*, n.s., 19, no. 3 (September 1984): 355–370.

Tsouvala, Maria, Vasso Barboussi, Natalie Zervou, and Irene Loyzaki. "Opening Plenary Panel: The State of Dance Studies in Greece." Opening plenary session at "Cut & Paste: Dance Advocacy in the Age of Austerity," the 2015 Joint Conference of the Society of Dance History Scholars and the Congress on Research in Dance, Athens, Greece, June 4, 2015.

Tucker, Sherrie. "When Subjects Don't Come Out." In *Queer Episodes: In Music and Modern Identity*, edited by Sophie Fuller and Lloyd Whitesell, 293–310. Urbana and Chicago: University of Illinois Press, 2002.

Tuena, Filippo. *Le varizioni Reinach*. Milan: Rizzoli, 2005.

Tzartzani, Ioanna. "Embodying the Crisis: The Body as a Site of Resistance in Post-Bailout Greece." *Choros: International Dance Journal* 2 (Spring 2014): 40–49.

Vaillat, Léandre. *Ballets de l'Opéra de Paris (ballets dans les opéras; nouveaux ballets).* Paris, Compagnie française des arts graphiques, 1947.

Van den Toorn, Pieter C. "Neoclassicism and Its Definitions." In *Music Theory in Concept and Practice*, edited by James M. Baker, David W. Beach, and Jonathan W. Bernard, 131–156. Rochester, NY: University of Rochester Press, 1997.

———. "Politics, Feminism, and Contemporary Music Theory." *Journal of Musicology* 9 (1991): 275–299.

Van Steen, Gonda. "'The World's a Circular Stage': Aeschylean Tragedy through the Eyes of Eva Palmer-Sikelianou." *International Journal of the Classical Tradition* 8, no. 3 (Winter 2002): 375–393.

Vian des Rives, Régis. *La Villa Kérylos.* Paris: Les Éditions de l'Amateur, 1997.

Vuillermoz, Émile. "Salamine." *Candide*, no. 276 (June 27, 1929): 15.

Weil, Henri. "Hymne à Apollon: Inscriptions de Delphes, nouveaux fragments d'hymnes accompagnés de notes de musique." *Bulletin de Correspondance Hellénique* 17 (1893): 569–583.

Weil, Henri, and Théodore Reinach. *Hymne à Apollon: Inscriptions de Delphes, nouveaux fragments d'hymnes accompagnés de notes de musique, par Henri Weil. La musique des hymnes de Delphes, par Théodore Reinach.* Paris: Thorin et fils, 1894.

Wells-Lynn, Amy. "The Intertextual, Sexually-Coded Rue Jacob: A Geocritical Approach to Djuna Barnes, Natalie Barney, and Radclyffe Hall." *South Central Review* 22, no. 3 (Fall 2005): 78–112.

West, Martin L. *Ancient Greek Music.* Oxford and New York: Oxford University Press, 1992.

Wiegman, Robyn. "The Times We're In: Queer Feminist Criticism and the Reparative 'Turn.'" *Feminist Theory* 15, no. 1 (2014): 4–25.

[Willy] Gauthier-Villars, Henry. "Deux Ballets Russes de Musiciens Français." *Comœdia Illustré* 4e année, no. 18 (June 15, 1912): [s.p.].

———. *The Third Sex* [1927]. Translated and with an introduction and notes by Lawrence R. Schehr. Urbana and Chicago: University of Illinois Press, 2007.

Wilson, Nick. *The Art of Re-enchantment: Making Early Music in the Modern Age.* Oxford and New York: Oxford University Press, 2014.

Withers, Debi. "Kate Bush: Performing and Creating Queer Subjectivities on *Lionheart.*" *Nebula* 3, nos. 2–3 (September 2006): 125–141.

Wolf, Stacy. *A Problem Like Maria: Gender and Sexuality in the American Musical.* Ann Arbor: University of Michigan Press, 2002.

Wood, Elizabeth. "Sapphonics." In *Queering the Pitch: The New Gay and Lesbian Musicology*, edited by Philip Brett, Elizabeth Wood, and Gary C. Thomas, 27–66. New York and London: Routledge, 1994.

Yatromanolakis, Dimitrios. *Sappho in the Making: The Early Reception.* Hellenic Studies Series 28. Washington, DC: Center for Hellenic Studies, 2008.

INDEX

Note: Page number followed by *"f"* and *"ex"* refers to figure and example

danse d'école, 81, 104
and Delphic Festivals, 127–28, 135–37
documentation of, 14–15, 145
Emmanuel and aesthetics of ancient,
80, 82–84, 92–94, 99–100
Palmer Sikelianos and, 108–9
performers' role in, 11
in *Prometheus Bound*, 123–26
re-enactment of ancient, 106,
115–18, 152
Dance Your Ph.D. competition, 79
La danse grecque antique (Emmanuel),
80, 83–84, 86, 88–94, 100–105,
118, 119*f*
Daphnis et Chloé (Ravel), 19, 100, 108,
117, 118
Daudet, Alphonse, 61, 173n47, 174n56
Daunt, Yvonne, 183n81
Davis, Natalie Zemon, 14
Dayton, Ohio, 48, 51, 60–61,
170n6, 190n39
Debré, Michel, 47
Debussy, Claude, 81, 98–100
d'Eichtal, Eugene, 39
DeJean, Joan, 174nn56, 61
Delphi, 107–8, 156
Delphic Festival(s)
abandonment of, 136
archaeologically correct elements in,
134, 135
author visits site of, 156
founding of, 107, 111, 120
photographs of, 130, 131*f*
purpose of, 185n48
re-enacted performances at, 115
Second, 126–29
Delphic hymns to Apollo, 26–27, 156.
See also *Hymne à Apollon* (Fauré
and Reinach)
Delsarte, François, 57, 186n73
Delsartism, 57, 63
Delvair, Jeanne, 58
Denk, Jeremy, 139, 140–42
Dermoz, Germaine, 58–59
Diaghilev, Sergei, 103, 115, 117, 118
Dialogue au soleil couchant (Louÿs), 58
Dialogue of the Dance (Lucian), 94

Dinshaw, Carolyn, 66
Don Giovanni (Mozart), 140–41
"drag, temporal / archival," 175n77
Dubois, Théodore, 38
Duncan, Irma, 92
Duncan, Isadora, 89, 90–91, 101,
117, 124–25
Duncan, Penelope (née Sikelianos),
58, 60, 61*f*, 62–63, 113, 121–22,
125, 174n58
Duncan, Raymond, 58, 60, 120,
121–22, 124

early music movement, 6–7
Elgin Marbles, 2, 135–36
elocution, 56–57, 63
Emmanuel, Maurice. See also *Salamine*
(Emmanuel); *La danse grecque
antique* (Emmanuel)
and aesthetics of ancient dance, 80,
82–84, 92–94, 99–100
collaboration between Marey
and, 84–88
La danse grecque antique, 80, 83–84,
86, 88–94, 100–105, 118, 119*f*
Debussy and, 98–100
education and scholarship of, 82–84
organization of material of, 179n41
Prométhée enchaîné, 177n7
reconstructions of Palmer Sikelianos
versus, 124
and scholarship versus
performance, 105–6
Epstein, Louis, 69–70
Équivoque (Barney), 58–65
erotohistoriography, 144–45
eurhythmic dance, 19, 81, 90, 92, 93,
95, 103–04
Euripides, 99
experimentation, in Belle Époque, 11–14

fandom, 30, 166n35
Farge, Arlette, 145
Fauré, Gabriel. See also *Hymne à Apollon*
(Fauré and Reinach)
La bonne chanson, 38
Cinq mélodies "de Venise," 38

Pratsika, Koula, 118
Prométhée enchaîné (Emmanuel), 177n7
Prometheus Bound
   as collaboration between archaeology
      and performance, 116
   critical responses to, 134–35
   documentation of, 129–34
   film of Palmer Sikelianos's staging of,
      127, 130–32
   music for entrance of Oceanids
      in, 130*ex.*
   music for first chorus in, 130*ex.*
   Oceanids from Palmer
      Sikelianos's, 128*f*
   Palmer Sikelianos's approach to, 117
   and Palmer Sikelianos's musical
      training, 112
   photographs of, 132, 133*f*
   reconstruction of music and dance
      in, 123–26
   re-enactment of, 118–22
Psachos, Konstantinos, 125–26, 127
pseudo-nostalgia, 65
psychology, 93

queer musicology, 52–54
queerness and queer temporalities and
      spaces. *See also* lesbianism
   of Barney, 5, 49, 65–66, 67–68,
      174–75nn67, 68
   of Palmer Sikelianos, 5, 55, 111
   of Salomon Reinach, 190n36
   in temporal re-enactment, 175n77

Rambert, Marie, 60
Ravel, Maurice, 42, 117
reading, paranoid and reparative modes
      of, 4, 154–55
re-enactments, 8–11
   versus historical interpretation, 161n31
   of Hodson, Nijinsky, and
      Roerich, 115–18
   as knowledge-seeking process,
      108, 113–14
   Palmer Sikelianos's approach to, 117
   of *Prometheus Bound*, 118–22

queerness in temporal, 175n77
   of Sappho, 75
   Schneider on, 66
Reinach, Adolphe, 165n10
Reinach, Béatrice, 165n10
Reinach, Bertrand, 165n10
Reinach, Fanny, 165n10
Reinach, Joseph, 25
Reinach, Léon, 165n10
Reinach, Salomon, 25, 145–53, 165n10,
      190nn32, 35, 36
Reinach, Thédore. See also *Hymne à
      Apollon* (Fauré and Reinach)
   career of, 25–26
   collaboration between Fauré and, 26
   and construction of Villa
      Kérylos, 21–23
   and Emmanuel's *Salamine*, 80–81,
      95, 96–97
   lifestyle antiquity of, 113
   and neoclassicism, 24–25
   and 1911 edition of *Hymne à
      Apollon*, 39–41
   and performance of *Hymne à
      Apollon*, 29–32
   reconstructions of Palmer Sikelianos
      versus, 124
   and scholarly voyeurism, 151–52
   significance of works of, 23
   in Villa Kérylos, 44*f*
Renacle, Jeanne, 29
Renan, Ernest, 82
reparative mode of reading, 4, 154–55
reparative musicology, 3–4, 155
reperformances, 8–11, 136, 155
repertoire
   versus archive, 8
   of Barney, 73
   as musicological resource, 72
   and scholarly voyeurism, 152
   works informed by, 8–11, 50–51
Reynolds, Margaret, 75
Rite of Spring, The [see *Le Sacre du
      Printemps*],115–117
Rodriguez, Suzanne, 55
Roerich, Nicholas, 115–16